*AuthorHouse™*
*1663 Liberty Drive*
*Bloomington, IN 47403*
*www.authorhouse.com*
*Phone: 1-800-839-8640*

*Published by AuthorHouse 5/29/2012*

*ISBN: 978-1-4772-1007-9 (sc)*
*ISBN: 978-1-4772-1008-6 (e)*

*Library of Congress Control Number: 2012908839*

*Any people depicted in stock imagery provided by Thinkstock are models, and such images are being used for illustrative purposes only.*
*Certain stock imagery © Thinkstock.*

*This book is printed on acid-free paper.*

*Because of the dynamic nature of the Internet, any web addresses or links contained in this book may have changed since publication and may no longer be valid. The views expressed in this work are solely those of the author and do not necessarily reflect the views of the publisher, and the publisher hereby disclaims any responsibility for them.*

# X-Treme Muzzleloading:
## Fur, Fowl and Dangerous Game with Muzzleloading Rifles, Smoothbores and Pistols

By

Wm. Hovey Smith

# Table of Contents

***The author with a Cape buffalo taken during his 2009 Safari.***

# *Introduction*

On my first exposure to muzzleloading guns in the 1950s, I was very interested in their differences in design, how to shoot them and how well they shot. Twenty years later I was satisfied that they would indeed "go bang," and if I did my part, would shoot holes in targets with monotonous regularity. The question, "Would these guns hunt?" consumed more of my attentions in the mid-1980s. Answering this question brought me to the point that I have gun hunted almost exclusively with muzzleloading firearms for the last thirty years.

Pistols are small, portable and challenging to shoot. Consequently, the first black-powder gun that I took into the woods was a replica .36-caliber brass-framed Confederate revolver. While living in Arizona, I purchased an original rifle made by Alonzo Seldon in Whitehall, New York. Typical of the type, this was a half-stocked rifle with a .45-caliber barrel. The first game that I bagged with it was a Georgia beaver.

Although the Seldon rifle shot well enough to win a number of target events, I retired it after the drum blew out of the barrel during a match. Seeking to replace the gun, I purchased a .45-caliber Mowrey and later a flintlock Thompson/Center Arms Hawken rifle. It was with these two rifles that I took my first few deer with front-loading guns. It wasn't the equipment or the lack of deer that prevented me from killing deer sooner, my problem was that I had to age sufficiently to learn the patience to sit for hours in a deer stand and let the animals come to me.

As years passed, more of my time was spent writing for various publications, and I became increasingly specialized in covering black-powder guns and hunting with them. As a practical matter, I soon realized that I did not have to kill the biggest, baddest or mostest critters in the woods to sell articles about my hunts with an increasingly wide sampling of muzzleloading guns. Almost every hunt found me taking a different gun. Proceeding on this path had me hunting armadillos with a Japanese matchlock, squirrel with a percussion single-shot pistol, deer with an outrageously long flintlock handgun and shooting swan with a flintlock musket stuffed with steel shot in addition to hunting with each year's new crop of in-line rifles. These experiences culminated with an African safari in 2005 where I took five species of plains game using a muzzleloading rifle, smoothbore and pistol (Chapter 8) which was followed in 2006 with a South Dakota buffalo hunt (Chapter 19) and a Cape buffalo hunt in 2009 (Chapter 20).

With increasing frequency my articles about muzzleloading guns, black-powder hunting and wildlife cookery appeared in a variety of magazines including Gun Digest, Blackpowder Hunting, Muzzle Blasts, Chevy Outdoors, Dixie Gun Works Black Powder Annual, Safari, Fur-Fish-Game and a number of others. My writing became known for featuring unusual hunts and guns. I became a Senior Writer for Guns and Gear Magazine and specialized in covering black-powder guns and hunts and in 2007 became the black-powder editor for Gun Digest.

Not only do I hunt, but I also cook and eat what I shoot. In my previous books, Practical Bowfishing, Crossbow Hunting and Backyard Deer Hunting: Converting deer to dinner for pennies per pound, I have included chapters on cleaning and cooking game (see concluding pages for information on these titles). This book continues that tradition, and a number of new recipes are offered. These hunts and the preparation of the muzzleloading guns provided the experiences on which this book is based. This book is not to record my accomplishments, but rather to illustrate to the reader the wealth of hunting opportunities that exist with all sorts of muzzleloaders. While the popular TV and magazine media almost exclusively focuses on deer hunting, there is much more to muzzleloading hunting than taking an in-line rifle out for a few days during the black-powder deer season.

The thrill of watching an animal feed closer until it finally comes within the 25-yard sure-kill zone of a flintlock pistol is far more exciting than potting that same doe on the other side of the bean field 150-yards away. I invite anyone to tell me that killing a North Carolina swan dead in the air with a black-powder shotgun was not one of their most memorable hunting experiences (Chapter 11).

During the closing decades of the 20th Century, I came to know some of the pioneers of the modern muzzleloading era including Val Forgett, Turner Kirkland and Tony Knight. Each contributed much to the wealth of muzzleloading guns and hunting opportunities that we have today.

I have also worked with many editors who have influenced my writing and been good friends. Among these are George "Butch" Winter, Ken Warner and Eric Bye. Thanks are also due to Balazs Nemeth, the editor of the E-magazine, "Blackpowder No. 1," who designed this book in exchange for adapting some of the stories for his publication. He lives in Hungary, and his interest and participation in this book is an example of the world-wide appeal of muzzleloading guns.

Wm. Hovey Smith
Whitehall, Sandersville, Georgia
August, 2011

*The author shooting the Austin&Halleck 12-gauge bolt-action muzzleloading shotgun.*

## Chapter 1. Small game

State fish and game personnel readily agree that hunters are not taking full advantage of small-game hunting opportunities. Deer hunting, especially trophy-deer hunting, has captured the imagination of many hunters to the extent that they infrequently consider other opportunities. Often the only other times they venture fourth to sample other game is on the opening weekends of dove, turkey, pheasant or duck seasons. Otherwise, their attentions are focused on deer.

Small-game hunting allows the modern hunter to make the closest approach to a time when the hunter had the woods to himself, and he could practice his hunting skills without much concern that someone had already beat him to his favorite spot. Doing these hunts with a muzzleloading rifle, pistol or smoothbore adds an additional challenge to the hunt and firmly reconnects the hunter with sport. The hunt becomes more than killing X-number of pieces of game, and how the game is taken assumes equal importance.

I cannot claim that a squirrel stew made from seven squirrels taken with as many shots with a flintlock rifle taste any better than that made from squirrels shot with a modern rifle, but I do take more pride in presenting a flintlocked stew to my dinner guests or consuming it myself. I also find that the guns' accomplishments take on special meanings. I don't often name my cartridge guns, but many of my muzzleloading rifles have names. Bess, Cantank, Little Flint and Tage have taken their places in my gun rack and in my affections. The more primitive they are, the more likely that I have hung some sort of moniker on them. Although I did not name these guns out of strong feelings of tradition, hunters like David Crockett named their guns too. He called one of his rifles "Old Betsy." This particular gun was a gift from the people of Tennessee, and it may now be seen in The Alamo where he died fighting for Texas independence.

Squirrels

Increasing populations of grey squirrels in the eastern part of the nation have reached the point that in many communities they are considered pests. No one minds watching their acrobatics as they negotiate telephone wires when they cross roads or burry acorns in the yard, the troubles arise when they decide to move into houses. They also feed quite happily at bird feeders and are ingenious in discovering ways to get at this free bounty of seeds.

Because Georgia's squirrel season opens on August 15, my first hunts with any new muzzleloaders are often after these arboreal rodents. While it is traditional to use .32 and .36 caliber rifles on squirrels, I have also employed .45 and .50-caliber guns using round balls. As with any shooting at targets in trees, care must be taken to insure that there is a back-stop to catch the balls. Even the .50-caliber guns do not destroy much useable meat as I aim for the rib cage; and body shots, although messy, do not destroy the front or hind quarters.

On one occasion I was walking home from deer hunting and had a .75-caliber round ball and 100 grains of FFg black powder in Bess, one of my smoothbore guns. A squirrel was feeding on the ground, and I decapitated it with the ball. This was admittedly over-kill, but I felt that I might as well do something useful with the ball as the gun needed to be unloaded. On the other end of the size spectrum, I have also finished off squirrels with a .22-caliber percussion North American Arms revolver shooting 4 grains of FFFFg black powder.

Muzzleloading smoothbore muskets and shotguns also have squirrel-killing potential. With cylinder-bored guns using 4s and 5s, the problem is that patterns are so loose that a crippled squirrel will often be the result, and it helps to have a dog to tree the animal while the hunter reloads. Demeter and Diana, my Labs, have become expert in spotting squirrels, pointing them and recovering them once they are hit. Choked muzzleloading turkey guns used with optimum loads are as effective as any cartridge shotguns on squirrels.

A variant of still hunting squirrels consisting of walking, stopping, listening and spotting them when the woods are wet enough to move quietly through the leaf litter. On these hunts Demeter walks behind me and only moves forward if she has a strong scent or sees a scurrying squirrel. Once she came to a solid point and was apparently fixated on something about four-feet off the ground that I could not see. Sure enough, there was a squirrel hiding in the thick cover. On another occasion, she dug one out of a hole by a stump. When the leaf cover is too dry to move quietly, I often sit by a den tree at first light and wait for the activity to start. This may take some time as on cold days, as squirrels may not move until about 10 AM when the sun has penetrated the forest.

Hilly country provides some of the best opportunities for rifle-hunting squirrels. Even if the rodents are in the tops of the trees, there will often be sufficient relief so that these tops will be below the hunters standing higher on the slope. This way the lead balls will hit the ground and not go flying to hit a person or someone's house, cow or car.

Squirrel activities vary depending on the types and locations of their food sources. Early in the season they will be found cutting pine cones. Next, they will work on hanging grapes as these ripen on their vines in the trees. Once the acorns fall, many squirrels will be found nosing through the leaves on the ground. They feel more secure if there is some overhead cover such as vines, briers or low shrubs. This is the optimum time to pistol-hunt squirrels. One of the best is Tradition's Crockett .32-caliber single-shot pistol loaded with a round ball and 20 grains of FFFg black powder. This load will work on squirrels and game up to the size of coyotes. A muzzleloading pistol also provides a rapid follow-up shot if necessary to finish a crippled animal.

*The Ruger Old Army with some Georgia squirrels and its trophy alligator.*

Problems with many percussion revolvers is that they do not have adjustable sights and don't shoot to the point of aim. It is not uncommon for a percussion revolver to shoot more than a foot high. This makes hitting a small animal very difficult at any but point-black range. Ruger's now discontinued Old Army revolver has an excellent set of adjustable sights and in my opinion was the best percussion revolver ever made. I have shot many squirrels with this gun as well as taken rabbits and alligators. I describe alligator hunting in detail in my book Crossbow Hunting. The revolver is used to provide a finishing shot through the brain at a range of a few inches. I once owned a .31-caliber replica Colt pocket pistol that did shoot to the point of aim. I unwisely sold it, and have regretted that decision every since. It was a fine small game gun and killed better than a Smith & Wesson .22 LR Kit Gun.

Squirrels formed a large part of the diet of early settlers, and they remain good eating today, although many modern hunters turn up their noses at them. Among the most adamant detractors were a visiting pair of Irish hunters who so distained the gray squirrels that had been imported into their country that they called them "tree rats" and considered them unfit to eat. Before they left I fed them a pot of squirrel stew which they much enjoyed. When I told them what it was, they said that they thought they were eating chicken.

Gray and fox squirrels are a bit of trouble to clean, but they are worth the trouble as they yield an excellent meal as stews or fried and steamed until they are tender. Some commonly used and family-tested recipes are found in Chapter 26. Both the experiences of bagging squirrels with muzzleloaders and eating the harvest are worth doing.

*Rabbit, Bess and Ham Bone, the beagle.*

Rabbits

While squirrels are very often considered rifle game, rabbits are mostly thought of as more suitably taken with shotguns. As might be supposed, I very often hunt rabbits with muzzleloading shotguns and muskets loaded with shot as well as with rifles and pistols. Each is best done during a different time of the year using different hunting techniques.

Early Fall brings rabbit season in most of the country. In some areas some snow has already fallen, but generally the trees have turned and the leaves have just started to drop. There remains areas of thick cover that are best worked by eager beagles who like nothing better than squirming under the vines after the bounding bunnies (Chapter 10). Most of the time the shots will be at a fleeing rabbit, although occasionally they will pause for a few seconds offering a sitting shot.

The hunter needs to place himself on the rabbit's back trail so that when the rabbit circles it will pass within range of his scattergun. Some shots will be quite close, while others will be farther out. A modified-choked gun works reasonably well, although the best of all is a double-barreled gun that is choked cylinder and modified to cover both close range and moderately distant shots.

Muzzleloading shotguns with choked barrels can make excellent rabbit guns if care is taken to develop appropriated loads. By far, 12-gauge guns are most commonly available. Typically, these guns shoot reasonably with about 100 grains of FFg black powder, two felt Wonder Wads over the powder followed by 1¼-ounces of lead 6s and a thin over-shot card. Overloads of powder or shot yield blown, hollow-centered, patterns. I have also used red Winchester plastic wads for 1¼-ounces of shot in some of my guns with good success. Experimentation and pattern shooting is necessary to achieve optimum results.

Ex-military muskets, or their replicas, make excellent scatterguns. The .75-caliber Brown Bess and its variants are 11 gauge, but may be loaded with 12-gauge wads. Other .69 caliber muskets, such as the U.S. Springfields, are 14-gauge and will accept, and shoot well with 16-gauge wads. In addition, wads in odd-size gauges, such as 11, 14 and 24 gauges, are available from Dixie Gun Works and other sources. I have used both plastic and fiber wads in these guns with success. As with all muzzleloaders, the barrels must be scrubbed with soap and water, but the plastic fouling from the wads comes out as soft strings.

Another type of shotgunning for rabbits is appropriately called "rabbit stomping." Here the hunter goes out in the late afternoon to hunt the thickest ground cover he can find, walks through it kicking brush piles and shooting the rabbits as they flush. Young planted pine plantations often offer excellent rabbit-hunting opportunities. The thicker the ground cover of vines and briers, the better the hunting will be. This was very close range work. As a teen, I found that few things worked better than a double-barreled .410. Very often the rabbit would only be seen for an instant and shot at ranges of 20 yards or less. With cylinder-bored muzzleloaders, charges of no. 4 shot often provide even patterns that are not too destructive at close range. Even 20-gauge muzzleloaders will suffice for this very close range work using between 60 and 70 grains of FFg black powder and 1-ounce of 6s.

During the dozen years I spent in Alaska, I often used the same techniques and .410s on snowshoe hairs. Although the snowshoes were large, they were not difficult to kill when temperatures were below zero, and I was busting them out of snow-covered willow thickets. For this hunting I also used a small set of snowshoes to keep me from having to "post-hole" my way through drifted areas.

Western jackrabbits were the ideal targets for muzzleloading rifles. They were big, commonly would be spotted sitting in their forms under some small brush and would remain still while the rifleman prepared his gun and made his shot. The big jacks were tough, but the young rabbits are fine eating. One summer when working in Utah's Henry Mountains, I enjoyed quite a few meals from young jackrabbits smothered in gravy and onions.

Muzzleloading handguns may also be used on jackrabbits, but my favorite time and place to pot rabbits with pistols is in February in the Deep South. By this time even the blackberry vines have lost their leaves, and it is possible to spot the rabbits sitting in the middle of their thorny refuges. Even when flushed, the rabbits would usually only run to the nearest thick place and sit again. By the third flush they would often sit long enough for a shot. While almost any reasonably-accurate muzzleloading handgun would do for this work my favorites were Ruger's Old Army, Traditions .32-caliber Crockett and Thompson/Center Arms' now discontinued Patriot and Scout pistols.

*A nice bag of quail with the Austin & Halleck 12-gauge bolt-action muzzleloading shotgun.*

Upland birds

Upland species of North American birds very greatly in size. They range from the diminutive, but very numerous doves, through the quails and progressively increase through members of the grouse family that culminates in the king of North American game birds, the wild turkey (Chapters 3 and 12). All are enormous fun to hunt, most are fine eating and they can all be taken with muzzleloading guns.

In some western states it is legal to shoot grouse with pistols, and I have eaten many ptarmigan and spruce grouse in Alaska and Montana that were gathered with a pistol. Mostly though, these birds are considered shotgun game and either choked or unchoked black powder shotguns can serve well to shoot a meal of quail to be served with grits and gravy or prairie chickens with bread stuffing.

Cylinder-bored guns can work very well to take close-flushing preserve-raised quail and pheasants. On wild flushing birds, particularly pheasants, some heavy loads and tight chokes will be needed to bring them down cleanly. Once in West Virginia I was hunting preserve-raised pheasants, but they were not holding for the dogs and would typically run and flush 20-yards (or so away) from the gun. By the time I got the Knight TK-2000 mounted and was tracking the birds they had nearly doubled the distance. What the birds were not aware of was that I was sending 1½-ounces of 5s after them powered by 120 grains of FFg and shot through a tight turkey choke. Every bird that got up was folded by this heavy charge.

Switching game, guns and location, I used an Austin & Halleck 12-gauge shotgun with 100 grains of black powder and 1¼-ounces of 8s fired through an improved cylinder choke to down eight consecutive quail with the furthest being killed dead at 35 yards. This gun also has interchangeable chokes. The following Spring and Fall the same gun was employed to shoot snow geese and prairie chickens.

The Knight and Austin & Halleck guns represent the most effective muzzleloading shotguns yet developed. The TK-2000 is an unabashed turkey gun capable of shooting 120 grains of FFg black powder and 2¼-ounces of shot. This very heavy shot charge shoots tight patters, but shoots low. It is best used with either the adjustable rifle sights on the gun or with a scope. For wingshooting, the iron sights make it slow to use. For more general work I remove the rear sights and load it with 1¼-ounces of shot to produce a moderately-recoiling load that patterns to the point of aim.

As received, the Austin & Halleck is a very light-weight gun and uncomfortable to shoot with anything heavier than 1 1/8-ounce loads. This is a fine combination for eastern grouse and woodcock, but the gun is too light to comfortably handle the heavy shot loads needed for waterfowling, pheasant or the heavier western grouse. I added weight to the gun by drilling a hole in the stock

*African Guinea fowl and francolin with Davide Pedersoli slug shotgun.*

and pouring it full of lead shot and by replacing the polymer ramrod with a steel rod. These steps yielded a gun that was much softer on the shoulder while handling a charge that later proved to be very effective on turkeys, prairie chickens and snow geese.

Double-barreled muzzleloading guns are something like consecutive children. They may be joined by genetics, but you are very fortunate indeed if they have the same temperaments. Similarly, one barrel of a double gun may shoot well with one load, but the other may not pattern nearly so well with the same components. The slug shotgun that I used in Africa shot round balls very well from both barrels (Chapter 8), but only one of the two non-choked barrels would shoot reasonable shot patterns. Although I had two loads in the gun, I might as well have been pouring the second barrel's load of shot on the ground. When both big and small game are in season, I often carry this gun with one barrel loaded with shot and the other with ball, making it truly a ball-and-shot gun.

Varmints

Generally considered as uneatable, what constitutes a varmint is generally up to the individual, place and common culture. When I was a boy the principal that applied was that if you were not going to eat it, you did not shoot it. Now illegal, but not then, we even dined on winter robins taken with a Daisy BB gun. Nowadays, we have varmints aplenty that we did not have when I was a boy. In Central Georgia we have coyotes and armadillos which were not present when I was growing up. These, added to our native populations of poisonous rattlesnakes, copperheads and water moccasins, now provide year-around shooting opportunities for muzzleloading hunting.

I have arrowed, crossbowed and muzzleloaded armadillos, but the most fun I ever had was taking them with a Japanese-pattern smoothbore matchlock loaded with a 50-caliber round ball. This is an unusual firearm in that it has little more than

*Japanese matchlock with armadillos.*

a stick for a buttstock that is held to the cheek when it is fired. The entire gun is mostly barrel, and looks more like an enormously long sword with a slightly bent handle than a firearm. The first step in preparing it to shoot is to blow up a hot coal on the end of a nitrated cotton cord that is three or so feet long. This cord is fixed in a cock, and when the trigger is pulled the burning cord falls into a pan of priming powder firing the gun – sometimes. As it turned out on my hunt, it took five attempts to successfully take the first armadillo with the gun and three attempts for the second.

My conclusion was, "The matchlock is an ideal gun for the person who wants the maximum hunting experience, but does not want to be bothered with cleaning much game." Besides armadillo, I have taken squirrels and rabbits with Tage, as I call the gun, and it and I still go deer hunting at least once a year. We haven't been successful yet, but someday we will.

Most of the time that I am in the woods, I am armed with a muzzleloader. During the summer months this is very likely to be a pistol. A problem with pistols is that they are very unhandy to carry in the hand. Some, like the Ruger and Thompson/Centers' Scout and Encore, have factory-made holsters. Other outsize and unusually-shaped handguns do not, and I have often sewn holsters for these guns from fabric or deer leather. Thus carried, the pistols are conveniently available to take a variety of game.

Animals that I have taken with my muzzleloading handguns include snakes, beavers and even a bobcat. The last was taken while deer hunting with a 12-gauge smoothbore pistol loaded with a patched round ball. This unlikely gun was

*Rattlesnake with CVA .50-caliber Hawken pistol*

made up by attaching a Thompson/Center muzzleloading turkey barrel to a pistol stock and installing the improved-cylinder choke. This combination offered excellent iron sights and enabled me to work up a load of 85 grains of FFg GOEX black powder to power the big ball. The bobcat was first spotted about 100 yards away. It happened to be hunting in my direction. When it stepped from behind a brush pile some 15-yards away, I shot it through the shoulder killing it instantly.

Precision shooting at long-range targets under low-light conditions requires the use of an accurate scope-sighted rifle. Coyote hunting provides useful off-season practice for deer hunters who may use the same loads, or even develop better ones, that they used the previous year to take their deer. Good optics that will keep their zeros despite power-level changes are a necessity as is a solid rest. Besides providing exciting hunts, taking an occasional coyote helps the environment and makes it more likely that a hunter will be able to make a long-range shot on big deer when the opportunity presents itself.

*Small game hunting with muzzleloaders greatly expands the potential uses of all black-powder guns. Depending on the game and state laws, muzzleloading rifles, pistols and shotguns can be used to hunt something in almost every state. Hunting small game provides an opportunity for the hunter to learn his gun/s and increases the potential for later successes on larger game species.*

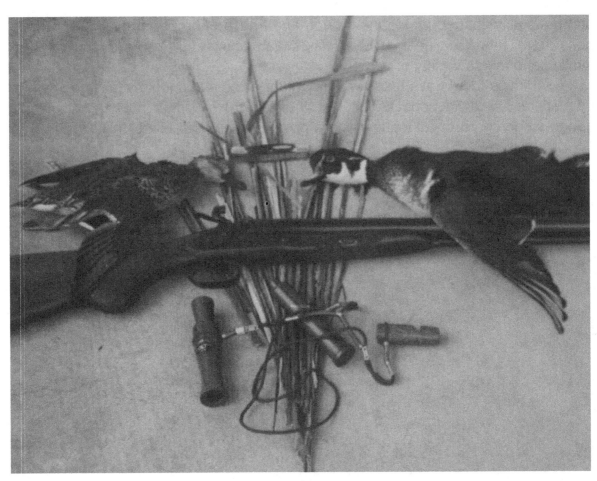

*Davide Pedersoli slug-shotgun with drake wood duck and greenwing teal – typical Central Georgia ducks.*

# Chapter 2. Waterfowling

For someone who was always fascinated by waterfowl hunting and the stories connected to it, I grew up in a miserable place. My typical Georgia hunts consist of eight attempts during which I might shoot three times and bag one wood duck or Canadian goose a season. Yet, each year finds me cutting a new path to my duck hunting spot up one arm of a mile-long pond, launching my boat and hoping for foul weather days that will coax the birds to fly at less than stratospheric heights. Even under these tough conditions, I most often use muzzleloading guns.

Fortunately, my working life in Minnesota, Alaska and Arizona exposed me to much better waterfowling opportunities, and the late Buzz Downs of Tucson taught me much about decoying and hunting ducks on Arizona's stock tanks and reservoirs. I was still using cartridge guns and went through the transition from lead to non-toxic shot with these guns.

*Photo of "Buzz" Downs with a 16-gauge Model 12 pump that I lent him after his favorite 12-gauge Model 12 featherweight was taken from his hunting truck .*

Ultimately, I sold my Winchester Model 24 double Duck Gun and Model 12 pump Duck gun and purchased a Mossberg 835 pump which would chamber the 3½-inch shell and throw enough steel shot to be effective on ducks and geese. However, this synthetically stocked aluminum-framed gun was so light, that I could not shoot full-powered loads without taking more punishment than I desired. I solved this problem by replacing the wooden rod in the magazine tube with a length of ½-inch steel re-bar wrapped in electrical tape and pouring a mix of lead shot and beeswax into the hollow buttstock which was tamped down with plastic grocery bags. These steps made the gun much kinder to shoot and consequently more effective on game. I later used a similar technique on Thompson/Center's Black Mountain Magnum 12-gauge shotgun and Austin & Halleck 12-gauge muzzleloading shotguns to tame them.

Three requirements for all varieties of waterfowling guns are that they throw enough weight of large shot to be effective on the fowl, that they are reliable enough to shoot in bad weather and that they shoot to the point of aim. If all three of these criteria are met, the guns will bring home ducks, geese and even swan year after year.

As they became available, I used steel, bismuth and HeviShot in my waterfowl loads. With bismuth shot it is not necessary to use a plastic wad to protect the bore, but bismuth usually patterns better if a plastic wad is used. Steel and HeviShot loads in plastic wads often provide better patterns, and wads are necessary to protect the bores from the abrasive effects of the hard tungsten-containing HeviShot. For the non-deforming steel and HeviShot, it is best to use modified standard chokes or chokes designed for these types of shot. The bulk HeviShot that I use is irregular, poorly sized and the pellets are not well shaped. Nonetheless, this shot penetrates well and kills effectively.

Waterfowling is best done with 10, 11 and 12 gauge muzzleloading guns. Smaller gauges will work on close-range birds, but it is the 1¼-to-1½-ounce loads of coarse shot that provide consistent kills. For 10, 11 and 12-gauged guns my first trial waterfowling load often consists of 100 grains of GEOEX FFg, a ¼-inch over powder card, two lubricated felt Wonder Wads, a plastic shot cup with a split 20-gauge fiber wad in the bottom to reduce its capacity to 1¼-ounces of no. 4 shot, a measured charge of 1¼-ounce (by volume) of HeviShot and a thin over-shot wad. This load is adjusted up or down to obtain better patterns and hit the approximate point of aim.

Different species of waterfowl require different aiming techniques. On small ducks, like teal, it is fine to aim at the body of the bird, pull ahead and shoot. When taking on the progressively larger geese and swan, aim at the vulnerable head and neck. The head on a swan is about as large as the body of a green-wing teal and behind it is a yard of neck. Hits in this area, even with relatively puny steel 4s, will likely break the neck and down the bird. HeaviShot 4s, will do an even better job. This is a better alternative to blasting at the body of these huge birds. Steel pellets hitting the body may break a wing, but will often not penetrate sufficiently to kill the bird.

Cylinder-bored muzzleloaders

Cylinder bored waterfowling guns require special treatment because the loads and hunting tactics need to be different than those used with choked guns to obtain more than haphazard results. These are close-range guns typically limited to a maximum range of 35 yards, and most of these shotguns and muskets pattern best with no. 4 or larger shot. Plastic shot cups help even out the patterns and improve results by delivering a sufficient number of shot to decisively kill the bird. Of course, a lucky hit can always bring down a duck; but the conscientious waterfowler should work towards increasing those odds.

Dense shot kills, and although steel shot may pattern well and draw feathers, the denser bismuth and HeviShot have markedly superior results – well worth the added price. Other more dense shots such as HeviSteel and tungsten-polymer or tungsten-bronze mixes are sold in loaded shotshells, but not presently in bulk. While the shot from a few $3.00 shells can be salvaged for that once-in-a-lifetime hunt for swan or sand hill cranes, these other specialty shots are very expensive to use very often.

My waterfowling with cylinder-bored guns has been an evolutionary process with load development sometimes extending over a period of years. Bess, which is a Dixie Arms Company Indian Gun, is an adaptive design of the British Brown

Bess Musket with a shortened browned barrel. Both the short barrel and less reflective finish appealed to me for waterfowling as did the fact that the gun's massive cock used a 1-inch wide flint to scrape sparks from an equally huge frizzen. With this much rock-to-metal contact I thought sparks were apt to fly and that this gun could be depended upon to fire under most conditions. It also had a stock that fit me fairly well. The first time I picked up the gun, I was looking straight down the barrel which gave me the immediate impression that I could kill ducks with it.

I ordered 11-gauge wads from Dixie Gun Works and found that 12-gauge plastic wads would easily slide down the bore. To make sure there was a gas seal I also loaded 20 grains of Cream of Wheat between a .125-inch over-powder wad and the long, pink MEC wad that was designed to hold 1¼-ounce of steel shot.

Among this gun's first trips (out was a hunt on Georgia's Oconee WMA where I had been lucky enough to draw one of five public blinds. On this particular January hunt the water had frozen around the planted corn back of the blinds, and I had to break ice to set my decoys. One drake wood duck flew over the nearest row of corn some 30-yards away. I swung on the bird and pulled the trigger. I was rewarded by the sight of the bird falling beneath the smoke cloud. Persephone, my Lab, saw the bird fall too. She bounded after the fowl, chased it down through the corn and brought it back still alive. I believed that I had hit it with the fringe of the pattern, and subsequent patterning demonstrated that this load was shooting about a foot low at 30-yards.

*A pair of banded giant Canadian geese taken on the wing with one shot when my partner flushed them from a stock pond.*

With that same gun and load I also took a pair of Canadian geese from a stock pond. I walked over the top of a dam and flushed the birds. Holding now in front of and above the lead bird, I pulled the trigger. To my surprise not only did that bird fall dead, but the other one came down wounded. My partner, shooting from across the pond, managed to finish off the second bird with multiple shots from his Remington 870. Bess' work was culminated when I took a decoying swan at Lake Mattamuskeet, North Carolina, with a single shot (Chapter 11). The huge bird was hit from beak to feet with a charge of steel 4s and killed dead in the air.

I was much less successful with similar loads fired from Davide Pedersoli's Mortimer Flintlock Fowler. This was an elegant gun with a late-period flintlock featuring a waterproof pan and roller-bearing frizzen. I could only load the 12-gauge MEC wad that I used in Bess down this gun's tight barrel by using a steel ramrod. Once I even capsized a duck boat in a shallow pond filled with freezing water while attempting to reload it. Not only this, but to secure reasonable patterns I had to reduce the shot charge to 1 1/8-ounces of shot. I did manage to kill a giant Canadian goose with this gun, but it took two shots to finish it.

A number of years later after HeviShot was introduced, I revisited this gun. This time I loaded 100 grains of GOEX FFg, a 12-gauge over-powder card, two Wonder Wads and a plastic shot cup without a gas-sealing base. This plastic cup was one of 1,000 I had purchased from Herter's decades before. These cups were designed to hold 1 5/8ths ounces of shot, and I put a cut-off section of 20-gauge wads in the base to reduce their capacity to 1¼-ounces (by volume) of the new HeviShot. This combination was easy to load and worked. Using this gun and load I shot and recovered five out of five snow geese on a spring hunt in Manitoba. Mortimer had redeemed itself, and I have since used this same load in a percussion .75-caliber musket, Davide Pedersoli 12-gauge double and Austin & Halleck's in-line shotgun.

With all of these shotguns, I have found that it is often beneficial to load the equivalent of 100 grains of GEOX FFg for the first shot and then reduce the charge by five grains for subsequent shooting. Higher pressures are generated by shooting through the fouled barrel and reducing the load delivers more consistent patterns.

One advantage of using a cylinder-bored gun is that these barrels may also be loaded with round balls and used on deer and other game. Davide Pedersoli takes advantage of this and offers a slug shotgun with a fold-up sight. I have used this gun to take a wildebeest in Africa one day and then shot birds with it the next day (Chapter 8). With my particular gun I found that one barrel shot patched round balls significantly better than the other while the other barrel preferred shot charges. This would be ideal in areas where big and small game seasons overlapped and close-range shots at either might be offered or in Africa where a big, nasty beastie might be behind the next bush.

Hunt tactics needed for cylinder-bored guns require that hunters position themselves so they can shoot the waterfowl at close range. Hunting small-water

*The author standing in flooded timber waiting for the evening flight of ducks.*

areas in blowing snow or in fog can be good. Lay-out blinds sitting in the middle of a decoy spread in cut corn or other crops can be very effective in getting geese and ducks to approach close to the guns. Flushing waterfowl from small stock tanks or waterholes can also be successful as may be walking the edges of meandering creeks. Sitting in blinds or standing in flooded timber with a few decoys in front of you can work if the birds are inclined to come in, but will require many hours of patient sitting unless weather conditions are favorable.

Areas where I have had good hunts with these cylinder-bored guns have been in the Horicon Marsh area of Wisconsin, the Manitoba farming country west of Winnipeg and less frequently at Lake Mattamuskeet, North Carolina. The latter is a fine place to take a swan with your musket, but duck shooting is a sometimes affair (Chapter 11).

Choked muzzleloaders

Adding some choke to the muzzleloader's barrel increases the gun's effective range by about 10 yards and evens out the patterns. Some cautions paradoxically come as too much choke can be deleterious because non-compressible loads of steel or HeviShot can seriously damage the delicate barrel threads on interchangable chokes or the game may be too close for tight chokes to be of much use.

On one goose hunt at the Horicon Marsh, the other hunters were using full-choked semiautomatic waterfowl guns, but the honkers were coming right over our heads. I had better luck on a shot-for-shot basis with my cylinder-bored 1842 British musket than they did with the cartridge guns. Their guns shot so tight that they were punching holes in the air around these very close birds or, if they hit them, were practically blowing them to pieces.

The almost universally used screw-in chokes are of enormous help in more nearly fitting the gun to existing hunting conditions, and a double barrel with two choke options is an excellent selection for the black-powder waterfowler. As always with any shotgun, assume nothing. Pattern the gun with the hunting load and believe the patterns. Some choked barrels may shoot far off the point of aim. In this case try another choke until one is found that is more nearly compatible with your gun. It is also not unusual for one barrel of a double gun to shoot to a different point than the other. A person skilled in choke grinding can correct this situation by preferentially relieving one side of the choke to redirect the shot charge.

When cleaning the gun after each shooting session, don't forget to remove the chokes and clean and relubricate the threads before reinstalling them. Failing to do this can result in corrosion damage to these nearly hair-thin threads.

Some excellent examples of choked muzzleloaders using sidelock actions are Davide Pedersoli's 12 and 10-gauge Turkey and Trap guns which are sold by Cabela's and Thompson/Center Arms' now discontinued Black Mountain Magnum 12-gauge shotgun.

In-line shotguns

More in-line shotguns of either bolt-action or drop-barrel persuasions are being offered to the black-powder hunter each year. The unfortunate aspect of this is that these guns do not have a very large market. It is easy for the bean-counters to persuade management to discontinue an otherwise excellent gun because its limited sales potential does not appear to justify development and advertising costs. Thompson/Center Arms' excellent System 1 with interchangeable rifle and shotgun barrels succumbed to this line of reasoning.

Although the first in-line shotguns used no. 11 caps for ignition, later versions progressed to the more powerful musket caps and still more potent 209 primers. Knight's excellent TK-2000 offers the option of also purchasing bolts and breech plugs that will allow all three ignition systems to be used as well as their Full Plastic Jacket holders for the 209 primers which makes these guns nearly weatherproof. Another advantage is that the Full Plastic Jackets are much easier to handle with gloves or cold fingers than any previous ignition system.

Thompson/Center's most recent shotgun offering is part of their Encore system which uses the same frame to mount pistol, rifle, shotgun, muzzleloading or rifle barrels and forends. This 209-primed muzzleloading shotgun barrel is very short, only 24-inches, and the gun has considerable recoil and devastating muzzle

*The author with a swan taken with heavy loads from the iron-sighted Knight TK-2000 shotgun held here by his friend Billy Krantz.*

blast when used with a 1¼-ounce waterfowl load. As a specialized turkey gun where only one shot may be fired every week or so, it works as designed; but it does not do well as a potential waterfowler. I pity the other guys in the blind if someone cuts loose with one of these guns. With another 6-inches of barrel and some added weight it might have some possibilities, but not at present.

After removing the rear sights and filing down the front sight to a block, the Knight TK-2000 did pattern to the point of aim with a charge of 100-grains of FFg and a plastic wad containing 1¼-ounces of shot. Loaded with HeviShot this combination was very effective on ducks and geese. This gun's swan was taken while the gun was still wearing all its sights and with a load of 1½-ounces of HeviShot. Waterfowling with an iron-sighted shotgun is a slow affair for a methodical shooter. By the time I pulled ahead of the huge swan, aligned the sights and fired, the bird was said to be a full 40-yards away. My blind partners had already decided that I had passed on the bird because I was standing in a strained position with one foot on the seat while attempting to shoot over the brush wired to the back of the blind.

As a result of my shot I had blood flowing from my nose, a gash in my thumb and my glasses were knocked off. I was pushed off my one-footed stance on the seat by the gun's heavy recoil. The swan hit the water about the same time

I collided with the front of the blind. When I examined the bird, I found that the shot charge had caught the swan in the head and neck with all the shot hitting in what appeared to be a 10-inch group. Not counting the exit holes, no less than 17 shot struck the bird. If I were going to pass shoot geese or sand hill cranes from a more stable shooting position, I have no doubt that this load would kill as well as any cartridge gun.

Austin & Halleck's 12-gauge shotgun is an adaptation of their 50-caliber bolt-action rifle. The action is the same but the barrel is considerably lighter making it nearly ideal for the grouse hunter, but too light for waterfowling. Despite the usual opinion that bolt-action shotguns are poorly balanced, the A&H swings and handles well. On my gun I increased the weight to 7¼-pounds by boring a hole in the maple stock and adding a charge of lead shot and substituting a solid steel rod for the plastic ramrod. After transferring the fittings from the original rod to my replacement, I had a serviceable ramrod and had added some needed weight to the front end. The result was a very well balanced gun that was a pleasure to shoot.

This gun proved itself on a spring snow goose hunt in Manitoba where it took five blue and snow geese with as many shots. I also used the same choke to take a turkey and an interchangeable improved-cylinder choke to shoot quail. The gun impressed me as being a well designed, nice handling and good-shooting shotgun. One added attraction is its full ventilated rib which makes this gun's sight picture identical to that of most modern cartridge shotguns.

Break-open muzzleloading shotgun designs, looking much like the break-open single shot cartridge shotguns from which they were derived, are now being sold by several makers. Rossi, North American Arms, CVA, MDM and Traditions all offer break-open muzzleloading rifles with interchangeable barrels, and it does not take too much engineering to also offer a muzzleloading shotgun barrel. The temptation is to make these guns as light as possible as turkey guns are carried much, but shot little. However, waterfowlers need weight to tame the recoil from repetitive shots. Substituting a solid steel rod purchased from a hardware store for a ramrod and refitting the ends combined with adding some lead shot to the buttstock can make these guns much more user friendly.

Taking up the challenge of black-powder waterfowling requires a time commitment to develop good loads. The loading information that I have given will provide a good start, but is generalized. Proceed cautiously, pattern the gun; and soon some loads will emerge that will shoot well enough to bag close-range ducks. More experimentation with different powder charges, wads and shot will give improved results and extend killing range. Each shot is a custom load, and may be designed to provide optimum results for a given type of waterfowl: be they swift-flying teal or a plodding swan.

Handle what few muzzleloading shotguns that can be found in retail stores, and if a gun has obvious appeal purchase it along with the accessories needed to make it shoot. Market realities are that any particular gun may only be offered for a year or a few years. This is no real problem as a well-maintained gun will last for generations.

Shotgun pairings with individual shooters is a very person thing. Should you be fortunate enough to find a muzzleloading shotgun that shoots and kills well, let not blood, friendship or money part this gun from you. No amount of money will ever be able to replace that gun once it is gone. Another gun, even of exactly the same model, may never shoot quite as well.

As the majority of these new muzzleloading shotguns offer only a single shot, it often takes a little mental transition for cartridge-gun users to learn to wait for an optimum shot opportunity. Occasionally, my hunts have become one-shot affairs because I left a vital shooting component at home and arrived at the blind with my only load being the one that I had preloaded the night before. At home my shots at ducks and geese are so uncommon that this is not a particular disadvantage.

On one hunt with a Thompson/Center Black Mountain Magnum sidelock, I found when I was on the pond that my shooting bag with all my reloading stuff was still on the kitchen table. Drat! Fortunately, I still had a musket primer in my hunting coat, so I would have at least one shot.

Once I have a hunt plan I try to stick with it. On this day I paddled my Stealth boat into the weeds on a channel in hopes that a pair of geese that I had seen would return along the same flight path that they used the previous day. I sat, waited and fumed at my stupidity; but nothing happened. At any rate, I would wait until at least 10:00 O'clock before I pulled out. Finally, "Honk, honk, honk," from up the creek. They were on their way, but coming from the opposite direction. Changing positions and kneeling in the bottom of the boat I waited. They came, swung in front of me and I had a shot opportunity at about 25 yards. I picked out the lead goose, swung ahead of its head and fired. Well hit, it tumbled into the water on the other side of the brush and expired. Luckily, no follow-up shot was necessary.

I have often said, "If there is anything that takes more junk to do that black-powder waterfowling I don't want to do it." Things that must generally be had are the various licenses and stamps, boat, motor, trailer, paddles, life preservers, Coast Guard required signals, motor, gas, oil, plug, decoys, spare line, anchor, rope, extra weights, camo, lunch, drinks, wet-weather gear, treats for dog, dog vest, calls, knife, boat tools, spare sparkplug, duck tape, boat boots, bailing cup as well as the powder, shot, wads and primers needed to service the gun. If nothing else, it is a good mental and physical exercise getting all this "stuff" to where it needs to be in the pre-dawn darkness.

In spite of everything, and the generally miserable weather, is all of this fun?

"Yes. It is."

"Does muzzleloading simultaneously increase the fun and aggravation quotients?"

"Yes. It does."

After fighting the weather and overcoming the innate difficulties of duck hunting, taking any legal bird with a black-powder gun measurably increases the satisfaction and pride of the entire experience. Not only this, your efforts provide a direct link between you and your hunting companions to a time when waterfowl darkened the skies and hunters shot until they either had enough or had exhausted their supplies.

There may be some good natured banter along the lines of your simultaneously killing and smoking your ducks, but you will have earned the right to take justifiable pride in successfully waterfowling in "the old style."

Thoughts on individual guns

*The author with a CVA Trapper and swan walking out from a blind on North Carolina's Bodie Island.*

The now discontinued CVA Trapper 12-gauge single-barreled percussion muzzleloader is a light-weight gun with a "European modified" choke. The gun has a thin wooden stock that is uncomfortable to shoot with anything but a mild load of powder, 60-80 grains, and 1 1/8-ounce of shot. Used with steel shot it was a marginal killer on ducks and swan, except at extremely close range. A swan hit with a load of bismuth shot had to be run down and clubbed with the gun.

Davide Pedersoil's Mortimer 12-gauge flintlock is a well-balanced fowler. This handsome gun worked best with a load that consisted of 100 grains of GOEX FFg and 1 ½-ounces of HeviShot (by weight, 1¼-ounce by volume) contained in a plastic wad. This gun has a very tight cylinder-bored 12-gauge barrel. It is possible to use a steel ramrod to force some wads down the bore, but the preferred method is to employ an over powder card, a plastic shot cup for 1 5/8ths ounces of shot with a bit of plastic bagging stuffed in its base to take up the excess room, a load of 1½-ounces of no. 4 HeviShot and a thin over-shot wad. So loaded this gun is effective on close-range snow geese and other fowl, but patterns thin very quickly beyond 30 yards. During cleaning, the vent-hole liner must be removed to keep wet residues from accumulating in the gun's subchamber.

I have shot an original Indian-made back-action .69-caliber (14-gauge) Brunswick smoothbore musket imported by Atlanta Cutlery from the Royal Armory of Nepal (Chapter 12). After considerable cleaning, replacing some parts and reproofing, this gun was taken out for small game and waterfowl hunting. With a load of 80 grains of FFg and 1 1/8-ounces of HeviShot contained in a 16-gauge shot cup, the 14 gauge was effective enough to take quail, pheasant and a turkey. In this load I use 14-gauge card and fiber wads and a 30-grain charge of Cream of Wheat between the powder and the plastic wad. The old war horse had a very hard life, and I have since retired the gun and given it to a friend. Atlanta Cutlery does not recommend that its collector's guns be shot, and none should be fired without careful examination and reproofing.

Davide Pedersoli's 12-gauge double-barreled percussion Ball and Shot gun (photo at head of chapter) has a flip-up sight and is designed for use with either a patched round ball or shot. It is effective at close range with a load of 100 grains of FFg and 1 ¼-ounces of bismuth or HeviShot contained in a red Winchester AA wad. This load functions reasonably well with the wad loaded directly over the powder, but shoots tighter patterns if a card wad, filler wad, Cream of Wheat and plastic wad system is used. I usually start out with the more complex load and use only the wads when the shooting gets heavy. When loading, load one barrel at the time and drop the ramrod down the other barrel to keep from double charging a barrel.

Dixie Gun Works' .75-caliber (11-gauge) Indian Gun is a shortened, browned version of the Brown Bess flintlock musket used during the Revolutionary War. This gun is robust, sparks well and kills with authority. I load 100 grains of FFg for the first shot and then reduce the load to 95 grains for subsequent shots. Then comes a thick over- powder card, a ½-inch 11-gauge fiber wad, 20 grains by volume of Cream of Wheat, a plastic shot cup with 1¼-ounce of bismuth or HeviShot and a thin 11-gauge over shot card. This gun kills very well with this load.

Another Nepalese relic is the Indian Pattern 1842 .75-caliber musket originally made for the British East India Company. This gun is the percussion version of the flintlock Brown Bess, and I use the same load described above. Thus far this gun has killed squirrels, pheasant and geese, made a clean kill on a giant Canadian goose at 30-yards, and taken a swan.

Thompson/Center Arm's Mountain Magnum 12-gauge shotgun has interchangeable chokes and works well after it had been modified by adding about two pounds of lead shot and melted beeswax to the hollow buttstock to balance the otherwise barrel-heavy gun. Using the improved-cylinder choke, 100 grains of FFg and the card-fiber-Cream-of-Wheat wad column, with a shot cup and 1¼-ounce loads of HeviShot, this gun makes a very effective waterfowler. I would like a few inches more barrel length, but this gun is short enough to work well in a duck blind or for shooting in tight areas.

Knight's TK-2000 can take a charge of 120 grains of FFg and 2¼ ounces of shot. It has a set of adjustable iron sights so that the gun can be sighted in for turkey shooting. Aligning these sights is too slow for any but the most deliberate aiming at high-flying birds. For ordinary duck and goose hunting I removed the rear sight and filed down the front sight base to make the gun a more natural pointer. After taking these steps, I found that the gun shot best with 100 grains of FFg and 1 ¼ ounces of no. 4 HeviShot contained in a plastic shot cup. This load rocks geese at a full 40 yards with most shot completely penetrating the body.

Although a bolt action, the now discontinued Austin&Halleck's 12-gauge shotgun is fast and has excellent handling characteristics. As received it weighed only about 6 pounds and was too light for a full 1¼-ounce 12-gauge load. If grouse hunting or turkey hunting in steep country, the lack of weight is welcome, but not for waterfowling when more shots opportunities will be offered. To increase this gun's weight I added sufficient lead shot to the stock and made up a steel ramrod to bring the gun's total weight to 7½-pounds. These additions to both ends of the gun preserved its excellent balance and made the gun much more shooter friendly. I discovered that its modified screw-in choke worked best with a load of 100 grains of Hodgdon's TrippleSeven powder, an over powder card, and a shot cup with 1½ ounces of HeviShot with plastic bag filler as described for the Mortimer flintlock.

The firing pins on the A&H guns are tiny and the bolt spring is weak. On both the shotgun and rifle versions of this gun I had to add washers behind the springs to develop sufficient bolt velocity to reliably fire the hard Remington 209 primers. In one case it was necessary to drill the relatively soft stainless steel bolt and installed a hardened steel firing pin. Thus modified both the rifle and shotgun became reliable performers.

Some lessons learned

A. Don't overload your cylinder-bored shotguns. Almost without exception shotguns ranging from 14-10 gauge will shot best with charges of between 80-110 grains of FFg or Pyrodex RS and 1 1/8-1 ¼-ounces of shot. Overloading with powder or shot will result in hollow-centered patterns.

B. In developing a load it is more important to have one that hits to the point of aim, rather than attempting to launch a maximum charge of shot that may pattern well, but strike low on the target. To successfully shoot ducks you will often have to get on the bird and shoot – right now. In such cases you don't have time to remember to hold 2-feet high on a crossing shot to center the duck in your pattern.

C. Use plastic wads and shot cups to protect the barrel from abrasion and improve the pattern. There will be some plastic residue remaining in the barrel, but this scrubs out easily with Dawn dishwashing detergent and water. Yes, this is non-traditional, but it is an absolute necessity to keep the hard HeviShot from abrading the barrel. Bismuth is softer and may be used without a plastic wad. In some guns barrel steels are hard enough to be able to take steel shot without using a protective shot cup.

D. A complex wad column with multiple components is helpful in keeping the barrel clean enough to shoot all day and to improve patterns. Very often I will load something like the following: powder, a thick nearly ¼-inch hard card wad of proper gauge. This wad has been lubricated slightly with Thompson/Center's Bore Butter and the powder "crunched" when loaded. The over-powder wad is followed by a ½-inch fiber wad that is also lubricated with Bore Butter. If the plastic wad has a concave cup at the bottom, I load 30 grains of granulated Cream of Wheat to help expand the shot cup in the typically somewhat oversize barrel i.e. using a 12-gauge plastic wad in an 11-gauge barrel. Following this I drop the shot charge, which is retained in the barrel by an over-shot wad (if not too dry a square of folded corn leaf works well). Do not use newspaper as wadding unless you want to set the woods or your blind on fire.

E. Hands down, HeviShot even in relatively low-velocity loads of about 900 fps., is so much more effective than anything else that it is worth the price. Loose HeviShot may be purchased from Cabala's for about $75 for 7 pounds. I most often buy no. 4s, which kills as well as, or better, than lead 2s. Many of the shot will be out of round, have tits attached or be over or under sized. Density is more important than looks, and this shot patterns well and KILLS. Many times I have had no. 4 HeviShot completely penetrate a goose at 30 yards. The look of tungsten-containing-heavier-than-lead shot is improving and Winchester now loads its turkey loads with perfectly round tungsten-containing shot. However, this shot is not yet available for bulk purchase.

F. Choked muzzle-loading shotguns enable a hunter to shoot a heavier load and kill at longer ranges; but the problem is that these heavier loads most often pattern well below the point of aim.

G. Choked tubes and choked barrels can be altered to change the strike of the pattern. This process will open the choke slightly, but careful work can move the pattern a foot or so at 40 yards. The metal is removed on the side of the barrel and in the direction that you want to direct the charge of the shot.

H. With HeviShot use no 4s for most shooting and an improved cylinder or a weak modified choke.

I. If you are shooting a percussion gun and the gun's hammer is large enough to work with them, musket caps greatly ease reloading, as the larger caps are much easier to handle with cold fingers. If you must use no. 11s, the best are CCI's Magnum no. 11 caps. The most efficient way to handle these tiny caps is with an in-line capper. Fumbling with a box in the dark and cold is a great way to dump its entire contents in the bottom of your blind.

J. If dampened, caps can be dried by setting them out in a warm room and their effectiveness will be fully restored.

K. For waterfowling 10 and 11-gauge cylinder-bored guns are preferred over 12 and smaller gauges. With proper chokes (usually improved cylinder to modified), 12-gauge guns are satisfactory. The smallest gauge shotgun that can be recommended for even close-range ducks over decoys is the 14-gauge (.69-caliber smoothbore).

L. The killing shot on swan and geese is to aim for that enormously long head and neck. Bismuth and HeviShot 4s can break a swan's neck at 30 yards, but a shooter cannot put enough steel shot into the body of a swan to cleanly kill the bird. Steel -shot shooters who take body shots most often have to break a wing and chase down the bird to collect their swan.

M. I have left the most important thing for last. You absolutely must pattern your muzzleloading shotgun to have any idea of how far you load will kill or even tell if you have a load that will half-way shoot. If you don't have the time to do this, then don't use muzzleloading scatterguns until you do. Some muzzleloading shotguns will kill as well as, or even better than, many cartridge guns; but you must pattern your loads.

Where do I get the stuff?

Dixie Gun Works of Union City, Tennessee, is the best supplier of all gauges of fiber and felt wads. Cabala's now sells bagged HevyShot as well as plastic shotgun wads for common cartridge gauges. Many of the larger sporting goods stores sell components for 12-gauge shotguns that will work in muzzleloaders.

It is more trouble to use a black-powder shotgun, but go smoke yourself a fowl. You will be very pleased that you did.

*I have likely published more on black-powder shotgunning with more muzzleloaders than any other writer in recent decades. My shotgunning articles have appeared in Muzzle Blasts, Blackpowder Hunting as well as in many more general-interest outdoor publications. On the largest of all fowl, an ostrich, I elected to use a black-powder rifle instead of a scattergun. It is ironic that the shot that I took was in shotgun range, had I taken an appropriate black-powder shotgun.*

*Sharon Henson turkey hunting with a .50-caliber, CVA Youth Model side-lock muzzleloader. Muzzleloading rifles may be used in many states, such as Georgia.*

## *Chapter 3. Turkey hunting*

If the waterfowlers' rationality can be questioned for going through all they do for the chance to bring home a few ounces of duck meat, turkey hunters are even closer to losing their sanity. Each time a hunter goes out in the pre-dawn light, he knows that the odds are stacked against him. The probabilities are that he will not even see a legal bird, or if he does, that he will not have a shot. This is particularly aggravating since domestic turkeys don't have the sense that God gave geese, but the cagy wild toms are all-to-often able to outfox us.

I, and millions of other hunters, have turkey fever every spring. Each year bring renewed hope that this year I will be able to take my three Georgia toms with whichever hunting tools I happen to use that year. These might include muzzleloading rifles (legal in Georgia and some other states), muzzleloading shotguns (legal in all states), muzzleloading pistol (legal in some states) or maybe even a crossbow (legal in some states) or bow (legal in all states). Not only are Georgians blessed with a mid-March to mid-May turkey season, but all I have to do to hunt them is to walk out my back door and turn right. One fall I counted 21 toms in my food plot, and surely I should have been able to get one with my muzzleloading shotgun the following spring. Right?

Shotguns

Not necessarily so. That year, after some dozen hunts, I finally bagged my home-grown turkey with my designated "turkey killer of the year," an Austin & Halleck 12-gauge bolt-action muzzleloading shotgun. I used the same load of 100 grains of TrippleSeven, .125 over shot card, 20-grains of Cream of Wheat filler, plastic shot cup, 1½-ounces of HeviShot 4s, and a thin over-shot card that I had worked up for duck, goose and swan hunting.

After the first 10 hunts, I drew the charge, cleaned and reloaded the gun. From a mechanical point of view, a hunter can get away with keeping a clean and freshly loaded gun for several days with a charge in the barrel. If the gun has been shot, even if only once, the charge must be fired or drawn and the gun cleaned and freshly reloaded to keep the barrel from corroding. Even so, black powder is hydroscopic. In a humid climate it will absorb atmospheric water and corrode a chamber if left in a gun barrel for weeks.

As I live alone and am religious about never having a capped gun in the house, I keep my unfired muzzleloading guns loaded during turkey season. Anyone with a spouse, kids or friends trafficking through his home would be taking a grave safety risk by doing the same. To remind me which guns are loaded, I

***Austin&Halleck 12-gauge bolt-action shotgun with a Georgia turkey.***

leave the ramrod in the barrel so that it sticks out. I also make sure that there is not a charge in a barrel, before I reload any gun.

On my 13th hunt the Austin & Halleck and I were successful in taking a tom from my food plot (Chapter 12). Persistence, rather than skill, was apparently the most important factor.

The previous year on the same food plot at very nearly the same location I was hunting with a Brunswick smoothbore .69-caliber (14-gauge) musket which came to me via Nepal. This was an original gun purchased and sold by Atlanta Cutlery and imported into this country as an historical relic. This gun had apparently been made in an Indian arsenal as it had only Indian-character markings. Many of these guns were hard used, stored badly and unsafe to shoot. My gun was uncleaned and nonfunctional when it was given to me. I cleaned the gun, replaced a cracked mainspring, and got it ready to hunt (Chapter 12).

After re-proofing the old gun, I cautiously worked up a load of 80 grains of GOEX FFg, a 14-gauge over-powder wad from Dixie Gun Works, 20 grains of Cream of Wheat filler and a 16-gauge plastic Remington wad loaded with 1 1/8-ounce of Knight's hard lead no. 5s. After patterning the gun, I found that my sure-kill range was about 25 yards. This musket, as might be suspected, used a musket cap which provided prompt ignition to the powder charge.

On the third day of Georgia's season, I sat on my food plot. Dawn came and there were no turkey noises. Finally at 10:00 AM I saw a long-bearded tom approaching my decoys. I was 10-yards back in some young pines with the Brunswick smoothbore across my lap. The tom never strutted, but did turn away, temporally blocking its vision. I raised the gun, and when its head appeared between the rows of small pines, I fired. The bird, taken at 20-steps, went down hard.

I consider the 16-gauge as about the lower limit of practicality for turkey hunting with a muzzleloading shotgun. With a choked barrel and loaded with 6s, a 20-gauge might be used for 20-yard birds, but the small amount of shot rapidly runs out of pattern density and energy for sure kills. To be sure, 20-gauge guns can, and have, killed turkeys, but the muzzleloading version with only 1-ounce or less of shot puts the added burden on the hunter to wait until the bird is very close.

Something to watch for with muzzleloading shotguns is when a gun that is carried for some hours, the constant back-and-forth movement of the shot can cause the over-shot card to become dislodged and the shot to dribble out of the barrel. Checking the load with the ramrod might not do any good if a plastic wad was used because the ramrod end will contact the ends of the wad petals and stand at the "loaded" height above the muzzle. When such a load is fired, there will be more smoke, less recoil and a running turkey unless fortune smiles and the bird's neck is broken by the plastic wad. Check your loads periodically even if it means drawing a wad with a worm, pouring out the shot and putting down a newly-measured load of shot and following the shot with a new pair of tight-fitting over-shot wads.

Field expedients that I have used for over-shot wads include folded sections of half-dry corn leaves and cut-out pieces of Styrofoam drinking cups.

Rifles

*Remington Model 700 ML with a Georgia turkey*

I am an equal opportunity turkey slayer and have taken toms with .36, .45, .50 and .54 caliber muzzleloading rifles. Most of these have been percussion sidelocks, but they also included a Markesbery in-line and a scope-mounted Remington Model 700 ML. Except for the Remington in which I used a solid copper saboted bullet, the other guns were loaded with round balls.

It is generally unappreciated that patched round balls can be shot with a high degree of accuracy from barrels with as fast a twist as 1:22, provided that the powder charges are reduced to around 55 grains in .45 and .50-caliber rifles. In fact, most muzzleloading pistols employ a fast twist to eek maximum accuracy out of the round-ball load.

My first efforts to take a turkey with an in-line rifle was with a Markesbery .45-caliber gun which I loaded with 50 grains of FFg and a patched round ball. This scope-sighted gun shot with good accuracy, and I had visions of being able to take a turkey at 100 yards with this outfit. After more hunts than seemed really necessary, I had my opportunity when a group of jakes came to water at a tiny water-filled basin at a reclaimed kaolin mine. The jakes, as teen-agers of any species often are, were constantly moving which prompted me to rush an 80-yard shot. One of the birds was more or less sideways and I tried for it. Taking aim, I squeezed the trigger. The gun fired, feathers flew, and so did all the turkeys. When

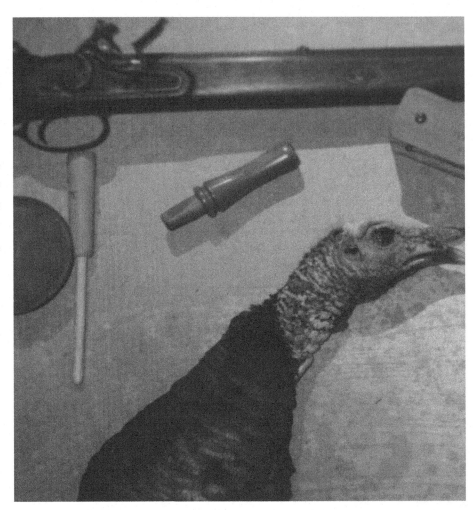

*A turkey that was taken with the Lyman Deerstalker flintlock and the turkey and crow calls used on that hunt.*

I approached, I found a number of cut breast feathers and the jake's beard on the ground. The ball had trimmed the front of the breast, cut off the beard and the bird had escaped minus a few feathers and a scrap of skin, but was otherwise no worse for the event. This is as close to "catch and release" turkey hunting as I have ever come.

On another occasion, I was using a Lyman .50-caliber flintlock Deerstalker rifle. This gun featured a 24-inch barrel and would not completely burn heavy charges. In this gun I loaded 85 grains of GOEX FFg behind a patched round ball. I was set up on a steep hillside overlooking the swampy bottom of what was aptly named Reedy Creek. I called, and a turkey answered. This one sounded like it would come to me, and I could hear it approach as it made its way up through the dry leaves. I saw the tips of its tail feathers first and swung my gun into position to rest on my knee. When the bird came into view it was in full strut. I aimed the peep and blade front sight at the center of the breast and pulled the trigger. Again, both feathers and the turkey flew.

Looking at the site where the turkey was shot, I found breast feathers and cut wing feathers. Apparently the turkey had been swinging its body from side to side as it strutted, and my ball had passed through the meat on one side of the breast and exited the bird cutting off some flight feathers on the wing, but never reaching the bird's vitals. I spent the remainder of the afternoon attempting to relocate that bird. I flushed it from the top of a tall pine and it flew deep into the swampy bottom. From this event I learned to either shoot for the neck or head of an oncoming bird or wait until it turns to offer a shot through the fist-sized area of the turkey that contains its organs.

Writers often receive guns for a limited period of time, and it was time for me to kill something with the Remington 700 ML. This now-discontinued muzzleloader used the Remington bolt and trigger assembly combined with a muzzleloading barrel and breech. It was also pre-drilled for mounting a scope. Although I had tried several times to find a deer to shoot with it, I had not been successful. I had sighted in the gun with a Remington's solid copper saboted hollow-pointed bullet for my deer hunts and would use the same load on the turkey.

At this time I had not established any food plots. My best opportunity was to call in some turkeys from their roost trees on a nearby pond and hopefully coax one to close enough for a shot. I had tried this tactic before and had a mad hen stand 7-feet away and talk to me. Dawn came, and I called. There were responses from three roosted toms and I shut up. After they had all flown down I called again. There were a couple of gobbles, but nothing sounded close. The toms were servicing their hens and paid no attention to this apparent hen that had gone up the side of the hill.

Attempting to close the distance was impossible. My only chance was to wait until the hens started coming up the bank to begin feeding. Perhaps a tom will be trailing the hen. About 40-yards away I could see one hen's head and then another. A line of hens was working up the slope. I had only a narrow shot window through the low brush. I watched. Hen, hen, hen, TOM. As soon as his red waddles cleared the brush I started my trigger squeeze. This time fate, chance, my hunt plan and my scope sights were all appropriately aligned. The turkey was killed instantly. The hollow-pointed copper bullet had created a ragged 2-inch cavity through the toms' lungs and back. I had my bird and the Model 700 was sent back with a turkey feather in its box.

Seen in retrospect, the scope helped considerably in permitting me to pick out a shooting lane and to also positively identify a tom. The deer load of two 50-grain Pyrodex Pellets and nearly a 300-grain bullet was more powerful than necessary for turkeys, but it sure worked.

I once bought a .45-caliber flintlock Kentucky rifle from Navy Arms Co. with the expressed idea of having a gun that I could use to take small game, turkeys, hogs and close-range deer. Using 85 grains of GOEX FFg, a Wonder Wad and dose of Cream of Wheat with a canvas-patched round ball, I had a load with which I killed squirrels and two deer. When spring arrived, it was time to take Cantank, as I had named the gun, turkey hunting.

To help cover the shiny brass work that made the gun so attractive to my wife, I purchased a slip-on elastic gun stock with a camo print. It was necessary to cut a portion of it away to allow the flintlock to function, but the sock effectively hid the shiny brass. Although this rifle has gone on several hunts, I have yet to pull its trigger on a tom. I am sure that I will someday. If I can take seven squirrels with seven shots, I can certainly kill a turkey with it when one presents itself.

Smaller caliber rifles in .32 and .36 caliber can also be used for shooting turkeys. One very handy gun is Thompson/Center Arms' now discontinued Senica rifle which was made with interchangeable .45 and .36 caliber rifles. This little gun was relatively short barreled, light weight and had set triggers. Once when carrying the .36-caliber rifle I spotted a flock of turkeys emerging from the fog. Both they and me were alerted at about the same instant. I threw up the gun, picked out the tom, set the trigger and fired. With the explosive sound of the shot, the entire flock flew. I had hit the bird, but apparently in a spot that was not immediately fatal. Returning to the house, I let Demeter, my Lab, out of the pen and she and I returned. Employing her super-sharp sense of smell, she quickly found the tom 30-yards away in some thick brush. This was another occasion where one of my dogs found game animals that might have otherwise been lost.

Before using a muzzleloading rifle for turkey hunting, consult the regulations to insure that it is legal. As the foregoing has demonstrated, almost any rifle will serve.

I have often been asked why not load shot in a .58-caliber rifle instead of a round ball and use this gun to kill a turkey. The answer is that the shot will spin out of a rifled barrel, and the pattern will be so dispersed that the chances of achieving killing hits at ranges of more than a few yards are slim. There have been historical oddities such as rifled barreled guns with screw on chokes for stabilizing shot charges, but none are in common use today.

Handguns

Turkey hunting with muzzleloading pistols is permitted in some states, and one practitioner of this art is Jan Chase who has taken these birds with two different styles of percussion revolvers as well as a percussion dueling pistol. For each years hunt she sets a new challenge for herself which included a World Slam including the Osceola, Eastern, Rio Grande, Gould's, Merriam's and Ocellated turkeys plus a hybred – all taken in 1995. Following this, black powder hunting consumed more of her interests, and she took a double slam in 58 days with muzzleloaders and handguns in 1998. She followed this in 2002 with a Grand Slam with a Davide Pedersoli dueling pistol.

Jan's activities during 2006 including recovering from a serious back injury that resulted from a 1994 fall from a tree stand. Although her leg, which was broken in numerous places and required the installation of pins and braces while it healed, had recovered; more problems developed with her back. Sixteen surgeries followed and an electrical implant was put in her spine which allowed her to start

*Jan Chase and turkey taken with a replica Remington muzzleloading revolver.*

the 2006 season in a wheelchair. She quickly recovered and was able to complete the season on foot. The plucky lady continued her hunts with the aid of her husband Tim and managed to take three of the four-bird slam during the Spring. That Fall they completed their quest for a black-powder revolver slam by taking a Merriam's, marking Chase's 12th Grand Slam.

Although she did take her Osceola with a Colt-pattern replica pistol, her favored revolver is a Remington replica made by Davide Pedersoli. Husband Tim worked up loads and sighting information for the gun in 10-yard increments out to 40 yards. His best load was 26-grains of BlackMag3 powder and a Speer 143-grain .454 round ball, a Wonder Wad and a with a thick glob of Thompson/Center's Bore Butter lubricant over the ball. This load just fills the chamber, and Jan says that it gives 1½-inch groups at 50-yards. This is a remarkable group for a percussion revolver. With this pistol and load she took her Eastern with a 40-yard shot through the neck.

Because of their light weight and small sight radiuses, pistols are much more difficult to shoot than rifles and shotguns. My preference in muzzleloading revolvers is for good sights over authenticity, and I like Ruger's Old Army with its excellent adjustable sights. The Ruger has sufficient power to take on turkeys, deer and hogs with well-placed shots, most percussion revolvers are too puny for hog and deer hunting. Steel-framed revolvers using Hodgdon's TripleSeven powder may be used for close-range hunting.

Pyrodex pellets are also available for muzzleloading revolvers. These are convenient and make reloading a snap by eliminating the need to measure charges for each chamber. They require the same through cleaning with soap and water that is needed when black powder or Hodgdon's new TripleSeven black-powder substitute is used.

It is common for replica percussion revolvers to have one of more chambers that shoot to a different point of aim. A good practice is to mark the nipple of the worst-shooting chamber and carry the hammer down on this chamber's uncapped nipple. Carrying with the hammer down on an empty chamber is an absolute requirement for single-action pistols, including the percussion varieties. Since one chamber must be empty, it might as well be the one that produces the worst groups. A small dot of red nail polish applied to the base of the nipple is all that is needed to identify this chamber, or one can even leaving the nipple off that chamber.

Since only a single shot opportunity is usually offered on a turkey hunt, single shot pistols may also be used. Some good candidates are Thompson/Center Arms' Encore 209X50 muzzleloading and Scout muzzleloading pistols and Traditions' Buckhunter Pro. These guns may be fitted with scopes. Almost any other gun that can accurately shoot a .44 or .45-caliber ball and 30-to-40 grains of black powder will serve. Shot placement, as always, is more important than power, and scopes and crisp triggers are helpful in making good hits.

Primitive hunting methods

Turkeys are tough to hunt, and those who enjoy using primitive means to take these magnificent fowl have their work cut out for them. Toms can be bagged with homemade calls and cylinder-bored shotguns, but the potential for success can be considerably enhanced by also applying some modern knowledge about turkey behavior.

Call makers Harold Knight and David Hale combined their nearly 80 years of turkey hunting experiences to find a way to simply explain why turkeys act differently in different states at the same time of year and why their behaviors change during some states' long seasons.

"From hunting them in different states during different times of the year, you would never know they were the same birds," Hale explained. "About every 15 days turkeys change the way they act and the way they respond to calls. It is a whole new deal every 15 days. Harold and I have identified five different transition periods and plotted the dates when these transitions typically occur in different parts of the country. A hunter can take our Gobbler Guide and check the dates for his hunt in another state and find out how the turkeys will be acting, how to hunt them and what calls to use."

How does this help the hunter who wants to use primitive techniques?

There is one transition period, "Period 3," when the hens are nesting that tom turkeys are responsive to almost any kind of call. The sexed-up toms want to

46

breed hens, but most of the hens are hiding in their well-concealed nests incubating their eggs. The last thing the hens want to do is to attract potential predators by bringing attention to themselves. During this time the desperate toms will respond to almost anything that sounds like a willing hen.

Give or take five days to make allowances for unusual weather, this magic period occurs in the Southern part of the U.S. from April 4-10, in the nation's midsection from April 19-May 3, and in the Northern part of the country from May 3-May 18. States with one-week or 10-day turkey seasons often try to have the seasons during these optimum periods, but hunters in states with a two-month season, like Georgia's, will see most of the five transitions.

One year, on a bet, I called up a tom by rattling stones in a tin can. The loud noise and rhythm of my simulated gobble brought a long-bearded tom running. He apparently thought that another tom had taken his hens and came ready to fight. I have had even better success with wing bone and slate calls which mimic "hen talk." I made these calls using parts of turkeys that I had shot and things that I picked up on my travels through the woods.

Making your own wing-bone calls

Wing bone calls are probably what come to most hunters' minds when someone speaks of a primitive turkey call. Originally developed by the American Indians, the classic wing bone call uses three sections of bone taken from the wing bones of a wild hen turkey. A problem is that in many states it is illegal to shoot hens, and the only available wing bones from wild birds come from buzzard-picked road kills and other less than savory sources – none of which I care to put in my mouth.

I make my wing-bone calls from two bones from a wing of a tom turkey. These give a somewhat lower pitch than hen-bone calls when the end of the largest bone is cut off to give a trumpet-shaped opening. If the bone end is drilled with three holes instead of being cut off, a higher-pitched yelp can be obtained. In addition, the sound can be further modulated by cupping the hand over the end of the call.

Just as the human arm has a single large bone in the upper portion and two smaller bones between the elbow and wrist, the turkey wing has the same three bones. In making a wing-bone call from a hen, all three bones are used. The ends of all bones are cut off, the bones boiled and the marrow removed. The flatish end of the smaller bone is used as the mouthpiece. It slides into the other "forearm" bone which slips into the larger wing bone. The friction-fit bones will not be air tight, but a mix of flour paste and wetted newsprint can be used to seal the joints. It is best to let the bones cure for 30-days before applying the cement to allow for shrinkage.

The bones from a tom's wing are larger, and I use only the two "forearm" bones, instead of all three. As before, the bone ends are cut off, the bones boiled, the marrow removed, and the bones allowed to cure.  The flat-shaped end of the smallest bone is used as the mouthpiece and slid inside the smaller cut end of the other "forearm" bone. As wings come in pairs, two calls can be made from one turkey. One call can be made with an open "trumpet" mouth and the other drilled with three 1/8-inch holes to have two different sounding calls.

Yelps can be made with the tom wing-bone call by holding the tip of the call with the thumb and forefinger, inserting the mouthpiece between the lips and sucking in sharply. The less bone that is held between the lips the higher the pitch; but a point is reached when the amount of lip on the call is insufficient to prevent air leakage. Using the fingers as a stop helps keep the tone of the call the same throughout the calling sequence. A key-key-run can be done with a hen wing-bone call, but the tom calls cannot reach these high notes. They are best used for yelps. A fast series of yelps simulating cutting by an old hen will sometimes provoke an answering gobble. No turkey call works every time.

Homemade slate calls

A shell from the common Southern box turtle makes a good sound chamber for a slate call. I am fond of turtles and would not kill a turtle for this purpose. I use dead turtles' shells I find in the woods. There is no reason why the shell of any turtle could not be used so long as it is small enough to be conveniently carried - a size of about 2½-3 inches seems to work best.

Old fragments of roofing slate are fairly abundant and these splits can be shaped with a file so there are sufficient contact points (four is ideal) to hold the slate firmly in the shell. Friction alone is usually sufficient to keep the slate in place, but a little glue can also be used. If you wish to avoid using glue, drill a hole through the slate and shell and secure the slate to the shell with a rawhide thong that is knotted at both ends. Twisting the knot on the back of the shell applies more tension, but be careful not to break the brittle slate.

Shaping the slate is done with a file. Surface irregularities can be removed by filing the slate and using medium-grit sandpaper to finish the striking surface. Sand the slate in one direction so that the striker will have a constant-friction surface capable of yielding repeatable tones. Higher-pitched calls will result from dragging the striker across the slate's surface close to its edges and lower-pitched calls from working the striker nearer the center of the slate.

A traditional striker can be made by using a hickory stick about seven inches long and 3/8ths-inch in diameter. Two inches of the end of the stick is inserted into a 3-inch section of dried corncob. The end of the stick is rounded, but not pointed, and roughened with medium-grit sandpaper. Although the slate surface itself can be used in wet weather, tonal quality decreases dramatically if the wooden striker is damp or wet. Synthetic strikers are available that will give the call an all-weather capability.

Although crude-appearing, the turtle-shell slate call can give as good a result as any commercial slate call. The tonal range is excellent, the call has good volume and it is rugged enough to be constantly used. I prefer my turtle-shell slate call to any others for dry-weather use. As the particular shell I used was sun-bleached white by the time I recovered it, I painted it with a black and green pattern to help conceal it. Fresher shells will already be naturally camouflaged.

Turkey wings

One item that goes with me on every hunt is the tip of a dried turkey wing. The wing section contains ten primary feathers that are about 18-inches long. This wing is used to simulate the fly-down noise of a hen and to make "scratching" sounds in the leaves.

The only preparation needed is to take the wings of a freshly killed turkey and clip off the tips holding the last primary feathers and store it in a warm, dry place for six weeks. A little salt or borax on the cut surface will keep insects away until the wings have cured. If wetted they need to be dried out again to prevent decomposition.

Provided that you know how to time your hunt, the effective range of your gun, where your patterns are hitting and your calls; your dream of taking a turkey using strictly primitive black powder guns and techniques can be realized.

*There are turkey killers and there are turkey hunters, and I suspect that I belong more to the " turkey killer" category. I have called in birds, but I am as likely to take one late in the season by "foul ambush" as by using more traditional methods. Nonetheless, I have managed to place more than a few turkey-hunting and turkey-cooking articles in publicatiolns over the years. Perhaps one of the more unusual was "Airboating for smokepole turkeys" in the September, 2003, issue of Airboat World.*

*Cantank, a Navy Arms Company .45-caliber Kentucky rifle and its second deer.*

## *Chapter 4. Deer hunting*

Deer hunting has evolved into a nearly all-year undertaking. Spring and summer are spent getting food plots ready, scouting, buying new four-wheelers, putting up deer stands and watching the newest crop of deer videos and TV programs. For the sake of variety some of these shows will even feature hunting with the newest in-line muzzleloaders made by their sponsors. The Fall is spent searching for that elusive trophy buck and perhaps taking a doe or two for the freezer. Then follows, hopefully, a trip to the taxidermist and a brief recovery period before the deer hunting cycle repeats itself.

Even before most states adopted separate muzzleloading seasons or offered management hunts where only muzzleloading guns were allowed, there were some hunters who preferentially used the old-time guns and replicas to take their game. They were interested in recapturing the spirit of past times when game was nearly limitless and the forests were all their own. Yet another faction was interest in bagging trophy animals for the black-powder categories newly established by hunting organizations such as the Safari Club. The most rapid expansion of muzzleloading hunting came as state-by-state special seasons were adopted that allowed deer and other big game animals to be hunted with black-powder guns prior to regular gun seasons. Hunters quickly saw this as a way to spend more time in the woods when they were less crowded and the game was not nearly so spooked.

Concurrent with this increased level of muzzleloading activity, simpler to use in-line guns became more popular. Some of these guns looked much like the cartridge rifles hunters were accustomed to using, were easier to manipulate and became more reliable performers in all weather conditions. In states where they were allowed scopes could be attached. The only disadvantages that muzzleloaders had over cartridge guns was that, for most shooters, their range was limited to about 100 yards, they had only a single shot and they still needed to be cleaned just as carefully as traditional guns.

Change-ups for black-powder deer

Some claim, with a degree of validity, that the modern scope-mounted in-line muzzleloader is too much like a modern rifle, is nearly as capable, and taking a deer with these guns has lost something of the mystique and drama of hunting with more primitive black-powder guns. The common link between the new in lines with the older side-lock guns is that the majority of designs offer only one shot and take longer to ready for a second shot than semiautomatic, pump, lever, bolt-action or even single-shot cartridge rifles.

This is what Thompson/Center Arms' former CEO Greg Ritz was fond of calling, "the single-shot challenge" which is the necessity of making a precise, deadly hit to take full advantage with what is likely to be the hunter's only shooting opportunity. This is an added burden on the hunter, and being restricted to one shot is the most that some muzzleloading hunters are willing to accept; much less fiddling with loose powder, patched balls and percussion caps.

I am not a traditional black-powder purest, and any year might find me having used an in-line rifle, a flintlock fowler, percussion musket and a muzzleloading revolver. Among the more unusual animals that I have taken was a 10-foot alligator that was finished off with a percussion pistol after it had been arrowed with a crossbow. Using older-technology black-powder guns necessitates taking more time to learn the gun, how it shoots, what loads it likes and how to, and not to, manipulate the gun in the field. Using side-lock guns is more trouble, requires more skill and provides a considerable increase in satisfaction when a deer is taken with these more primitive shooting systems, even if it takes several trips to finally succeed.

Why do it? Shouldn't the ultimate aim of the deer hunter be to shoot as many deer as possible in the shortest possible time?

That is the approach that usually holds sway in the mind of a young hunter on his first hunts. The urge to shoot more and kill more is very strong. Usually after a few years when the hunter has taken a number of deer, the quality of the trophy assumes more importance than the number of deer killed. It is during this period that "the hunt" rather than "the kill" becomes more important. To have hunted hard, skillfully and well emerges as a satisfying end in itself. The taking of game is

*CVA .50-caliber Hawken pistol.*

reduced in importance; although bringing home an animal is irrefutable proof of success.

To have prepared well, hunted hard and failed is no shame; but to have prepared well, hunted hard and succeeded is an emotionally glorious outcome. To have taken a deer with a primitive, short-range hunting tool elevates both the quality of the hunting experience and the intrinsic value of the outcome. The most lasting trophies of the hunt are not those on the wall, but are those in the mind that are cemented in memory by a mortar mixed from trial, failure, unanticipated events and ultimate success.

Close-range techniques

Handgunning has always had a special place in my heart. I enjoy the convenience of carrying a comparatively short-barreled gun and appreciate the challenge of being able to effectively use a pistol to take game. In the military and as a civilian shooter in my 20s and 30s, I spent hundreds of hours on the range with a variety of centerfire and rimfire pistols. I never shot cartridge handguns competitively, as I found it more challenging to attempt to better my last score than against others. I instantly appreciated the hunting potential of Thompson/Center Arms' Contender single-shot pistol with interchangeable barrels and purchased no. 1618 while I was a graduate student in Alaska along with .22 LR, .22 Jet and .44-

Remington Magnum barrels.

Even before this I had been shooting replica percussion and flintlock pistols, but it was not until the purchase of the Thompson/Center Scout in 1995 that I owned a muzzleloading handgun that was sufficiently powerful to reliably take deer-sized game. In the meantime "old 1618" had mechanically failed, and T/C replaced it with a new gun under their lifetime warranty policy. I also bought a 14-inch .44-Remington Magnum barrel for the new pistol.

"What better way to compare the capabilities of these guns than by taking them on a deer hunt to the National Seashore on Georgia's Cumberland Island and killing deer with each of them," I thought. This hunt is restricted to handguns, black-powder guns and bows. This was also a hunt where multiple deer and hogs could be taken. I applied for the 1996 hunt, was successfully drawn and proceeded to work up loads for both pistols.

Complications arose. Because of a delay in approving the National Budget, there was doubt until I received a call from a park ranger two days before the hunt that it would actually take place. I quickly packed and got my camping gear ready for a three-day wilderness adventure. In addition, Georgia was experiencing the coldest January in 80 years. Temperatures were expected to drop to nearly 0 degrees on the coast. From my years of living in Alaska, I had the good cold-weather gear and an Arctic-weight sleeping bag that many of my fellow Georgians had no reason to possess.

My late wife Thresa had considerable trepidations about my going on the trip, but I could not be persuaded to stay at home as this hunt had now taken on the status of a quest. It was going to be a hard hunt because it was in a designated Wilderness Area and hunters had to walk to their stands and drag their animals back to camp. These conditions were slightly mitigated in that the camp had running water and a walk-in cooler for the deer and hogs.

Thirty-mile-an-hour winds combined with the cold froze the salt-water marsh

*Bess, a Dixie Arms Works Indian Gun is a derivation of the Brown Bess musket of the Revolutionary war.*

surrounding the island. These conditions were so brutal than a number of hunters never left camp. First with the muzzleloading Scout and the following day with the .44 Magnum Contender, I took two nearly identical deer. Both were killed with a single shot, and the 85 grains of FFg and 370-grain Thompson/Center .50-caliber MaxiBall fired from the Scout appeared to put the deer down more decisively than the .44 Mag. The 30-odd hunters on the island only killed seven deer, and I had shot two of them. I was very pleased with my successes.

As the majority of muzzleloading rifles are single-shot guns, it is often prudent to also take a single-shot pistol as a back-up gun. One that I often carry is a CVA .50 caliber percussion Hawken with a replacement musket-cap nipple. The replacement musket-size nipple uses a larger cap that is easier-to-manipulate than the tiny no. 11 in addition to providing a little extra velocity from the 65-grains of FFg fired from the 10-inch barrel. For faster loading and increased penetration I also use a 245-grain Buffalo Bullet BallEt which is a hollow-based Minie ball bullet that requires no patching.

This pistol is carried in a homemade bag holster sewn from deer hide so that it can accompany me as I climb into tree stands or pursue game on foot. There are three types of opportunities where this gun may be effectively employed. 1. The first is when a deer walks up under the stand and the hunter cannot turn around in the stand to use his rifle; however, the deer can be taken with a one-hand-held pistol. 2. A second chance is provided by having a pistol when a hunter misses his first shot, but the confused deer comes closer to the stand while it attempts to identify the source of danger. 3. Finishing a crippled deer is a typical use of a "back-up" handgun, and the CVA pistol has worked very effectively to kill deer that were down, but not dead.

Once my brother-in-law wounded a deer. He and his hunting buddy had searched for it all morning without success. I brought my canine deer recovery team, Demeter, Saladin and Ursus, to assist. After trailing another deer, I brought them back and put them on fresh blood. This trail led through the creek bottom and a series of beaver ponds that were partly blocked by blown-down trees.

I clamored over, through and around the trees, briers and cane thickets in a vain attempt to keep up with the dogs. Once I sunk nearly to my knees in a pond. Ultimately, the dogs stopped and began barking. I knew that they had the deer at bay. My first sight of the dogs revealed Saladin standing to one side and barking, Ursus on the other; but my view of the deer was completely obscured by the root ball of a blown-down oak.

After climbing up on ball of the tree and standing very unsteadily on two flexing roots, I had my first view of the deer. The buck was laying with its hindquarters in the water, but its head was still up while it attempted to hook Demeter who was standing in front of its nose. I dared not use the buckshot-loaded muzzleloading 12-gauge that I carried for fear of ricocheting shot hitting the dogs. I put the shotgun down and pulled out the pistol. The deer's head was swaying from side to side, and I was moving up and down on the springy roots.

Lining up the sights with the neck I slowly squeezed the trigger and got off a shot when the sights and the deer's spine were in alignment.

When I shot, the deer's head immediately fell. The shot had penetrated the spine and ended the animal's struggle. At least this was one deer that would not go to the coyotes and buzzards. I rested for a few seconds before giving a call to my brother-in-law and his buddy who had been following the chase in the comparatively clear woods above the swamp.

"Hey fellows. My dogs found this deer. I killed it. Now you come down here and get it!"

The load I used in the CVA pistol is reasonably powerful, but must be employed at close range, preferably within 25 yards. Even at this comparatively close distance the bullet strikes 6-inches high. Knowing the precise range and holding well under the target are vital to making a successful shot.

Smoothbores

"Bess," which is a .75-caliber derivation of the British flintlock Brown Bess musket from the Revolutionary War period, is one of my favorite guns. If I were going to be buried with a gun, I would like Bess by my side. Equally effective with ball or shot, Bess has taken deer, geese, swan and small game as well as several deer.

Among the deer hunts that I have had with Bess, the first hunt was the most memorable. As usual, I had changed my stand location from where I had been sitting a few days before. This time I wanted to hunt from a tall pine in an area of rank second-growth shrubs and saplings. This stand was selected because I would have chances at deer walking down a field road about 35-yards away or moving along intersecting game trails that passed near the pine.

Before dawn I had walked about a mile from my house pushing my Tom Cat tree stand, gun and pack on my homemade "deer barrow" that I had built from a section of aluminum ladder and the wheel from a kiddy bike. Arriving within 500 yards of my tree, I dismounted my equipment, put it on my back, walked to the pine and climbed the tree. Access to the hunt area had been successfully completed, and I was up my tree at daylight.

My hunt plan was that I would attempt to ambush a deer as it came up from the pond a quarter-mile below to feed on acorns dropping from the upland oaks. It was starting to be a long sit by 10 O'clock, and although I had brought a cushion, I was starting to get somewhat butt sore. Finally, I spotted a bit of a deer's back as it walked down a trail. Swinging the gun around to that side of the tree, I prepared for the shot. I had checked the prime in the pan about 30 minutes before, so I knew that the charge of FFFFg was dry and properly positioned. I held the trigger and pulled back on the massive cock. When the hammer was all the way to the rear, I released the trigger and eased the cock forward until it caught on the sear's full-cock notch. The only sound heard as the gun was readied for the shot was that of the deer's hooves softly striking the ground.

I cheeked the gun firmly and lined up the front sight on the deer. When the sight's blade pointed between the top of the shoulder and the spine I pulled the trigger. There was no delay. The gun fired instantaneously. The doe collapsed on the spot, and quickly breathed its last.

A rush of emotions came over me. Bess had done very well, and I was proud of her. I was pleased with myself that the hunt plan had successfully come together and had honest pride in my accomplishment. Before too long I had the stand, Bess and the deer strapped on the deer barrow for the return trip home.

To prove that my success with Bess was not an accident, I needed to take another deer with the musket. My opportunity came when I hunted on Tom Veal's property in another county. I had unsuccessfully turkey hunted there the previous spring and found an outcrop of jasper exposed in a creek. Native Americans had also found this outcrop centuries before and the ground was littered with small flint chips where they had fashioned their arrow, spear and knife blades.

"Wouldn't it be a neat to take a piece of this jasper, chip a flint from it, put it in Bess and kill a deer using a flint fashioned from a rock taken from the same property?"

That concept was irresistible. I took a fist-sized hunk of jasper home, spalled off some flakes and made three rough flints that would fit the cock's jaws. As long as the flint was sharp it sparked well, but after only a few hits on the frizzen it needed re-knapping to renew the edge. Before the hunt, I carefully fitted a fresh homemade flint, wrapped it in leather and screwed it tightly in the cock taking care that it was positioned just back of the frizzen's face so that it would throw the maximum number of sparks as it scraped the steel.

I spent the previous night at Tom's house so that we could get off to a pre-dawn start. I had already set my climbing stand in a tree overlooking a deer crossing near a small waterfall. The evening before I had passed a shot on a buck that was standing 50-yards away. It was partly obscured by trees at what I considered the maximum sure-kill range for the gun, and I did not want to risk wounding it. Tom had plenty of deer, and I was sure that I would see another in a better shooting position if I were patient.

Almost as if it were following a script, a deer walked on a trail across the creek. Cocking the gun, I wondered if I had not been foolish to attempt to shoot this deer with an untried flint. This jasper was not as strong as the English flints and my hand-crafted flint might break when it hit the frizzen and not fire the gun.

Perhaps ignition was slightly slower than it would have been with an English flint, but the gun fired. The deer ran five steps, crashed into a tree and went down. Success is sweet. This was certainly not a huge buck, but it ate very well.

As might be reasonably concluded from these four examples, rifled pistols and smoothbore muskets or shotguns (with round balls) can be very effective. The restraints are that the game must be close which means that some shots must be passed that could have easily been made with a muzzleloading rifle.

Hunting with sidelock rifles

Sidelocks are muzzleloaders that "look like muzzleloaders." These are the guns of David Crockett, Lewis and Clark and the Civil War. They were effective hunting tools in their day and were capable of, and did, kill all of the world's game animals including bison and elephant. The key to successfully hunting with these guns was to use the appropriate weight of ball or bullet for the game. A .45-caliber ball when used in connection with dogs and horses was considered to be about right for deer hunting. Going upscale to .69-caliber was appropriate for point-blank shots on buffalo, and the new-fangled Minie-ball rifles in .58-caliber enabled the hunter to stand off at 70 yards or so and still obtain decisive kills.

These guns have limited range because of the steep trajectories of their slow-moving balls and primitive "iron" sights. With much practice, hits on game at 200 yards can be obtained, but the majority of hunters do well to restrict their shots to within 100 yards. Hunting close is no problem in the thick woods where I hunt in Eastern North America. Almost all of my shots are closer than 50 yards and many are within 20 yards. If I have to kill a deer at 100 yards I can by holding some 6-inches over my target to drop the bullet into the heart-lung area.

*CVA's .50 caliber double rifle is a gun that is suitable only for round ball or short elongate bullets.*

Flintlock rifles

Navy Arms Company's Val Forgett helped me select "Cantank,"(see photo at chapter head) which is a .45-caliber flintlock Kentucky rifle that I have previously mentioned in Chapter 3. I considered this rifle a traditionally styled gun that I could use for primitive flintlock matches at National Muzzleloading Rifle Association (NMLRA) events in addition to hunting small game, turkey, hogs and deer.

My first efforts in preparing the new gun was to thoroughly clean the barrel of all its shipping grease and smooth up the lock. Working on the lock required that I use fitted screwdrivers to remove all of the lock parts from the lockplate, inspect them under a hand lens for any metallic burrs and removing these burrs with a very fine stone. This work considerably improved the trigger pull and lock speed by removing these sources of mechanical friction. The frizzen and related components on the outside of the lock worked fine, although I did polish a rough edge on the frizzen spring that was scratching the lockplate.

Shooting came next. I had considerable problems discovering a good-shooting load that was potent enough to kill deer. As this gun's sights are adjusted by filing down the front sight for elevation and drifting the rear sight for windage, I wanted to develop one load and use it on everything. Ultimately, I succeeded with a charge of 85 grains of FFg, 20 grains of Cream of Wheat, and a lubricated pillow-tiking patch wrapped around a .440 round ball. After winning or placing in several events at a club match and taking seven squirrels without a miss, I deemed the gun and load ready for deer hunting.

While walking back from a morning's hunt with this gun I heard the sound of running hooves. I turned and saw two deer running at top speed directly towards me. I pulled up the gun and shot between the lead doe's feet. Five feet from the muzzle of the now empty gun, both deer made quick right-angle turns off the trail. These deer was so panicked, that I believe they would have run into me if I had not fired.

Shooting Cantank's two deer was fairly uneventful. Both were taken from tree stands. One was at about 20 yards and the other was at around 35. Both deer were drilled through the shoulder and both lungs. In one case the ball passed through the deer and exited through the rib cage on the opposite side and on the other deer it remained under the skin after punching through both shoulder blades. Although chewed up from its passage through bone, the ball retained most of its mass. This is exactly the performance that might be expected from .45-caliber round balls on does that weighted 80-90 pounds. Heavy deer are best shot with .50-caliber guns. They can be killed with .45-caliber round balls, but the shots are best restricted to the lung area to avoid going through the shoulder.

Lyman's Deerstalker is a different-appearing flintlock. It has a shorter, .50-caliber barrel; and I soon replaced the original coil-spring lock with an L&R leaf-spring lock made by Bob Cox in Sumpter, South Carolina. These replacement locks will fit a variety of guns including those made or imported by Thompson/Center, CVA, Traditions and Navy Arms as well as old and new style Lyman flintlocks. These RPL (replacement) locks are faster and more reliable than the original factory locks. They require hand polishing, bluing and some inletting because they use different internal designs to provide better functional characteristics.

After-market sights are one of Lyman's traditional products and, naturally enough, they drilled and tapped their guns to accept the company's adjustable peep sights. I installed these on my gun and was very happy with the result. Because of the Deerstalker's 24-inch barrel I only used 85 grains of FFg black powder which, at 50 yards, shot Thompson/Center MaxiBalls and round balls into about the same hole.

I then took the gun to Roger Kicklighter's Shoulder Bone stand on the Tip Top property and waited. At about 10 O'clock, a deer walked along the edge of a small clearing to my left and it appeared that it would also cross a road more nearly straight ahead of me. The noise that the deer made walking through the woods effectively covered the slight noise that I made as I shifted position to shoot. When the deer stepped into the road and its shoulder offered a clear shot I fired.

For a time I could see glimpses of the deer as it ran down the creek valley. I reloaded the gun and waited for a half-hour. I found that the deer had stumbled into the creek, attempted to climb the bank, made it out of the water and died. The 370-grain MaxiBall had passed through the 100-pound doe and was not

*Paul Presley with his first muzzleloader deer shot with a CVA Hawkin rifle that the author built from a kit.*

recovered. From the spot where it was hit to where it was found, the deer had covered about 50 yards – typical for a lung-shot deer.

Percussion Rifles

Double-barreled percussion rifles appealed to many Africa hunters during the mid-1800s. Then and now, doubles were expensive to make and regulate so that both barrels would shoot to the same point of aim. This is hard enough with cartridge guns that used precise amounts of powder and fixed-weight bullets and becomes very difficult when the powder charges and bullet weights may vary within wide limits.

Desire drives markets, and CVA had sufficient requests for a double-barreled rifle to have one made in Spain to serve the U.S. markets. CVA also had an added burden in that their guns at the time were aimed at low-end markets in line with their slogan, "the best gun for the buck." The result was that the CVA double rifle was built with locks using small components, barrels that were less than first quality and the gun was stocked with undistinguished wood.

To help resolve the problem of regulating the barrels, one muzzle was fixed in a steel collar and adjustment was provided for the other by Allen screws that used differential pressures on the muzzle to direct the strike of the bullet. After trying a series of projectiles, it became apparent that this gun preferred patched round balls, but it shot them very high. To make the gun shoot more nearly to the point of aim, I installed a tall front sight that helped to correct the problem so that one barrel, at least, could be sighted to hit dead on target.

Shooting the gun demonstrated that changing the powder charges caused the bullets to impact at different points. While it would be very desirable to use the same load for both barrels, I was prepared to use different loads if it was necessary to achieve optimum results rather than trying to remember that I would have to aim 4-inches low to hit approximately the same point with the other barrel. I had more problems regulating double guns in chapters 15 and 20.

With loads generating more recoil than was produced with 85 grains of FFg and a round ball, doubling became a problem. The result of the nearly simultaneous firings of both barrels was that the ball from the second barrel hit wildly off the target. The way to prevent this from happening was not to cock and cap the second barrel until after I had fired the first. Although slower that successively pulling two triggers, this was still a faster and quieter operation than reloading a barrel. The double gun, even with its management difficulties, still had significant advantages over a single-barreled gun.

By the time I had the gun ready for hunting, I had an invitation to hunt Tip Top Farm that had recently been purchased by friend Roger Kicklighter. I chose to put my climbing stand in a tree overlooking a creek bottom. Trees were scattered throughout the bottom, but there was much more brush on the hill slopes. After a four-hour sit a buck moved through the distant brush about 50-yards away. I shot my right barrel and the deer went down. I had apparently hit it in the spine.

As the deer was still moving, I cocked and shot the other barrel. This also hit the deer, but it was still not dead. Reloading both barrels, I used these to finally kill the animal. In the meantime, Roger was getting concerned that I had shot two or more deer. He was somewhat relieved that I had only killed one, despite taking four balls to do it.

What does this mean? The deer probably would have died within five minutes from the combination of the spine shot that immobilized its hindquarters and the second shot which hit both lungs. Rather than watching it suffer, I accelerated the process with two more bullets. Lung shots take time to work, and it may take several minutes before a lung-shot animal dies during which time it may run over 100 yards.

Although the proceeding two hunts happened to be with slow-twist (one turn in 66-inches) side-lock percussion guns that used round balls, many replica rifles use faster twist (one turn in 45-inches) barrels that can stabilize round balls or elongated bullets. One of my favorite fast-twist percussion sidelock guns is the CVA St. Louis Hawken .50-caliber rifle that I built from a kit. Although I did not have the skills or patience to build a percussion gun from scratch, I had no problem getting the wood finished on this gun and otherwise getting it ready to shoot.

The result was a gun that was not as heavy as the original Hawken rifle, but still retained sufficient barrel weight to hang steadily on target and a good set triggers. The rifle shot very well with a conical hollow based bullet that CVA first called the DeerSlayer and now known as the BuckSlayer. This 300-grain projectile propelled by 85 grains of FFg shot very effectively. Among its first trips was one to Georgia's Ossabaw island where it took a walking hog at 85 yards with an off-hand shot.

Because this gun is of a traditional pattern, I often loan it to others who want to try hunts with black-powder rifles. Another of my hunting buddies, Paul Presley, took his first muzzleloaded deer with this rifle with a clean neck shot at 30 yards. He actually muffed his first shot when the delicate set trigger discharged the gun before he was lined up on the animal. Set triggers take some getting use to, but once mastered they are great aids to off-hand shooting. The trick is to successfully use them the finger does not even go into the trigger guard until the instant that the hunter is ready to fire the shot. With set triggers, a delicate touch does the job, rather than the three-to-five pound pulls that are standard on factory cartridge rifles.

As with any new type of hunting tool, it takes practice to insure that you are really "masters of the gun," before taking it out to kill game. This requires more effort at the range than taking a gun out of a box, buying a box of cartridges and shooting a few tin cans to see if it is sighted in.

*Only in books does an author have the opportunity to discuss hunting with so many guns. With most articles it is more like, "get gun, hunt, kill and write it up"*

*with one gun and hunt being a stand-alone article. For those who miss this*
*approach I have individual hunts in chapters 10-20. Both writing styles have their*
*validity, but side-by-side comparisons of hunting guns need the space provided in*
*a book-length work.*

When this book was in its final stages I found two percussion revolvers, the Ruger Old Army and Cabela's Buffalo made by Pietta in Italy, that would develop the 500 ft. lbs. of energy that is gerenrally considered required for hunting deer and hogs when loaded with Hodgdon's TripleSeven powder. Both of these guns have steel frames and adjustable sights which give them increasing appeal as serious hunting pistols. For details see the 2013 Gun Digest Annual and my YouTube videos.

These are heavy loads best used in all steel solid-framed guns. Do not use in brass-framed percussion revolvers and only cautiously in Colt-pattern guns.

*Photo of Tony Knight with Ohio factory building in background with sign from original store in Missouri and in cart hunting on his own property.*

## Chapter 5. Hunting with Tony Knight

However far a hunter may roam, there is always something special about coming home and hunting with family and friends. Occasionally others may join the family group as I was privileged to do when I hunted with Tony Knight in Missouri.

"Of course, we will be hunting with my muzzleloaders even though the hunt will be during the regular gun season," Tony said. I was not surprised or inconvenienced by this statement since I hunt almost exclusively with muzzleloaders. "And by the way, we are trying to let our bucks grow, and we only shoot 8-pointers or better."

Northern Missouri in the area around Kirkville is becoming noted for big deer, and Tony's statement about size limitations did not bother me much. Over the years I have taken a large number of deer, but I have never killed a buck that I would mount. I had much rather take a fat doe for the freezer than the 8-pointer that might be trailing her.

If an enormous buck stood in front of my deer stand as if to say, "Shoot me," I certainly would; but the measure of its antlers, in my mind, would not make this deer more or less worthy than a similar-sized doe. Besides, the does eat better, and most landowners are very pleased to let a visitor help adjust the sex ratio by shooting does.

What I traveled from Georgia to Missouri to do was not so much to deer hunt, but to spend time with one of the pioneers of modern muzzleloading. If we had been shooting chipmunks and talking about the measurements of trophy incisors rather than about 140 and 150-class whitetails, that would have done as well.

Tony had a couple of Knight's new guns waiting for me – a .45-caliber Disc Extreme and a TK-2000 12-gauge shotgun which both employ the new Full Plastic Jacket 209-primer ignition system. This top-hat shaped piece of plastic contains the 209 primer and makes a weather-tight seal on Knight's one-piece nipple-breech plug. Combined with a tightly fitting saboted bullet or a plastic shot cup filled with shot, this is as nearly a water-proof load as can be managed with today's muzzleloading technology.

This system is being used on all Knight guns produced in 2003, including the entry-priced American Knight, which was formerly only offered with no. 11 percussion-cap priming. Kits containing new bolts and breech pugs are available to convert older disc or striker-fired Knight rifles and shotguns to the new system.

Why abandon no. 11 and musket cap ignition systems that have been successfully used since the 1840s in favor of a 209-primer system that must have a plastic do-whickey to fire? To answer that question you have to understand Tony Knight's vision of modern-day muzzleloading.

*Knight's first shop in northern Missouri .*

Where Knight rifles began

The red-painted tin-sided building with the hand-lettered sign "Knight's Guns and Archery Services" was a not too-auspicious new start for the then out-of-work railroad employee who had been downsized out of his 20-year job. Arguing against success was the fact that his business was located 20-miles from the nearest town and 8-miles from the nearest paved road.

As it turned out something more important was happening in this shop other than retailing a few guns and bows. Someone with an inventive mind, machining skills and a strong entrepreneurial spirit was listing to what disgruntled black-powder hunters were saying about the poor performance of their traditional muzzleloading rifles during hunts in Colorado and other states.

Tony was hearing things like, "I had this enormous elk in my sights at 40 yards and all I got when I pulled the trigger was loud pop." Or, "I could never get close enough to risk a shot. I would never trust that rifle beyond 100 yards, and here was this huge deer at 150. I just could not shoot, and I never saw the deer again." And worst of all, "I hit the deer, found blood; but we never recovered it."

Statements like this were transformed into the equivalent of engineering problems in Tony's mind and resulted in a stoutly-built, striker-fired muzzleloader that could take large charges of powder and propel strongly-constructed muzzleloading bullets at higher velocities for reliable expansion and deep penetration on western game.

Of course, there were influences from other people. Striker-fired and bolt action muzzleloaders mostly built up on cartridge-gun bolt actions had been seen occasionally at Friendship even before World War II and more commonly afterwards. Roy Weatherby was touting the benefits of higher-velocity hunting loads and magnum performance. Bullet makers like Nosler and Barnes were making premium-quality bullets that out-preformed factory soft-points and were more reliable than early protected-point designs. There was even a new black-powder substitute powder in development that would ultimately become the Pyrodex pellets that are so often used today.

Tony's genius was to take these separate ideas, combine them in the design of a modern scoped rifle, and make a muzzleloading hunting rifle that was more accurate, reliable, weatherproof and a more effective game killer than any previous commercial front-loading rifle. Improvements were made in all these categories with the original MK-85. As technology developed and the muzzleloading hunter was appreciating the advantages of better ignition provided by 209 primers and Pyrodex pellets, the rifle's design was changed to incorporate the new technologies.

A list of the considerations that were driving the development of the new generation of in-line muzzleloaders would include the following: magnum-muzzleloading performance, reliability, accuracy, weather resistance, ease of use, accuracy, customer-directed options and competitive pricing. The significance of all of the above is obvious with the exception of customer-directed options. Because Tony came from a background of custom gunmaking, he always felt that a customer should be able to get the best rifle he could afford with the features he desired.

For decades Knight rifles maintained a custom shop to accommodate special needs and also offers high-end-priced guns for those who want the best in-line muzzleloaders. The newest version at the time was the Master Hunter Disc Extreme which now incorporates a cryogenically-treated barrel for maximum accuracy, is supplied with both wood and synthetic stocks and has a new bolt that does not require tools to disassemble.

To return to the original question, "Why incorporate Full Plastic Jacket 209-ignition throughout the entire line of guns?" Said simply, Tony's designs are performance driven. The question in Tony's mind was, "The Full Plastic Jacket is more weather resistant and more effective than any previously used ignition system in muzzleloading guns, and why would, or should, any black-powder hunter settle for anything less than the most reliable ignition system that is presently available?"

*Knight TK-2000 12-gauge shotgun (top) and Knight Disc Extreme Rifle .45-caliber rifle (bottom) with both using plastic holders for the 209 primers.*

Guns and loads

On our hunt Tony was using an experimental version of the Master Hunter that I can't say anything more about, his brother John and son had .50-caliber Disc Extremes while I was outfitted with a .45-caliber Disc Extreme. The load I was using was two 50-grain .45-caliber Pyrodex Pellets and the 150-grain solid-copper Barnes bullet that Knight sells under the name of Red Hot Saboted Bullets. "Although we supply sabots for both two and three-pellet loads, a decently-placed shot with 100 grains of Pyrodex pellets will kill any deer we have," Tony said.

I had taken a Georgia deer at 137 yards with the .45-caliber Knight DISC rifle and CVA's 225-grain PowerBelt bullets the previous year (and later used a

275-grain bullet in this rifle on Kudu and Zebra (Chapter 8) in Africa). This bullet preformed well on the deer even though it hit a little far back and penetrated the paunch sending fragments through the liver. The deer was recovered 30-yards from where it was hit. Because of legal restrictions, I could not use the .40-caliber saboted bullets in Georgia, and I was very interested to see how the light-weight Barnes bullets would perform on game.

My first shot at a doe at 150-yards was a miss. I failed to compensate for 7-inches of bullet drop and the bullet never touched the animal. I saw small 4-pointers, several 6-pointers and one thin-racked 8-point buck during the hunt. I already had my "meat doe," and was holding out for a huge buck. Certainly they were there. Tony had passed on several nice deer because, "I've already got a house full of 140-class bucks. If it's not a 150 or better I won't shoot it."

From one stand I glimpsed a heavy-tined 8-pointer down in a brushy bottom, but it had not offered a shot. A few days later, I saw the buck again. This time it walked up from the bottom and was feeding on acorns 50-yards away. The problem was that I could not see quite enough of him for sure shot placement.

"This is the best chance I'm going to have," I thought. "If he walks down the ridge or continues in the direction he is going, I won't be able to see him." I could see the buck's shoulder behind a thin screen of leafless branches. I took a solid rest, aimed and carefully squeezed off the shot. The deer showed no signs of being hit, reversed directions, and was last seen bounding over the next ridge at full speed. A shattered dangling branch told the story. The bullet had not touched the deer.

Both Tony and I searched the spot where the deer was standing, walked along its escape trail and searched the next two valleys without ever finding a drop of blood. I was an unlucky hunter, and that was a lucky deer. Given the result it is obvious that I should have passed on the shot in hopes that the deer would present an unobstructed target that day or at another time. But I was running out of time. I had only one more morning's hunting before I had to leave.

My last hunting opportunity came the next morning when I was in the same tree. At 9 O'clock two does walked behind me. There was no buck following them, but there was a line of 10 does lead by an enormous doe. "This is the one," I thought. The doe was striding at a steady pace, but I could see an opening that she would likely pass through about 30-yards away. She was walking through the opening, but further up from where I was aiming. I moved the sights onto the deer and shot before she walked into a thicket.

The doe ran, limping on the nearside front leg. As I re-wiped the barrel with a spit dampened patch, dropped two pellets down the bore, started the stiff-loading saboted bullet and seated the charge, the other does milled around in confusion. I could have shot another, but I had already used my two non-resident deer tags, and I was certain that I had hit the deer.

Twenty minutes later I was on the ground and found blood and corn from a paunch hit. Drat! I purposefully burned up some time by walking back to the road

*Big Missouri doe taken with .45-caliber Knight rifle.*

to leave my hunting bag and cushion and give the deer time to stiffen up. Following the blood trail was fairly easy, although the unsteady doe left a trail with many right-angle turns as it stumbled along its way. Obviously the deer was hard hit.

On a slope above a steep ravine there was a larger flow of blood where the doe had stood for a few seconds while its life drained away. I felt remorse at making such a bad hit. Taking another step, I found the doe at the bottom of leaf-covered ravine hung up on some saplings. It would take more than one of us to move that animal.

Tony had already gone back to camp, but a radio call alerted him to bring the Polaris. I left my gun, camera and skinning tools on the ridge top and hung my orange drag sling to mark the spot. It took three of us to hump that deer into the carry basket of the four-wheeler and move it to a better spot for photos. "That's a huge doe," Tony said. She must weigh at least 185 pounds." Without question it was the largest deer I had ever shot.

I was again very pleased with the performance of the 150-grain Barnes bullet. It had broken ribs on the near side of the deer pulverized the paunch and lower organs into jelly and left a ragged 1½ inch exit hole. Not everyone makes perfect shots on deer, and the bullet had done everything that could have been reasonably expected of it.

With one deer already cut up, wrapped and frozen, I had my work cut out for me in getting the other deer cut up and frozen for the day-and-a-half trip back to Georgia. I left some of the larger roast for other hunters who had been less successful, and started back with two nice corn-fed deer packed in dry ice. My deer ate very well, but I don't know if the numerous other hunters I saw in Missouri and Illinois carrying their unskinned deer home on trailers in 50-degree weather faired as well. I had rather eat my deer than theirs.

Tony did not take a deer on that hunt although he saw one buck that he had his sights on, safeties off and finger on the trigger. He did not shoot, and later regretted his choice. Tony's son took a nice 11 pointer with his .50-caliber muzzleloader and Tony's brother John bagged an even larger deer. Both had hammered their deer with single shots from their .50-caliber Knight rifles. Everyone had opportunities at good bucks and I filled my tags. Tony was still looking for his 150-plus buck, but the Governor's Hunt was coming up in Iowa, and he would certainly have other opportunities.

The hunter returns

Hunting is a lot of things and part of it is living up to your own performance expectations. By not taking a reasonable deer, I felt that I had let my Missouri hosts down. When I was offered a return trip, I eagerly accepted. I had already taken three deer with the .45-caliber rifle gun by then and I knew all the folks, so something of the pressure was reduced. I could enjoy myself on this hunt, and it was a little less like work.

Finding my way back to the camp was hampered by the fact that a bridge was being repaired. I could see where I wanted to go on top of the hill, but I could not get there by vehicle. Walking up to camp, I found John, Tony's brother, and was informed that I needed to go up to the next crossing, and keep turning right which would ultimately bring me to the camp.

Plans for opening day were being discussed. Since no one had apparently taken the buck that I had missed the year before, I was eager to try for him again. The stand that I had used had been removed, but I had brought one of my climbing stands which I could mount on a nearby tree. I thought I remembered the way, but just to make sure I drove in and put my stand on a good tree that afternoon.

Leaving before dark, I drove my truck and parked it along the road before I started my mile-long walk to the stand. I found all my landmarks, relocated my stand on the ridge top and went up the tree. It was full dark, and I turned off my flashlight and waited. In the predawn light I opened the action of the Ultra Mag and installed a Full Plastic Jacket with its 209 primer. About 10- minutes after it became light enough to shoot, I heard the steady crunch, crunch, crunch of a heavy animal climbing the hill. My first glimpse showed me that this was a large buck with massive beams and five long tines equally spaced on either side of its rack.

That was all the trophy evaluation that I needed to do. Silently swinging the gun over to where I could sight in on the deer, I made sure that both safeties were off and raised the rifle to my shoulder. As the buck crossed the crest of the ridge, I saw that it would pass through an opening. I placed the crosshairs behind the leg of the deer when it cleared the last tree and squeezed off the shot. This time I did not catch any wood with my bullet, and the buck ran down the ridge crests after I shot. The blood trail was easy to follow. The big buck had run perhaps 60 yards,

*Trophy Missouri buck taken on second trip with Knight Revolution .45-caliber rifle.*

collapsed and slid down the steep ridge until he was stopped by a tree.

On closer examination, the deer was very big bodied and had well matched points. I may someday shoot a larger deer, but I doubt if I will ever take a more handsome animal. It finally scored 149 points. There were some bigger bucks in the area. Should I have held out for one? I could have, but I think busting this "big boy" during the first few minutes of the season was a prudent decision as hot weather depressed deer movement for the remainder of the week.

Getting him so early had another significant advantage in that the processor could have my deer cut up, ground and frozen for my trip home a few days later. I still had a doe tag and filled it before I left. I cut up and froze that deer in camp which provided me with a freezer full of excellent corn-fed deer for the coming year and finally, a deer to go on the wall.

*In 2009 Knight Rifles stopped production of all of its guns and started looking for a buyer to continue the brand. In March, 2010, the company was purchased by PI, Inc., a manufacturer of plastic products, located in Athens, Tennessee. PI's announced intention is to continue service and parts support for existing Knight rifles and resume production of at least part of the Knight line of guns in Tennessee. Tony Knight, although "retired," remains active in the industry as one of the nation's strongest proponents of black-powder hunting.*

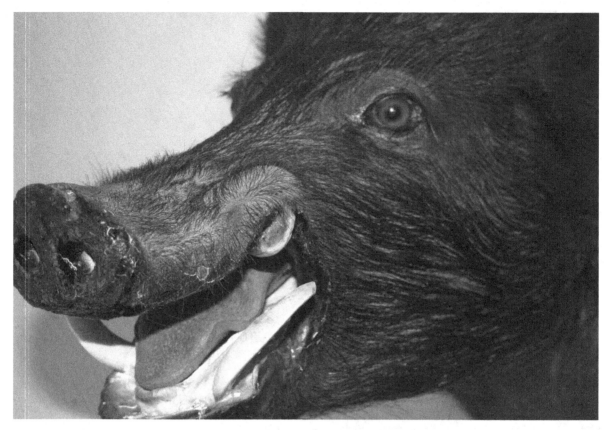

*Hogs like this one can provide a variety of muzzleloading hunting experiences wherever they are found.*

# Chapter 6. Going after hogs

Wild boars, hogs, warthogs, bush pigs, giant forest hogs and the javelina, their unrelated New World look-alikes, are among the most thrilling animals to pursue with black-powder guns. It makes no difference if the hunt takes place in Europe, Australia, Africa or in the Americas, going after hogs with a single-shot muzzleloader going to get the adrenaline surging and the blood pumping. All members of the pig family can grow into large animals. They are naturally well protected by a tough hide, thick gristle plate over the shoulders of the boars, a strong skill with a sloping head that can easily deflect straight-on shots and have good teeth coupled the will to use them.

Hogs prefer thick cover and their low profiles make them hard to spot. At high population levels they will be forced to forage in more open areas, but their strong preference is to move in fields and pastures only under the cover of darkness and often in heavy rain. Rain brings easy rooting providing an abundant supply of nutrishous roots and tubers. True omnivores, they will eagerly consume corn, grains, grasses, fruits, nuts, carrion, fiddler crabs, snakes, small animals and even each other. Sows are fiercely protective of their piglets, and a boar in an argumentative mood will take on all comers – be they other hogs or men.

The hog's anatomy is designed for protection. Its legs are comparatively short for its body weight making it difficult to be knocked off its feet. The bone structure is massive, stocky and well structured to absorb impact blows from other animals. The boar's gristle plate extends from the front of the shoulder to back of the shoulder blade. This spongy, fibrous material dissipates force, slows down projectiles and protects the heart-lung area. The spine is set very low at about the midline of the neck, and heavy layers of muscle protect it from above. The sloping forehead can deflect bullets and protects the animal's chest from a head-on shot. Once the animal weighs over 200 pounds, its body mass and low profile enables it to plow though thick brush that a man must negotiate on his hands and knees.

A hog's hearing is excellent and its sense of smell is probably even more acute than a deer's. Only in the vision department are man's natural senses superior to hogs. Needless to say, if a hunter is going to stalk hogs the best method is to proceed from downwind.

Although old boars may range by themselves, hogs prefer the company of family groups. Herds of hogs consisting of variously-aged individuals often forage together. These activities are accompanied by snaps, clicks, snorts, wheezes and grunts that are fully audible to hunters. Detecting hogs by the sounds they make while feeding and forging is one of the surest ways to find them.

Once they grow to over 200 pounds, few predators will take them on. North American alligators and mountain lions are effective predators where the animals' ranges overlap. Gators lie in wait concealed just beneath the water's surface waiting for its prey to come to water. When an animal approaches the alligator makes a lightning-fast strike grabs the hapless creature by the head and rolls until it breaks the neck of its prey. Once subdued, the unlucky critter is drug into the water so it can be stashed in a safe place until it decomposes enough for the alligator to tear it apart and eat it with its peg-like teeth. In California and Florida, the stealthy mountain lions have no problems taking medium-to-small size hogs.

Could one choose an animal to be if one were reincarnated, a hog would not be a bad choice. You would be well protected as a youngster, have a chance to eat a lot of good stuff, have ample opportunities for sex and once fully mature walk with the confidence that you are the biggest, baddest beastie in the swamp.

Muzzleloading smoothbores and hogs

Angry, snorting and popping its teeth, the 650 pound boar charged the three hunters. One of them had managed to put a ball from his cumbersome matchlock guns into the now enraged animal. Throwing down the now-useless gun he grabbed a spear and prepared to meet the animal's charge. The time was about 1610. The place was the historic Basque country in the Pyrenees Mountains between France and Spain where life and death struggles between man and the indigenous boars had occurred since the Stone Age.

Matchlocks, cumbersome, slow, unreliable and inaccurate as they were, helped even the odds between man and boar; but after, and if, they had successfully discharged their one shot these primitive guns were little better than clubs against a quarter ton of black furry. Typical supporting weapons included boar spears which were heavy pikes with crossbars on the shafts that served to both kill the boar and fend it off as it died. Also employed were boar swords with broad spear-tipped points and narrower upper blades designed to cut as long as they remained in the animal even if the swordsmen were tossed. Belt knives were reserved for last-ditch measures of self defense.

Matchlocks replaced the bow and crossbow as the preferred weapon for boar hunting because the heavy .75-caliber balls offered 1,000 pounds of shock on impact and better penetration than bow or crossbow arrows which transmitted less than 100 ft.lbs. of energy to the animal. Still, the hunting tool that offered the fastest kill was the spear because of its large dual-cutting blade and the leverage offered by a long shaft. Although spears could be thrown, their more accustomed use was to imbed the butt of the spear into the ground and use it as a pike. The hunters would surround the boar, the animal would be induced to charge and the hunter facing the boar would allow the animal to run into the spear. Once impaled, his companions would assail the animal and quickly kill it. Such hunts are still done in Germany with spears that are quaintly called "boar ticklers."

An unknown bladesmith in the French town of Bayonet observed that it was so cumbersome for a hunter to carry both a gun and spear that hunters often opted to use one or the other. He apparently reasoned that he needed to design a long knife that could be jammed into the muzzle of the discharged gun that would convert the (now useless) gun into a pike. These plug bayonets were instant hits, and were produced until the socket-bayonets were developed in the late 1600s. The socket bayonets had the advantage that they fitted around or onto the barrel so that it was possible to fire and reload the muzzleloader with the bayonet attached to the rifle and, equally important, would remain on the gun after a thrust.

*A plug bayonet (bottom center) and a variety of other edged tools used for hunting hogs.*

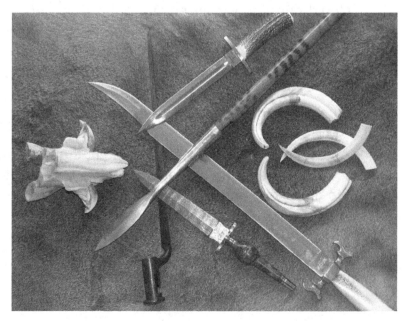

By the 1700s, bayonets were used by almost all of the world's military units simultaneously with their continued use for sporting purposes. Bayonets were also sold by custom gun makers as part of the accessory set offered with their firearms. Some of the finest surviving examples of bayonets were parts of these sets that were so highly decorated that they were considered as much works of arts as hunting implements.

In the 21st Century black-powder hunters are again facing hogs and other game with single-shot muzzleloading guns. To revisit this ancient technology I had a plug bayonet made for a replica flintlock .75-caliber "Indian Gun" marketed by Dixie Gun Works of Union City, Tennessee. Bess, as I called the gun, had previously taken ducks, geese and deer. The waterfowl had been shot with the now required non-toxic shot and the deer taken with a patched round ball.

The bayonet was made by Swedish knife maker Micke Andersson and features an 8-inch blade of forged Damascus steel and a tapered wooden grip made of a burr wood to fit into the muzzle of the gun. This is among the few plug bayonets made since the 1700s. It was time to put the old technology to the test. To work effectively, the bayonet had to be jammed into the gun's muzzle sufficiently for it to be retained during some fast side-stepping and thrusting.

To judge the plug bayonet's relative effectiveness, its penetration in block Styrofoam was compared with a spear thrown at five yards, a sword thrust at two feet, a knife thrust at two feet and a triangular socket bayonet affixed to an original 1842 British musket. After fixing the plug bayonet firmly in the muzzle I gave Bess a determined thrust, flexing the body and both knees forward. It was imbedded to the crossbar having penetrated 5¼-inches of Styrofoam and 3¾-inches of blade extended beyond the block.

This simple test indicated that the knife bayonet fitted into the muzzle and with a two-handed thrust behind it doubled the amount of penetration that might be expected from the hunter's knife or sword while keeping him further from the boar. Only the spear and triangular bayonet were more effective.

Just like the hunters of yore, if you are going to take on a big boar with a single-shot gun on the ground it is prudent to take along another back-up weapon for self defense. Even a dying boar can easily thrash a hunter before he expires. Have no doubt that he has the will and the equipment to do it. At the very least, spot a good climbing tree before you shoot. Can't climb, you say? Believe me, you will discover a facility for arboreal assent that you never knew you had when a big hog comes at you. There is nothing like incentive.

Muzzleloading handguns for hogs

Texas' Nail Ranch provided my first opportunity to take a trophy-size boar with a muzzleloading pistol. Previously, I had used a scope-mounted Traditions Buckhunter Pro to shoot a smallish sow during the last minutes of the last day of a hunt on Georgia's Cumberland Island. I was walking out removing flagging that some other hunter had put on the bushes. I heard a small noise and saw a sow crossing in front of me. I quickly raised the pistol, filled the scope with hog fur and sent the 240-grain saboted bullet powered by 85-grains of FFg on its way. The load was immediately effective and the 80-pound hog was down. This was a good eating-size pig and was excellent eating when I cooked it the following year.

I put the scope on the Buckhunter Pro because the iron sights could not be successfully adjusted. Using a scope enabled me to accurately zero the pistol with the load and added some needed weight to the gun. The downside was the scope slowed close-range shooting because of the need to make sure that the patch of red fur that filled the scope was located at a potentially fatal spot.

For the hog hunt on the Nail Ranch I chose to use Thompson/Center Arms' excellent adjustable iron sights rather than a scope. I also decided to develop a heavier load for the 15-inch barreled handgun. The 209X50 pistol version of the Encore uses a frame that will also accept rifle and shotgun barrels of either centerfire or muzzleloading persuasions. At present, rifle barrel chambers range from centerfire .22s to the .416s, and 20 and 12-gauge shotgun barrels are also available. There are also muzzleloading .50-caliber and 12-gauge shotgun barrels.

Thompson Center's CEO Gregg Ritz loves to hunt with the .50-caliber 209X50 muzzleloading Encore and has taken a variety of American and African game with the gun. To me, the highest evolution of the Encore system is its handguns. I like their looks, the way they feel and how they shoot. Esthetically, the rifle and shotgun versions of the Encore have never appealed to me. Have no doubt about it. These Encore rifles shoot very well, but in single-shot rifles, I prefer the Ruger No. 1 Single Shot.

A good-shooting load for the muzzleloading Encore pistol turned out to be two 50-grain Pyrodex pellets, a .50-caliber Wonder Wad and Thompson/Center's 370-grain MaxiBall. Using the Wonder Wad between the powder charge and the bullet increased the load's velocity by nearly 300 fps. This increase aids in both delivered energy and penetration. This load offered 858 ft.lbs. of muzzle energy and still retained 537 ft.lbs at 100 yards – about the equivalent of the .44 Remington Magnum with a 240-grain slug. However, the muzzleloader was shooting a larger diameter, tougher and significantly heavier bullet.

The shooting and carrying techniques that I used with the heavy, long-barreled Thompson Center handguns are different from those used with a conventional revolver or semiauto. The steadiest off-hand hold is with the grip held in the strong hand while the other hand grips the forend and applies forward pressure, as if to pull the gun apart. This stresses the muscles and reduces sight shake.

Thompson/Center makes a holster for the gun, which I used extensively in Africa. When I am pistol hunting with this gun I reverse it in my weak hand let the barrel rest on my forearm while the thumb hooks in my belt. This way I can raise the gun, sight and shoot without the noise resulting from drawing it from a holster.

Guide Brian Cope and I had been hunting the 56,000 acre Nail ranch in modernized cowboy fashion (Chapter 14). Instead of riding the trails on horseback, spotting game and then dismounting to stalk with lever-action rifles; we traveled the ranch roads in a four-wheel drive looking for game. Earlier that morning I had missed a running shot at a hog at about 50 yards. I had reloaded the gun with a fresh charge, but there was a lingering concern that perhaps the water of combustion from the first shot might spoil the pellets several hours later when we spotted the second bunch of hogs.

As we approached, the biggest boar in the bunch was busy trying to run off a smaller boar that had the audacity to pay some attention to a sow that the larger boar apparently intended to breed. While the hogs were distracted and the noise of our approach was covered by an approaching thunderstorm, I took a braced sitting position. I wanted the bullet to hit the rib cage, pass through the animal and imbed in the off-side shoulder. Cope stood by with a .270 and a bullet in the chamber in case "things got interesting."

When I shot, the hogs scattered and the big boar tore over the crest of a small rise, and passed out of sight.

There was little blood on the ground, but none was needed. When we crested a small rise we saw the dead hog. It had run a total of 30 yards. The boar weighed in excess of 350 pounds and we had to call for help to load it on the truck. The bullet penetrated some 26-inches of hog and was recovered from beneath the gristle plate on the off-side shoulder. It had expanded to about .75-caliber and retained 95% of its original weight. This was excellent performance for a pistol bullet in a big-game animal. I later used the same gun and load in Africa (Chapter 8).

When we returned to the ranch, the property's wildlife manager Craig

*Thompson/Center 209X50 muzzleloading Encore Pistol used to take a large boar hog at the Nail Range in Texas.*

Winters immediately asked how many shots it had taken to get this hog which was the largest one taken by the seven people in our hunting party. He was surprised when told that only one shot had been needed. His more accustomed result was that people would empty a cylinder or magazine full of bullets at a hog, some would hit it and the downed animal would still require a finishing shot.

As with any game shooting, precise placement of that first shot is the most important thing. Muzzleloading pistols teach this lesson very well. Most of the present crop of black-powder revolvers generate about as much energy as the .38 Special. The big Walker and dragoon pistols do have more power, but their primitive sights often pattern the light-weight balls so high as to make it difficult to hit with them under the pressure of a hunting situation. In addition, I consider a 60-grain load of black powder and a round ball marginal, at best, for hogs fired from a rifle and inadequate when shot from a short-barreled handgun.

Having a back-up shooter armed with a gun of sufficient power to stop a charging hog is good practice when hunting hogs from the ground. If the country is open enough and you are lucky, hogs may be shot from tree stands, but in the heavy cover hogs will often be heard passing nearby, but not seen in the thickets that they love. Watching trails in southern swamps where the mature hardwoods have opened the forest floor will sometimes be successful, but the great majority of the hogs that I have killed were taken while stalking on foot.

Muzzleloading rifles for hogs

Georgia's Ossabaw Island is one of my home state's premier hunting locations. This island is known not only for its overpopulation of deer, but also for its wild hogs. For years public hunting was offered for deer and in recent years wild hogs have also been put on the menu. These hunts have now become so popular that it takes three years to be drawn for one of the quota hunts.

On one hunt I wanted to take a .50-caliber CVA Hawken rifle that I had built from a kit. This gun came as a box of parts. Included was an unfinished but mostly inlet stock, a finished lock and barrel and a cast, but unfinished brass trigger guard and hardware. I finished the stock, polished the brass, glass bedded the rear of the barrel and smoothed up the lock. The gun shot very well particularly with a load of 85 grains of FFg black powder and CVA's 300-grain BuckSlayer hollow-based Minie-ball styled bullet.

The only problem that I ever had with this gun was that the water of combustion from previous shots would collect in the drum and yield misfires with the small no. 11 caps. To help overcome this problem I replaced the small nipple with one designed for the larger, and more powerful, musket caps. This helped, but did not really solve this problem. If the gun was fired once during the morning, care had to be taken to clean the barrel and dry the ignition passages. If this were not done the gun might not shoot when a big hog came in at dusk.

On this hunt I selected a long skinny parcel of land bordered on both sides

*CVA .50-caliber Hawken rifle that the author built from a kit and a Georgia hog from Ossabaw Island.*

by swampy reed-filled ponds. This was an old beach ridge and supported oaks, palmettos and other plants that hogs liked to browse. While scouting I saw a huge oak stump with a hollowed-out interior where hogs had obviously bedded for generations. When the tide was low the hogs moved out into the marsh to feed and returned to higher ground to rest when the rising water moved them out of the marsh. As the Georgia coast has 12-foot tides, this daily tide movement has a profound effect on coastal wildlife.

Earlier that day I had walked in to set my tree stand on a narrow neck of land thinking that this would funnel the amimals past me. I never got the stand in place. Walking in I spotted a herd of foraging hogs further up the road. As is often the case, I heard them before I saw them. I quietly dropped the stand and as the wind was in my favor, stalked the animals. All of these animals weighed about 50 pounds – ideal for something to cook in camp. Picking out one, I dropped it, cleaned it and drug it back to the road for pick up that noon. I selected a good spot for my stand in a palm tree for the afternoon hunt and hung it there.

Very often hogs move at about dusk, and as I was walking out, I spotted a 100-pounder walking across a cleared area at about 85 yards. Raising my gun, I set the trigger, aimed at the front edge of it shoulder and pulled the trigger. With the shot, the hog took two steps and fell. Taking two pigs in one day with a gun that I had a hand in building remains one of my most memorable hunts.

The Hawken-style rifle is my favorite design for off-hand shooting. Over the years I have taken a variety of game animals using Hawken-styled guns made by CVA, Thompson/Center Arms, Traditions and Sharon Rifle Barrel Co. If hunting in country where the vegetation is too thick for a shot from sitting or prone, these heavy barreled weight-forward rifles, particularly when equipped with set triggers, work very well. For this use they are far better than very light barreled in-line guns that must be shot from a rest to obtain accurate results beyond 30 yards.

Georgia's Bond Swamp National Wildlife Refuge on the Ocmulgee River south of Macon is exactly what you might think a Georgia swamp ought to be. It is on the floodplain of a major river and there are numerous sloughs, cutoffs and meandering streams snaking through the property. On the flat floodplain this is one area were the unwary can get lost in a hurry. There are few standout topographic features and only a railroad bed cuts through the entire property.

First opened to hunting in 1999, all of the refuge lies east of the Ocmulgee River. About 4,500 acres are periodically flooded river bottoms along with 2,000 acres of upland habitat north of Stone Creek and Georgia State Route 23. Although hogs and deer are Bond Swamp's most important inhabitants from a hunter's perspective, the swamp also has black bear, alligators, snakes, waterfowl and bald eagles among its wildlife.

There is limited access in the flat floodplain between Stone Creek and the Ocmulgee River. During low water the numerous oxbows and meandering drainages may be waded, but some are over 6-foot deep when bank full. In some cases the same creek may be crossed three times within 100 yards.

I was last drawn for a hog hunt on Bond Swamp in February of 2001. This was the second season that hunting was allowed in the swamp, and I, and most hunters, were seeing it for the first time. Finding areas with recent hog activity consumed most of my time. Some 400 hunters had tromped through the swamp during three previous hunts, and the surviving hogs had retired to the more remote parts of the refuge.

During the first two days I scouted the upland parts of the refuge, walked the trails and looked at the area along the Ocmulgee River. By the third day it was apparent that if I were going to get a hog, I would need to work the area between the Stony Creek and the River. Fortunately it had been a very dry Summer and the swamp was not completely flooded, and I could do the water crossings in my waders.

On my hunt, I kept checking my compass to keep going in a northerly direction as I slowly walked along. The wind was in my favor. At about noon, I saw three hogs bedded at the foot of a large oak. Raising the .50-caliber Savage Model 10 muzzleloader, I fired. The 300-grain jacketed .452 Hornady PTX bullet in an MMP black 50X.451 sabot propelled by a load of 49 grains of IMR 4227 at 2,047 fps. developed 2,792 ft. lbs. of muzzle energy. This load hit the hog's shoulder and

*Savage .50-caliber Model 10 ML and a Georgia hog from Bond Swamp.*

80

killed it instantly. It never rose from its bed, and this is among the most decisive kills that I have ever experienced with a muzzleloading rifle.

The Savage Model 10 ML and ML II are the only muzzleloaders designed to use some loads of smokeless powder. No other manufacturer recommends or condones the use of any amount of smokeless powders in their products as they may generate dangerous overloads. The 10 ML can also be used with loose black powder, black-powder substitutes or pelletized Pyrodex or TripleSeven powders.

After gutting the hog and cutting off the head and feet, I drug it northwards towards Bondview road. That proved to be more difficult than I had anticipated. I had to cross four water channels and go through some nearly impenetrable cane, briers and thick second growth before I reached the road. Even when on the road I was still several miles from my truck. Next time I will take in a pack, bone out the meat and not fight the long drag out. I started dragging at 1 P.M. and did not make it out to Bondview until dark. In retrospect, I should have retraced my steps and exited the way I came.

GPS units have much eased navigation chores in areas like this. Now I take one with me whenever I go into a new area and even use one on my own farm when I am on a blood trail after dark. Many miles of walking and dragging can be saved if the position of the dead animal can be precisely located and relocated as might be needed.

Savage's Model 10 ML II is a bit more convenient to operate since it no longer requires a primer carrier to hold the 209 primer. Cleaning requirements are not quite so pressing as with conventional black powder and black-powder substitutes, but the breech plug must be removed and cleaned periodically with smokeless powder use and after each day's shooting with black-powder substitutes or it will seize in the breech. I found that fouling would still accumulate in the bolt of the gun with the ML I model that I used, but this bolt is very easy to disassemble with an Allen wrench. The Savage rifle can easy mount a scope and has an excellent trigger. My limited personal experience with the gun was favorable.

Some state laws require black powder or approved black powder substitutes be used as propellants on primitive weapon hunts, but most regulations about hunting hogs are generally less restrictive. Before buying or hunting with a Savage ML 10, or any other muzzleloader for that matter, it is best to thoroughly research the regulations least you arrive at a distant hunt area with a gun that you cannot legally use.

*Anyone who hunts in North America in states where wild hogs are present needs to hunt hogs. Hog populations increase so rapidly that hunting, by inself, is not sufficient to adequate control the population. Trapping, baiting, night hunting and using dogs are all valuable tools that landowners need to utalize. Transferring wild hogs from properto to property is not a good practice as the hogs will roam to find the best available food sources.*

*Author on four-wheeler with Idaho black bear.*

## Chapter 7 America's Bruins

Although the grizzly population in the "lower 48" is much less than in the 1700s, it is slowly rebounding to fill wild habitats that are contiguous enough to allow the animals sufficient room to be relatively free from man-bear conflicts. Black bears have shown themselves to be much more adaptable, and their numbers are increasing almost everywhere within their historic range. The only place where black bears are not doing well is in the desert southwest where a decade-long drought is depressing wildlife populations. In eastern states where croplands have been increasingly abandoned or planted in trees, black bears, like the whitetailed deer, are repopulating their former habitats.

Ironically, the same week that I was on a Canadian bear hunt a 200-pound bear chose to stroll through my Central Georgia home town. I was not surprised as I had seen bear tracks on my farm 8 miles from town a few years before and clearly visible tracks preserved in a red-mud road the preceding spring on Buffalo Creek only a few miles from the city limits. After some difficulty, the wayward bear was tranquilized and relocated. So far as I could find out, this was the first bear seen in the town since early 1800s.

Most people think of eastern black bears in connection with North Carolina's Great Smoky Mountains National Park. There are estimated to be about 3,000 bears in the park and environs; but coastal North Carolina in the area between

Lake Mattamuskeet and the Alligator River hosts the state's largest population of 7,000 bears.

A few years ago an obese bear that weighed over 800 pounds was killed in eastern North Carolina. This monster lived next to a hog farm. When one of the hogs died it was put in a steel bin for the arbiter to collect on a periodic basis. The bear found this inexhaustible source of free feed and was apparently chomping down on a hog every few days.

Since the 1950s when a lot of marginal agricultural land that was put in the Soil Bank program and taken out of production, big game animals, like deer, have rapidly expanded their ranges. Deer were restocked from remnant populations from within the state and also imported from the Midwest and Texas. No attempt was made to restock bears, and their spread has been through natural increase. Although not repopulating as rapidly as the deer and turkeys, bears are looking for new areas to inhabit are generally working up major drainages and subsidiary creeks until they reach the fringes of populated areas. They quite happily reside in swamps and forests where sufficient food is available until they come into conflict with man.

Coastal Alaska and Canada have some very large black bears that have access to salmon runs with many huge bears coming from Vancouver Island, British Columbia. A reasonable argument can be made that these island bears, which have been separated from the mainland for over 10,000 years, are a remnant species from the Pleistocene when outsize animals like the super bison, giant ground sloth and wooly mammoth lived in North America.

Alaska also has an excellent population of black bears, particularly in southeastern Alaska where the rare blue glacier bear variant is found. Kodiak

*Bear Anchorage airport.*

Island is noted for its large population of its namesake bear which also roams the Alaska Peninsula. I frequently encountered these very large bears during the years I did exploration geology in Alaska. Happily, I never had to shoot one even though I carried a Smith and Wesson .44 Magnum on my hip every day. I made a pack with the bear clan. If they didn't bother me, I would not bother them. I kept my word, but it was sorely tested one day on the Alaskan Peninsula near Painters Creek.

I was taking a radiometric survey in a narrow creek valley. I was half-way up a steep slope when I looked down the creek and here came a cocker-spaniel-sized cub that was shortly followed by another.

"O Shit!" I thought. I drew my revolver and prepared to shoot if I needed to. Sure enough, here came momma. She had a head that was as big as a bushel basket. Handguns, even the .44 Magnum, are weapons of desperation against a large bear. The last thing I wanted to do was to shoot a brown bear with a puny pistol, much less one with two cubs. I had an aluminum notebook and raddled this against the side of the rock face. Momma bear looked up, spotted me and went, "Woof."

The two cubs scampered up the bare rock on opposite side of the creek wall immediately followed by the big sow. I breathed a sigh of relief. During eight summers of living and working in the Alaskan bush, I or none of my people ever had to shoot a bear. Once while we were waiting for a helicopter pickup four of us were standing on a gravel bar on one side of a shallow river. Three bears on the other side spotted and started over, apparently thinking that these bipeds must be black bears and a potential meal. We shouted and danced around, and once the bruins had identified us as human, they changed directions and went about their business.

Even when I was an Alaska resident, I never had a desire to take one of the big bears. While in the army or as a student, I did not have the money to do anything with a brown bear hide if I got one. I have since learned that brown bear makes good sausage meat, and Kodiak Smoking and Processing just off the airfield at Kodiak will turn your brown bear into something eatable should you kill one. Even so, it takes one guy a while to eat up 100s of pounds of bear sausage.

Carefully controlled hunting of brown and grizzly bears is done in Alaska and Western Canada and a few permits are sometimes issued in the "lower 48." These are spot and stalk hunts with either the spotting being done from a boat, as in coastal regions of Alaska, or on foot. This would certainly be an exciting and challenging hunt for a black-powder hunter. Don't take on one of these bears alone with a single-shot muzzleloader. The old African hunters had better sense, and you should emulate them and have a back-up shooter in case things go sour. Once that bear takes the first shot, they are very tough to put down and keep down. Stories are rampant in Alaska about hunters with .375 Holland and Holland magnums empting their magazines into one of these monsters still to have it come on to be finally killed by a fusillade of 11-15 shots.

If you are going to go after these big bears use a .50-caliber rifle, shoot a tough elongate non-expanding slug and aim to punch through the spine. Learn your bear anatomy so that shot can be precisely placed in the spine. The old timers shooting their .45-70s with 400 and 500-grain bullets had it about right. Heavy, hard, solid bullets will rake through any bear, but round balls and hollow points may not.

Lewis and Clark had great trouble with the big bears on their explorations through the west. Their round-ball rifles, even loaded with double balls, were not very effective against the aggressive plains grizzlies. The Indians had given these huge bears a wide berth, and Lewis and Clark's party of explorers learned to do the same. The lesson here is for modern black-powder hunters to use heavy, elongate bullets of large caliber and shoot very, very carefully.

The principal caution to black bear hunters in parts of Montana, Wyoming and Idaho is to make very sure that the bear in their sights is, in fact, a black bear and not an immature grizzly. Black bear can have different color phases including brown and blondish colors with or without some white splotches in the neck-upper chest area. Mature grizzlies have prominent humps on their back, dish-shaped faces and less pointed snouts that the black bear. The hunter has to make sure that that light-colored bear that he has his sights on is not an immature grizzly whose body size is not large enough to be instantly recognizable.

Muzzleloaders for black bear

Muzzleloaders for deer and black bear are generally grouped into the same class of firearms. Indeed, it is often the case that the same load that has proven to be effective against deer in the 200-pound range, will also work on black bear. The size of an average Idaho black bear is 167 pounds and those on the west coast probably average out to be somewhat over 200. To give a margin of safety, I would use bullets in the range of 275-grains in .45-caliber in-line rifles and go with 300-

*A variety of traditional or in-line muzzleloaders may be used for black bear as in this Winchester Apex in-line rifle.*

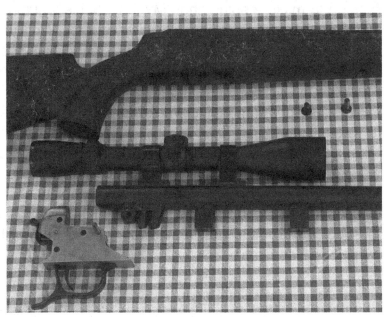

grain projectiles in .50-caliber guns. Charges of 100-grains of black-powder equivalent loads are generally sufficient to drive these bullets through a bear at any reasonable angle.

Within 50 yards, any smoothbore gun in .69-.75 calibers will reliably take black bears if loaded with 90-to-120- grains of FFg black powder. The key is to get close and place the ball through the animal's large lungs. It will react much like an arrow-shot bear and in most cases will need to be trailed. These slow moving slugs disrupt large amounts of tissue and make a bleeding wound that takes some time to kill.

If the bear goes down instantly, suspect a near-spine hit that may not be fatal. Reload quickly and approach the downed bear with caution. If it shows any signs of life shoot it again from a safe distance. Bullet holes in bear hides are easily patched, but bear holes in human hides are not so easy to repair.

A wounded bear, even a black bear, is a dangerous animal. Follow ups are difficult because even a fatal hit will yield little blood because the loose hide shifts to cover the bullet hole. In many cases the shot will be at a down angle, and the entrance hole may be high and blood will collect within the body cavity and nothing but a few fine drops may be found on the ground.

The only muzzleloading handgun that I would recommend for black bear is the Encore 209X50 with a load of 100 grains of Pyrodex or TrippleSeven pellets and a .370-grain Thompson/Center Arms MaxiBall. I have used this load to take a large hog (Chapter 6), warthog and to finish off a wildebeest (Chapter 8), and I have no doubt that it would also work on bear. As with any handgun, the bear must be close and the shot precisely placed for sure kills.

Average-sized black bear are still within the kill capabilities of a .50-caliber round-ball rifle loaded with about 100 grains of FFg., although a .54-caliber round ball will penetrate better. A problem with round-balls is that once they enter an animal they may be deflected along a variety of travel paths and not travel straight enough to make a spine shot. My first choice would be a .54 Hawken-style rifle if I were hunting in dry weather in thick country. With this gun I could be assured of making a good off-hand shot if one presented itself. In southeastern Alaska's rainforest and snow, ignition reliability wins over authenticity, and I would choose an in-line rifle and find a rest before I shot.

Light-barreled in-lines may be reliable, easy to carry but take much too long to "steady down" for precise shot placement. If you have ever wondered why it takes so long for a TV personality to make a shot on a piece of game, is that he is waiting for his barrel to quit wobbling long enough to put the bullet where it needs to go. There is a compromise between portability and shootability. In modern times the balance has swung in the direction of increasingly lightweight, but more difficult to shoot, rifles. Take that rest away, and many hunters are in trouble with their wispy-barreled rifles.

Bear hunting strategies

*Glassing for bears in Idaho.*

Bears can be hunted using variations of three basic techniques. These are: spot and stalk, over bait or with dogs; although not all are legal in all areas and the laws may change. If any black bear hunting is allowed at all, spot and stalk hunting is legal. Here the hunter walks or rides and periodically glasses open areas hopping to see a bear moving through a clear area, size it up and intersect it somewhere along its route. In the open country of the west, many bear will be seen, but some will be too far to reach and retrieve on foot. Good optics are a necessity to judge the size and condition of a distant bear and it is not unusual to employ both a spotting scope and binoculars.

Vehicles are usually used to get to the general area while horses or four-wheelers are often employed to take the hunter to the ridge tops where he can slowly walk and peer down into off shooting valleys to spot his bear. So far as spotting and shooting a bear, this can work very well. The problem is getting the bear out of the hellish hole that he has rolled into after the shot. Sometimes this takes several men, four wheelers and wenches to extract a big bear from the bottom of a deep canyon. Horses sometimes shy from the scent of bears and refuse to carry them. They may consent to pull them on the end of a rope, but if the animal has a wild-eyed you-ain't-going-to-put-that-thing-on-my-back look you had better pay attention.

Problems arise when one is hunting in a wilderness area where vehicles are not allowed and the hunter must haul the bear to some distant check station. The best approach is to take a couple of strapling young guys along with you who don't know any better and pay them off with two cases of beer. The second best approach is to always hunt uphill and stay reasonably near trails. If you deviate from the trails, prowl through relatively clear woods. Listen for your bear. Much like hogs, you may hear the bear before you see it. Once shot, roll the bear down to the trail, put in on a sled or slide sheet and drag it along the road back to wherever you have your vehicle.

An instrument that I have used to recover a variety of game is a simple plastic sled designed to be towed behind a snowmobile. It is very light weight, rugged enough to drag over cypress knees and will hold a 200-pound animal. It was periodically sold by Sportsman's Guide, but now appears in the L.L. Bean catalogue. Even more compact are heavy plastic sheets fitted with grommets. These are rolled up and put under the bear prior to dragging it. This protects the hide and also helps keep trash out of the body cavity.

If all else fails, the bear can be skinned on the spot and the hide carried out in a pack. I hate to abandon bear meat when the animal has been feeding on green matter, acorns, fruits and berries. These black bear are delicious eating and better tasting than the average deer or cow. The taste of the meat is entirely different when the animal is feeding on salmon or carrion.

Dog hunting bear is an exciting hunt for a young guy who is sound of lung and fleet of foot. The dogs are put fresh bear sign and off they go. There may be false starts, back trailing and multiple chases during the course of the hunt. A short dog hunt would be a four-hour chase before the animal is treed. More commonly, it can take six or more hours of travel through hellish swamps or steep canyons before the animal is finally bayed. Epic chases have lasted for days. Ultimately, the animal goes up a tree or into a cave. The hunters arrive and the bear is shot and recovered. To keep weight down dog hunters will often use heavy caliber handguns or .44 Remington Magnum carbines. With careful shooting these will work as will typical deer rifles or the muzzleloading Thompson/Center Encore pistol mentioned earlier. The principal problem is giving the hunter calmed down enough and rested enough so that he can make an accurate shot. If he can't see because his glasses are fogged and can't hold the gun steady because his heart is pounding, he cannot be expected to shoot well.

Getting the body and emotions sufficiently under control to make a shot while the dogs are howling, the men are shouting and all hell is threatening to break loose will take a few minutes. Take those minutes, make a precision shot and bring the animal down out of the tree. Almost without fail, the bear will still be alive when it reaches the ground, and the dogs will be on it. After the shot grab a speed loader and immediately start reloading to kill that bear as fast as possible. The objective is to hit the bear's spine or brain and not shoot one of the dogs. This takes some calm and deliberate activities on the part of the hunter in a situation that is anything but calm.

The downside of dog hunting is that the bear up the tree may have cubs or be too small to shoot. If so, everyone packs up and begins the weary trip home. It is guaranteed to have been an exciting and challenging hunt and the houndsmen-guides will have earned their fee if a bear is taken or not.

Shooting bear over bait is traditionally done in Canada and is also legal in some U.S. states. This is not as much a "sure thing" as might be expected. Very often small bears will come into the bait while there is still shooting light, but the

*Bait stations for bear.*

trophy-size bruins will hang back and only come after dark – precisely the same time that the hunters have come down from their stands and are walking out.

A real difficulty is sizing up the bear. Two-year-old bears are like gangly teens. They have long legs for their body size and erect closely-set ears. These are fairly easy to eliminate as not being shooters. The older the bear's get the more rotund they appear to be. The ears are set wide apart on a very round head, their bellies are low and their legs are comparatively short for their body size. The difficulty come distinguishing these bears from one-year-olds what have the same body profiles, but are much smaller. The way to prevent shooting one of these small bears is to compare its size with the bait barrel or something else in the food pile that has known dimensions.

Even though shots will be at close range, typically from 20-to-35 yards, scopes are an aid in shot placement at dusk when the larger bears typically appear. Often they will circle the bait before coming in. They are also use to checking out the tree stand to see if it is occupied, and sometimes it is prudent to put up a new stand near a bait that is active, but often hunted. If you are in camo and still, the bear may not see you. Once satisfied that the stand is empty, it will start to feed on the assorted stale donuts, meat scraps and other goodies that have been put out for him.

Most bears are shot in fading light and the task of following one up with a flashlight at night is nerve-wracking. If a death moan is heard, that is a good indication that the bear is dead. Still this trailing process is something to be done by more than one person and with good lights. It is possible for a lung-shot bear to go 100 yards or so, although most will be found within about 30 yards. Wounded bears will often head for the nearest water and use existing trails rather than plowing through thick brush. Go armed, proceed cautiously and don't expect much blood sign even from a well-hit bear.

*I like the diversity of black-bear hunting, the opportunity to use different types of muzzleloaders as well as working with some unique meat products. The big brownies do not appeal to me, but I suspect the nation's increasingly abundant black bears will provide materials for future hunts.*

*A victory pose after taking five species of plains game using a muzzleloading rifle, smoothbore and pistol.*

## Chapter 8. Africa: Taking on plains game

The dream of someday going on an African hunt is a persistent, but all-to-often unrealized, dream for many American hunters. The usual excuses are: "I don't have the time. I don't have the money. Wait until my son/daughter gets out of college." Ultimately, these will be replaced by, "I can't physically do the hunt anymore." Although the last statement may not be necessarily true, this is a hunt that is best done while you are physically able to enjoy it.

With rising energy costs, increasing costs of African hunts and the relative fall of the dollar against many of the world's currencies, it will be almost invariably true that next year's hunt will be more expensive that last year's. If you must, sell the extra car, sell the lake home and get some extra cash and go. Don't wait. The general frailty of the human condition is that next year may be too late. Go now.

George "Butch" Winter, a friend and long-time editor of Dixie Gun Works Black Powder Annual, had two unrealized dreams. He wanted to do hunts in Africa and Alaska before he died. His African hunt was done while he was suffering from colon cancer, and he became too ill to travel to Alaska to have his planned hunt in "The Great Land."

Butch's death impressed upon me the imperative to go on my African hunt. (Now!) In many ways I needed to get away. The previous year had been tough.

Thresa, my wife of ten years, had just died after a year-long battle with pancreatic cancer. This had been a real struggle for us both, particularly during the last months of home hospice care. This was not all bad because we had a chance to say our good bys, and she died at home with me and her son by her side as she wished. Still, it was tough.

With no more reasons for me to remain at home and psychologically needing a change, it was time for me to go somewhere and do something different. Fulfilling my dream of an African hunt was not exactly done under doctor's orders, but it would certainly have a beneficial result in helping me get through my grief as well as improving my physical condition after being mostly sedentary for much of the previous year.

Planning for the hunt

Some basic choices need to be made 8-12 months before the hunt. The first is what class of game do you want to hunt. For a first African experience a hunt for "Plains Game" is generally recommended. Typically a plains game hunt will include animals like greater kudu, zebra, wildebeest, impala and warthog with some substitutions allowed depending on the area that is hunted and the game that is available. More of the smaller antelopes might be included as well as the oryx if the hunt is in the dryer areas where these animals are found. Besides the animals on the "hunt ticket," many more may be seen and taken at extra costs.

Hunts for the "big five" including lion, leopard, elephant, water buffalo and rhino can be arranged under various conditions and prices. Buffalo are most abundant, and at present a reasonable buffalo hunt can be arranged for about $12,000. In almost all of Africa the other game is taken by permit only issued by the various countries' wildlife management officials. These permits, by themselves, are quite expensive and run the costs of elephant hunts up to the $50,000 range. Most first-time hunters have resources that are more nearly like $5,000 rather than $50,000, and taking plains game is an excellent start for an African hunting experience.

A good pre-hunt preparation is to join the Safari Club a couple of years before your trip. Membership benefits include an excellent magazine and newsletters that not only provide familiarization with the game and hunting techniques, but also gives you the opportunity to purchase donated hunt packages at less than full price by attending auctions and other events. Total expenses for a plains game hunt from getting on the plane to hanging your trophies on the wall will be about $10,000 at current prices.

After making the decision on the game animals desired, the second decision is to where to go. Africa is a huge continent with numerous countries. Historically, and at present, some are closed to hunting and others are too unsafe to hunt. The Republic of South Africa has an established, stable safari industry based out of large private ranches. It is not unusual for a ranch to have 30,000 acres under 12-foot high rhino-proof electric fence. This provides ample room in which to hunt animals under wild conditions.

Since the interior of the country is semi-arid to arid, water from wells is very often maintained for the game and supplemental feeding is done as necessary to maintain the game populations at the desired levels. The game animals are restricted from migrating, and populations of most species must be controlled by hunting to preserve the habitat. Each ranch has an optimum mix of animals which might include 20 elephants, 200 buffalo, 1,100 impala, 500 wildebeest, 5 hippos, 8 lions and so on. Lion and leopard feed mainly on the abundant impala, but will take other species as opportunities develop. Besides the large mammals, there are also native birds such as Guinea fowl, francolins, ducks and geese which can provide interesting shooting.

South Africa is easily accessed from the U.S. with direct flights from Atlanta to Johannesburg, English is commonly spoken and the country has a long history of accepting American hunters. Accommodations on the ranches are very nice. Spouces may accompany their hunting partners at comparatively little additional costs and tours and other activities can be arranged for them.

Firearms selection

My hunt was unusual in that I chose to use a black powder handgun, smoothbore and in-line rifle. For the average hunter things are much simplified by taking a .50-caliber scope sighted in-line rifle to provide some reach and power along with a 12-gauge muzzleloading shotgun OR muzzleloading handgun. I had the most fun waterhole sitting with the pistol and bird shooting with the smoke-belching shotgun. Before doing anything, make sure you are following current regulations, and that the safari company can get the necessary shooting

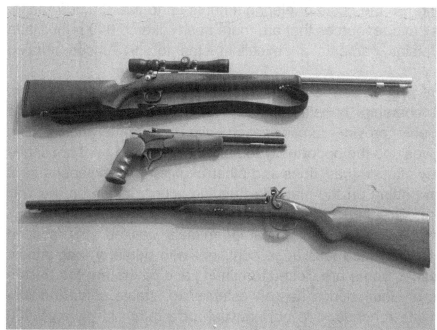

*Guns selected for the African hunt.*

92

components for you. Also, pay the $150 for having Air 2000 have your firearm import permits pre-approved. Be warned that mail is very slow in South Africa, and it may take a full month to get a letter to a person or company.

Muzzleloading bullets for plains game need to be heavy for their caliber to provide reliable penetration on animals like kudu and zebra. Bullet weights that perform well are often between 275-350 grains in .45-caliber and between 300-400 grains in .50 caliber using powder charges of between 100-150 grains. I worked up a kudu load and used it on everything to prevent having to remember hold-over or hold-under for different powder-bullet combinations. Shooting is very often at close range in the brusher parts of the country, and a sight-in distance of 50 yards is preferred. In the dryer parts of South Africa shots may be longer and a 100-yard zero would be appropriate. The safari company will provide guidance as to what ranges the animals are usually taken.

What to take

Once the safari company has been selected, they will send a list of recommended items. Since I was going to do this only once, I bought a set of Beretta Safari clothes and also took some light-weight camo jackets that I already owned. Two changes of clothes are sufficient as clothes will be washed every day. In brushy country it is better to choose a darker green-tinted outfit and for more desert areas the tans do quite well.

Professional hunters usually go out in shorts, tennis shoes with no socks and a jacket in the morning. African trackers go with long pants, and I would suggest that most American hunters do the same and wear high-topped lace-up boots. The PH's outfit is designed for quiet movement through the brush and they prefer to take the scratches and pricks of the various thorn trees than make the slight scratchy noises of fabric rubbing on bushes.

Camo patterns are not much used in South Africa, although almost any pattern that works well in South Texas will provide excellent concealment. While I was there it occurred to me that some of the mesquite-patterned clothing would blend in very well. I also took a camo head net for added concealment during waterhole sits. The apparent reasons that camo patterns have not caught on in Africa are that a hunter might be taken for a mercenary in some countries, and there is so much game that if a stalk is busted it is reasonably easy to locate another animal.

On a more personal note, tobacco products are difficult to get and if you have preferred brands, they had best be bought at the duty free shop before you depart. South Africa, like most of Europe, is not washcloth country, and if you use one you had best take it with you.

Getting the guns over

Anyone who hunts with black-powder firearms expects challenges. When I wanted to use a black-powder pistol, rifle and smoothbore for African plains game, I was presented a number of difficulties that put my possibilities of success into the damn-nigh impossible category.

The simplest part was choosing the pistol and load. I had already shot a 350-pound Texas boar with Thompson/Center's 209X50 Encore pistol using two 50-grain Pyrodex pellets and a 370-grain Thompson/Center MaxiBall.

This bullet penetrated 27-inches of tough hog, and the animal expired almost instantly. The load produced 1,022 fps. velocity and 858 foot-pounds of energy from the Encore's 15-inch barrel. At 100 yards the MaxiBall retained 537 foot-pounds, similar to the .44 Remington Magnum. I have also killed game with a T/C Contender .44 Magnum with a similar-length barrel. Although subjective, I think the heavier (370 grain vs. 240 grain) and larger MaxiBall kills better than the .44 Magnum.

Recently, I had been experimenting with Hodgdon's TripleSeven pellets and found these shot more accurately than the Pyrodex pellets. In addition, they gave less barrel fouling that cleaned up with a few water-soaked patches. Loaded with two TripleSeven pellets, a .50-caliber Wonder Wad and the 370-grain T/C MaxiBall, I could shoot 2-inch groups at 50 yards with the iron-sighted pistol.

There was no doubt that the .50-caliber Encore was going with me. One of the first problems was that a hunter may bring into South Africa only one gun of a given caliber. If I took a .50-caliber handgun, the regulations appeared to prohibit also taking a .50-caliber rifle.

My rifle would have to be downsized to .45-caliber, which is generally considered small for the kudu, zebra and blue wildebeest that I would hunt. Ultimately, I selected a Knight UltraMag using 275-grain PowerBelt AeroTip bullets. These were the heaviest .45-caliber PowerBelt bullets and had greater penetration than similar hollow points. I was assured by Big Bore Express' Michael McMichael that these bullets would work with chest-cavity shots.

Gun number three of my battery was a 12-bore double-barreled slug-shotgun made by Davide Pedersoli. This versatile gun can be used with either a 571-grain patched round ball or 1¼-ounces of shot. The Encore was to provide a back-up shot, if needed. I also planned to hunt warthog and impala with the outsize smoke-belching handgun provided that proper conditions presented themselves.

The initial response that I received from South African Airways was that only two guns could be taken per hunter. I was dismayed as one of the purposes of my trip was to do a DVD on hunting African plains game with a muzzleloading rifle, smoothbore and pistol. If only two could go, one important leg of my video was literally shot out from under me. Another agent gave the ruling that only two long guns could be taken, but up to five handguns; provided that they were designed for sporting purposes. My long-barreled single-shot muzzleloading pistol certainly qualified. As required for handguns by South African law, I obtained a letter from

Thompson/Center attesting to this fact and included a photo of me and my Texas hog.

Ernest Dyason, my professional hunter with Spear Safari, sent me copies of the South African form that I needed to temporally import my three firearms. This form may be filled out at Johannesburg, but as I had only two hours to catch my connecting flight, I contracted with Air 2000 Hunter Support to preprocess my paperwork.

Earnest informed me that he could, with great difficulty and expense, get black powder, no. 11 caps and 209 primers; but there was no source for TripleSeven or Pyrodex Pellets in South Africa. I asked Chris Hodgdon, and he confirmed that Hodgdon had no distributor in the country. If I was going to use the TripleSeven loads that performed so well in my gun, I was going to have to bring them with me.

Airlines will not fly with black powder (one exception is in Alaskan bush planes where an application has been made and the passengers and pilot agree). However, airlines will fly with ammunition provided that it is sealed in original factory boxes. Obviously, I needed to make "Cartridges for muzzleloading guns" using my components and put these into properly labeled boxes.

By happenstance, I fell into E-mail correspondence with Randy Smith, no relation, who had come to the same conclusion. In conjunction with White Rifles, he had made up labels for Hogdon's powders to be pasted on plastic ammo boxes. After changing the labels to reflect my components, I made up .45 and .50-caliber cartridges in plastic tubes for the rifle and handgun. These were declared as ammunition on the import forms.

This was not deceptive, as cartridges wrapped in paper and metallic foil were originally designed for muzzleloading guns. Only centuries later, was the name applied to what should more correctly be called "metallic cartridges."

SAS airline regulations required that I have three bags. One rifle case containing the two long guns, one with the pistol and a third with the ammunition, as it could not be included with the guns. This costs $125 for an extra bag. Once inspected at the Atlanta airport, the cases were locked and put on board. My flight had a stopover in the Cape Verde Islands, but the guns and I remained on the aircraft.

I can't say that getting there was half the fun, but it certainly was more than half the bother.

A South African hunt for plains game

Double-dog tired, leg cramped, over caffeinated and feeling like I had lived in my clothes altogether too long, I had finally arrived at Johannesburg for my first African safari. I kept reminding myself that my purpose was to take five species of plains game, kudu, blue wildebeest, zebra, impala and warthog, with three diverse black-powder guns.

Could I? The issue was still in doubt. Supposedly I was to be met by a representative of Air 2000 who was to have pre-cleared my paperwork for the in-line rifle, double-barreled slug shotgun and muzzleloading pistol that I would be using. I had read horror stories about taking up to five hours for hunters to process their guns, and I had only two hours to make my connecting flight.

Once off the jet way, I saw a fellow holding up a cardboard with my name on it. I felt like giving him a hug. "I've got your paperwork. We need to go get your luggage and guns. Then we can go through customs, and put you on your flight."

There was a hitch. I made it. My pistol made it. But the double gun case with my rifle and shotgun had not. The other hunters were standing in line with their guns. It was looking like I would have to spend the day at the airport until my guns caught up with me and lose a day's hunting. Then I saw my case being pulled across the floor by a porter. For unknown reasons, it had been taken to another part of the airport.

Having pre-approved paperwork eased my passage through gun registrations (two separate inspections and ledger entries), and I was hustled to the domestic departure gates. Finally, I was airborne once again accompanied by my three guns, pre-packaged "cartridges for muzzleloading firearms" and my luggage.

On arrival at Hoedspruit, the guns and paperwork were again inspected and recorded. I was relieved to be met by Ernest Dyason my Professional Hunter and owner of Spear Safari. It felt good to be finally loaded into the 4-wheel drive and began the two-hour trip to the 38,000 acre Thornybush Game Preserve where the hunt would occur. At this stage I was nearly brain dead after the 18-hour flight and the airport hassle.

The rolling dry country with its brushy cover looked much like the American southwest, but instead of mesquite and oaks there were acacias and marulas. Piles of elephant dung in the roads, hornbills in the trees and an albino lion on the other side of a rhino-proof electric fence reminded me that this wasn't Texas.

"We have some daylight so we can shoot your guns and get everything ready for your hunt tomorrow morning," Dyason said. "We will shoot from sticks." I did O.K. with the Knight .45-caliber rifle and 275-grain PowerBelt bullets and 150-grain charge of TripleSeven pellets, but I might as well have been throwing stones so far as work with the pistol and smoothbore went. Shooting from sticks felt so strange that it was not helpful. I had to increase my load in the smoothbore to 155 grains of German WANO FFg black powder to have the 571-grain patched round ball hit at about the same point of aim as my original charge of 120 grains of GOEX FFg.

After cleaning the guns, a fine supper and two glasses of South African wine, I was ready for bed. I was offered chicken and pork chops for the next couple of meals. I replied that I had not flown some 8,000 miles to eat chicken. "That's no problem. After tomorrow we will eat something of what you shoot," Dyason asserted. I hoped so. The way I was feeling, I would have felt fortunate to

*The author's first piece of African game was a mature kudu, which is a mule-sized animal, although considerably more handsome.*

have cleanly dispatch a trapped mouse – much less the kudu that we would attempt to find the next morning.

Awakening long before dawn, I assembled my rifle and got ready to go. My preloaded cartridges considerably eased the preparations. I found my rangefinder and camera, and slipped everything into my shooting bag. At daylight, I fired two 209 primers to clear the guns and loaded a fresh charge. As I had explained to Dyason, the guns would be carried loaded, but not capped until immediately before the shot.

"You have come at a good time," Dyason said. "This is among the first hunts of the season so we will be able to get close to the game. The kudu and most of the plains antelopes are also in rut. Sometimes kudu are very hard to locate. We will start with them. Once the kudu is in the bag, taking the other species will be no problem."

Not long after the safari car with me, Dyason, videographer Carl Zaayman and tracker John Chabalala left the camp compound; we crossed a deep wash and saw a kudu with tall twisting horns. We attempted to stalk it, but it heard us in the noisy brush and disappeared into the thick thorn. A half-hour later we saw another bull standing in a small clearing 70-yards away.

"That's a good one," Dyason assured me. "Shoot from the truck; we are not going to be able to get any closer." This was not the way I would have preferred to have done it. Nonetheless, the beastie was there and this trip was more about demonstrating black-powder technology than sport. I drilled the kudu through the shoulder hitting the spine. It went down immediately. I reloaded and gave it a finishing shot when we walked up.

Most African antelopes carry their spines lower in the body than North

American game animals. Although the result of the shot was acceptable, I should have aimed lower to catch the lung-heart area which is low and forward in the chest. The kudu weighed well over 500 pounds, and the safari car's wench was needed to load it. I had five days to hunt and five animals to take, but the first one was hanging in the meat house. We would have kudu shish-ka-bob for supper.

Day two was for zebra which I had also planned to shoot with the Knight rifle. We had not seen any the previous day although we had seen rhino, buffalo, giraffe, lion, leopard, warthog, impala, waterbuck, baboon, monkey as well as other antelopes and birds. Asked where the zebras were, Dyason said, "I have just not taken you to where they are. They like areas with more grass growing between the thorn patches. We only shoot the stallions, and I will pick one out for you."

"Good," I thought. "Zebra sexing is not among whatever few skills I possess." In videos, I could not tell the mares from the stallions.

We stalked one herd, but it winded us and moved off. This was no serious matter as we found another herd of eight animals less than an hour later. After several approaches on foot, the stallion moved into an open spot about 100-yards away. I was able to take a shot from sitting and hit it in the shoulder. It fell. As I reloaded, it got up and ran another 100 yards. There it stood discharging bloody froth from its mouth. A few seconds later, it collapsed and died. The bullet had penetrated both lungs, but did not exit.

It was now time to put the rifle away and take up the pistol. In the meantime I had also developed a load for the Davide Pedersoli smoothbore using the German black powder which Dyason had purchased. From an unsupported standing position, the gun put a left and right into the two-inch bull of the target at 30 yards. If I could get close enough, I was sure that either the smoothbore or pistol would do the work. I suggested we try at a waterhole and built a blind at the water's edge. As it turned out, we had to relocate it in thicker brush six feet above the water level.

A parade of animals came in. These included zebra, giraffe, impala, black-backed jackal and wildebeest. We even had some ducks, Egyptian geese and a spoonbill for variety. That afternoon a boar warthog with good teeth came to drink. The shot was at about 50 yards. I felt that I could make a solid hit by resting my wrist on a branch that Dyason had cut for a shooting rail. Immediately after I fired, the warthog ran. I could see a white dot in the middle of the shoulder which assured me that I had made a good hit. There was a good blood trail, and Zaayman and I found it dead about 30-yards away. The 370-grain MaxiBall propelled by two 50-grain TripleSeven pellets had passed completely through the animal.

There was a possibility that we could have taken every species of game I was after at waterholes, if I had enough time. I set up on another waterhole for wildebeest, but none came in that afternoon.

On day four, the next to the last day for big-game hunting, we were on the road again. At this stage everything went - the rifle, smoothbore and pistol. I was

*Boar warthog taken with the .50 caliber 209X50 Thompson/Center Arms Encore muzzleloading pistol.*

ridiculously over-gunned, but I wanted to take advantage of whatever shot was offered with whichever gun appeared to be appropriate. A reasonable impala was spotted, and I tried for it with the pistol from the safari car. The animal left a slight blood trail and ran. We recovered it later that afternoon. My bullet had hit in the middle of the shoulder where I aimed, but I neglected to consider that the animal was facing away at a shallow angle when I fired. The bullet only hit muscle and a bit of the head. The tracker and I had got the animal up three times, but had no shot opportunity. Shinga, a trailing dog, found and held it until Dyason could kill it with a knife. This was one animal the hyenas would not get thanks to Chabalala's tracking skills and Shinga's speed.

Last day, last beastie, and the 12-gauge smoothbore had yet to take any game. There was only one animal left on my allotment, a blue wildebeest. The best chance seemed to be to use the safari car. We tried two stalks on a group of them, but could not get close enough. As it turned out the kudu scenario repeated itself,

*Double barreled 12-gauge slug-shotgun and blue wildebeest.*

99

and an ancient bull was spotted. "Shoot when it turns," Dyason said.

Cocking and capping the left barrel, I waited. Finally, it began to turn left, and I fired. The ball hit, and the animal went down.

"Shoot it again. It might get up." Dyason ordered.
Fumbling for a cap and putting it on the other nipple I fired another ball into the animal's chests as it lay on the ground.

"Good. That's got it for sure. I don't know how many spine-shot wildebeest that I have seen get up and run. The spine is carried so low under the hump that most hunters don't break it with their shots. They just hit the tip of a vertebra and the animal goes down to run off a few seconds later. You did good. Take your pistol and give it a finisher."

A shot with the 370-grain MaxiBall busted through the sternum and cut the backbone. This bullet was recovered as was a round ball which had its diameter increased by about 30 percent due to its passage through the animal.

When I had done my part, the guns and loads that I used had performed very well on plains game. Does this imply that any and all muzzleloaders will do for African game? No. It does not. Only the heaviest of .45-caliber bullets should be used propelled by 150-grain powder charges. Pistol bullets must be tough, of heavy caliber and non-expanding for maximum penetration. Round ball smoothbore loads must be of large caliber and delivered at close range.

Now that the work of the trip was done, I could take the slug shotgun out for birds. The freshly killed impala 100 yards from the camp gate was an indication that this was not just another grouse hunt. As Dyason approached the kill a baby leopard broke from a patch of grass and ran into deeper cover.

"Momma is just a few yards away," Dyason casually remarked. "Take a picture if you want and we will leave. We don't want to disturb her."

You damn well better believe that I did not want to disturb her.

Marita Dyason warned me when I booked the safari that they had birds but, "they are runners and we don't have good shooting. There are places in the agricultural areas where shooting can be very good, but not here. If you are content to take the odd bird or two, then bring your shotgun; but don't expect very much."

Not very much by South African standards translates to this North American grouse hunter as abundant. We had been seeing from 50 to 200 game birds of various species every day. The larger birds included the helmeted Guinea fowl in flocks of from 6 to 30 birds, covies of coqui francolin containing 5 to 12 birds and pairs and groups of three to five Swainson's francolin with their white heads and red-circled eyes. In addition, there were six species of dove with one of the most abundant being the Cape turtle dove with its white-rimmed black collar.

I had only taken no. 5 shot for the Guinea fowl and did not have any 8s for the doves. Using Shinga we found some covies of various birds and tried for them. I did manage to shoot enough for the pot with the cylinder and cylinder muzzleloader. The bag included one Guinea fowl that I shot on the wing. I took five birds including one Guinea fowl, one Swanson and three crested francolins. This was enough for supper. I wished that I had a bit more choke in the tubes. The RWS caps I was shooting did not provide nearly the pressure of CCI magnum no. 11s, and I had to increase my powder charge to 120 grains of WANO powder to obtain a reasonable result.

Just as I began to feel like I was getting to know something of the where to and how to on the African continent's game, it was time to leave. I had met some good people, had a good time, eaten very well, gotten all of my animals and accomplished the objective of using a variety of muzzleloading guns.

Loads for larger animals

Cape buffalo, elephants and rhinos often require hits from several big, tough bullets to kill the animals. PowerBelt made a .50-caliber 530-grain dangerous game bullet with a steel point, lead midsection and plastic skirt designed for optimum penetration. The company's owner Michael McMichael uses this bullet with a stiff load of Hodgden's TripleSeven powder in Davide Pedersoli's Kodiak double rifle to take buffalo continuing the tradition of hunting dangerous game with double rifles.

A new double rifle was introduced by Traditions at the 2006 Shot Show. This gun is an over-under .50-caliber rifle built on a shotgun frame that employs 209 primer ignition. This gun appeared to have real potential for an African big game rifle, but no one I knew had a chance to use it. The gun was heavy which meant it had the mass to soak up the recoil from big bullets propelled by heavy charges. I thought that this gun would have a relatively brief production life because of its specialized nature and limited sales appeal. That proved to be the case. A year after I purchased the gun it was discontinued. It did get to Africa as related in Chapter 20.

Could my double-barreled 12-gauge slug-shotgun potentially work? I would not use it on this class of game. Smoothbore round ball guns for heavy African animals were historically 8-gauge, with the even larger 4-bore (gauge) being preferred for elephant. The 12-gauge round-ball guns were considered relatively puny, particularly in smoothbore, and are outclassed by the larger gauges and rifles shooting elongated bullets.

When the old-time African hunters when after buffalo and such with their single-shot muzzleloading rifles they had extra preloaded guns standing by in case a rapid follow-up shot was necessary. If you are tempted to do an all-muzzleloader hunt for dangerous game, it is prudent to do the same and practice with your gun bearer so that when he hands you the gun it is cocked and ready to fire.

*This is one of two Afcican hunts that I have made to date. As with most hunters, the first hunt is a "get aquainted" trip. The next hunt was after Cape buffalo (Chapter 20) with some side adventures for ostrich, and other game.*

*The result of the author's squirrel hunting experiences with from the top Tage, the Japanese matchlock; Mortimer, a Davide Pedersoli fowler; Thompson/Center Arms' Mountain Magnum shotgun and the Encore muzzleloading 12-gauge Turkey Gun.*

## Chapter 9. Squirreling with different guns

Arm weary from carrying the 8-pound, 9-ounce hunk of mostly steel and with only a few inches of smoldering match left, I began to wonder if taking squirrels on consecutive days with shotguns using matchlock, flintlock, percussion and 209-primer ignition was such a good idea.

Not just any squirrel would do for Tage, as wife and I called the .50-caliber Tanegashima-style Japanese matchlock. The squirrel would have to be cooperative enough for me to approach within 20-yards, blow up a hot coal, fix the match in the cock, pin the match into place, open the pan, raise the gun and pull the trigger. My load of 50-grains of FFg and 7/8-ounce (70-grains by volume) of no. 5 shot cushioned by two Wonder Wads over the powder and one over the shot fired from the gun's .50-caliber barrel dictated that the squirrel be as close as possible.

To say that Tage is awkward to use on moving targets is an understatement. All of the weight of the gun is held in the hands while a diminutive rectangle of wood is positioned against the jaw just beneath the cheekbone.

I take Tage out at least once a year to keep my hand in the technology. I had seen four squirrels, but none would stay still long enough for me to attempt a shot. In a thick tangle of vines and saplings, I spotted a busheytail trying to pick his way along some briers. The swinging, moving vines were delaying his progress, and I might have a chance.

After proceeding though the steps I have already described, I raised the gun and took the shot at 12 yards. The squirrel was hit hard, but recovered enough to make its way to the branch of a small cedar. I removed the smoldering match, pinned it to a nearby pine, and dug into my bag for powder, shot and wads while keeping an eye on the squirrel.

Reloaded and reprimed, I refixed the match in the cock, aimed at the squirrel and pulled the trigger. Poof! The pan powder flashed, but the main charge did not fire. I removed the match, hung it in a tree, reprimed the pan and teased a little priming powder down the long flash channel to the main charge. After blowing up a hot coal, I repined the match in the cock and tried again. Click! Although the end of the red-hot match was resting on top of the priming powder, the powder would not fire.

Four more times I attempted to get Tage to shoot, but it would not. As a last resort I held the gun with one hand against a vine, aligned the sights as best I could and dabbed the glowing match in the pan until something happened. In the process I got a nasty powder burn on one finger when the charge fired, but I did not care. The squirrel fell dead. Tage has triumphed. It had taken its squirrel, although not without some trouble.

I always claimed that the Tanegashima matchlock was the gun for the person who wanted a maximum hunting experience, but did not want to clean much game. Just getting the gun to fire on demand adds considerable spice to a matchlock hunt. Because of the danger of unintended discharges, which will happen, matchlock hunting is best as a solitary sport.

### Davide Pedersoli Mortimer 12-gauge

Obviously a hunt with a wheellock would have been next to follow the progression of firearm development, but since there are no readily available wheellocks on the American market, the next gun would be a flintlock. One flintlock shotgun, patterned after an English fowler, is the Davide Pedersoli Mortimer 12-gauge. This is an advanced design with a roller-mounted frizzen, waterproof pan and dog safety on the hammer.

This gun was designed for wingshooting, and I could anticipate making shots on running squirrels at close range. In fact, my first shots were at dove. When it took several strikes for the gun to fire, I realized that the flint was too short. I cut a small stick, positioned it at the stem of the cock and remounted the flint so that the striking edge lay immediately back of the face of the frizzen when the gun was at half-cock. This cured my ignition problem.

Mortimer is a bit finicky about what it likes to shoot. For small game I load the gun with a duplex charge of 25 grains of FFFg followed by 50 grains of FFg, a hard 12-gauge over-powder wad, a ½-inch lubricated fiber wad, 1-ounce of no. 5s and a thin over-shot card. Reasonable results can be obtained with 1¼-ounce loads if the powder charge is reduced and plastic wads are used. Attempting to produce stouter loads results in hollow-centered patterns that you could throw a goose through without nipping a feather.

Mortimer's first prize was a fat squirrel that was chattering at a crow from the top of a 20-foot pine. The distracted squirrel did not notice me until it was too late. I shot the squirrel at about 20 yards, and it fell to the base of the tree. The second squirrel was partly shielded by the limb that it was running along when I fired. The squirrel was hit, but not fatally.

Rather than stopping to reload, I followed the squirrel until it tried to hide by clinging to the other side of a small multi-trunked oak. When it stopped I reloaded – powder, wads, shot, over-shot wad, cleaned pan, wiped the flint and reprimed. When I moved around the trunk it struggled up the tree, and I took the animal with another shot at 15-yards.

Mortimer, and any cylinder-bored muzzleloader, needs to take beasties like squirrels within 25 yards. This typically means hunting thick cover on days when the forest is wet enough to allow the hunter to move quietly. Using Mortimer, I had seen five squirrels, and taken two with three shots.

## Thompson/Center Mountain Magnum 12-gauge

This was to be the day I hunted with T/C's Mountain Magnum 12-gauge side-hammer shotgun. I had already installed a slip-on pad to increase the length of the buttstock and had raised the weight of the gun to 7 lbs. 10 oz. by adding lead shot suspended in wax to the hollow stock. The modified shotgun fit me and handled very well.

I found that the gun would shoot a 1¼-ounce load to the point of aim if I used 90 grains of Hodgdon's TripleSeven powder (the equivalent of about 100 grains of FFg), a 12-gauge Wonder Wad over the powder, a 1 5/8-ounce shot cup with a cut 20-gauge wad inside to reduce its capacity to 1¼-ounce of shot and a thin over-shot card. This load was fired with the musket caps that I prefer to use on hunting guns.

Screw-in chokes can be purchased for this gun, and I chose to use the tightest-shooting choke I had – an extra-full turkey choke with a barrel extension and muzzle brake that was supplied with the T/C Encore shotgun. I probably would have been more successful with the modified tube as I missed one squirrel that was too close to take with that extra-tight pattern. Another squirrel passed four yards from the gun muzzle – too close for a shot.

Heavy thunderstorms associated with hurricane Isadore prevented me from

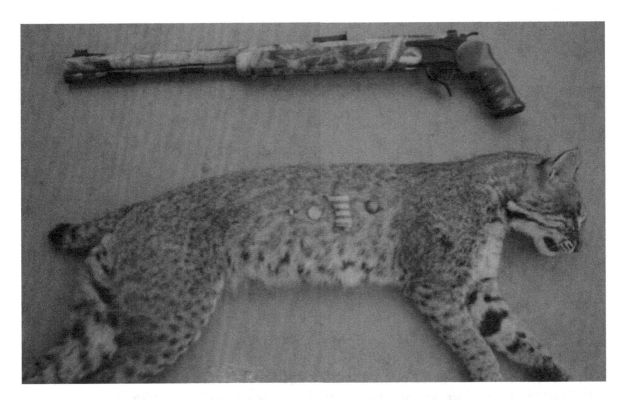

*While I had access to the Encore turkey barrel I outfitted the frame with pistol grip stocks and made a 12-gauge smoothbore pistol. This bobcat was taken at a range of about 15 yards with the gun. I later shot a deer with it and found that the charge was not sufficient to expand the ball, which cut through the animal more like an arrow than a bullet.*

hunting in the morning and part of the afternoon so the Mountain Magnum did not get a fair opportunity to show what it could do. This good-handling, good shooting gun would be my first choice among the four shotguns for squirrel hunting and wingshooting. This shotgun will also take turkeys very well, but is hampered by its lack of sights that prevent heavy loads to be zeroed to the point of aim.

The tally for the Mountain Magnum's abbreviated hunt was two shots taken, one squirrel missed and one brought home.

### Thompson/Center Encore 12-gauge muzzleloading shotgun

Muzzleloading and center fire Encore shotguns are best thought of as shotgun barrels fitted to rifles, which they are. The buttstock, while excellent for soaking up recoil from heavy loads, is inappropriate for wingshooting and the short 24-inch barrel reduces weight, but does not help the handling characteristics of the gun.

I chose T/C's maximum recommended load of 120 grains of FFg black powder, a plastic shot cup for 1 7/8-ounce of shot (the same 120 grain volumetric measure used for powder is used for shot) and a thin over-shot card. I prepared

## Table: Physical characteristics

| Name | length inches | weight lbs/oz | charge grains | shot oz | results |
|------|--------|--------|--------|------|---------|
| Tage | 54¾ | 8/9 | 50 | 7/8 | 1 squirrel/ 2 shots |
| Mortimer | 52¼ | 8/4 | 7 | 1 | 2 squirrels/ 3 shots |
| Mountain Magnum | 46 | 7/10* | 80** | 1¼ | 1 squirrel/ 2 shots*** |
| Encore | 40 | 6/12 | 120 | 1 7/8 | 4 squirrels/ 5 shots |

*Gun's weight increased by author
**Hogdon Triple-7 powder approximately equivalent to 95 grains of FFg.
***This hunt was delayed and later interrupted by hurricane-spawned thunderstorms.

some speed loaders with powder and shot in separate tubes, as I had none that could accommodate these large charges.

To give the Encore muzzleloading shotgun its proper due, the first four squirrels seen where killed with four carefully aimed shots. One shot at a moving squirrel was missed to make a total of four squirrels for five shots. The muzzle blast from the gun's short barrel was so severe, that I chose not to shoot the gun anymore without ear protection. For one shot at a turkey, it might be acceptable, but not for repeated shots at targets or game. This gun would be much more user friendly with 6-inches more barrel.

The hardly startling results of these hunts demonstrate that technological advances have made muzzleloading shotguns progressively more effective game getters. Choke boring has extended the range of gun by allowing heavier charges of powder and shot to be used while simultaneously achieving tighter patterns.

Glancing at the table quickly shows that the guns have become shorter, lighter weight and capable of giving acceptable results with increasingly heavy charges. This weight reduction is not all good because it has come at the cost of reducing the handling qualities of the shotgun to the point where they have become aim-and-shoot guns, just like rifles. This is acceptable for fixed targets like turkeys and squirrels, but not for flying game.

The best gun of the four for all uses is the modified Mountain Magnum with its added weight and lengthened buttstock. These alterations have much improved the gun. Installing adjustable sights, or a scope, would allow heavier shot charges to be effectively used for turkey hunting without having to remember to hold high to center the pattern on the bird's neck. The best of all would be optional barrels, a 30-inch one for wingshooting with another of the same length rigged for adjustable iron sights or scopes.

With the Encore shotgun, the pendulum has swung too far towards shorter barrels. That the 24-inch barrel is ballistically effective is not the point in question. The question is, "Will users, who need to hear what is going on while turkey hunting, remember to put in ear plugs before shooting?" The majority of the time they will not and could suffer hearing damage as a result. Five shots in an afternoon were too much for my ears.

Besides providing a tasty meal, these hunts served to refresh my memory on the operational characteristics of three guns, provide some new knowledge about a fourth, gave some good pre-deer-season exercise and renewed my acquaintance with some old-style, and favorite, firearms.

*A successful hunt with Roger Kicklighter, son Kevin and Ham Bone.*

## Chapter 10. Rabbits with Bess, bismuth and beagle

Stomping down briers while on a rabbit hunt with a tired 7-year-old, a beagle named Hambone that wasn't feeling well and hunting buddy Roger Kicklighter was not what I had in mind when I first charged Bess with 1 3/8-ounces of bismuth No. 2s. My intended quarry was geese, but geese were not to be this year – not because of any deficiency on Bess' part, but because of a lack of nerve on my part.

Despite her portly lines and homely appearance, I am fond of Bess, and we have experienced a number of hunting adventures together. I refurbished the Dixie Gun Works' Indian Gun after purchasing her at a club match. In my hands she has taken two deer, one swan, three geese, and ducks. The deer had been shot with .75-caliber round-ball loads, and the waterfowl were taken with steel shot. My original objective was to develop a more effective goose load using bismuth shot.

Even when shooting a flintlock, Federal law requires that nontoxic shot be used for waterfowl. Previously steel was the only acceptable substitute for lead, but the 1996-97 season was the first year that U.S. wildlife officials granted unconditional approval for bismuth shot. This metal is 23-percent more dense than steel, so I expected that a load of bismuth would transmit more impact energy to large birds like geese.

Trials of bismuth shot reported in several magazines were favorable, but for the first two years the shot was only available in no. 5 and smaller sizes. In 1996 a

*Bismuth shot in plastic jars with broken pellets (above) that were recoved from game.*

method was developed to form the balky material into larger pellets. Now loose no. 2 and BB shot as well as ammunition loaded with these shot sizes are available. The larger sizes promised to be as effective on geese as the no. 5 bismuth had been on ducks.

I remember how difficult geese were to kill with a 3-inch load of magnum lead no. 2s, and it was my hope the significant improvement bismuth loads offered over steel would be added insurance to help bring down these big birds. One goose I shot with Bess using steel shot was straight overhead. Roger saw the bird crump under the impact of the shot, but it continued to fly. The bird was crippled, and we recovered it later that morning. I felt there was a good likelihood a load of denser bismuth shot would have brought it down.

Four pounds each of bismuth BBs and no. 2s were ordered from Ballistic Products, Inc. The bill came to $72 after a writer's discount. This amounted to 56 cents an ounce for Bess fodder. If Bess needed it to do her job better, so be it. It was not as if I were going to shoot 500 rounds a day at trap. The cost for the half-dozen charges I might shoot at geese a year was an insignificant part of my costs per ounce of cooked goose, when you consider the annual depreciated costs of the gun, boat, motor and decoys to which are added the non-depreciatory costs such as transportation, food, licenses, scouting trips, etc.

First attempts

Many full-choked barrels are too constricted for good results with steel shot. Cylinder-bored guns like Bess have no such problems, and I developed steel waterfowl loads to use in both single and double-barreled muzzleloaders. Bess apparently preferred 90 grains of GOEX FFg, an 11-gauge over-powder card, 30 grains of Cream of Wheat filler, a MEC-122 plastic steel-shot wad, 1¼-ounces of steel shot and a thin shot-retaining wad.

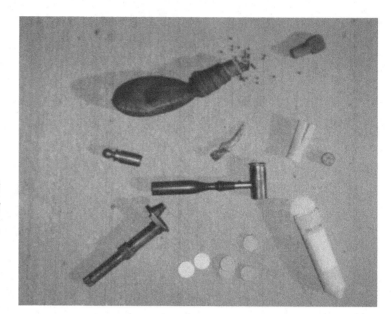

*Shooting accessories for a muzzleloading shotgun.*

Adapting my steel-shot load to bismuth only required placing a 3/8-inch Winchester molded fiber 20-gauge wad into the base of the MEC plastic wad to take up the excess space and filling the remaining volume of the wad with shot. This gave a reasonable load with 101 no. 2 bismuth or 52 bismuth BBs. The bismuth no. 2s penetrated 380 pages of the Thomas Register and yielded 50 to 70 percent patterns at 40 yards. The muzzleloading steel-shot load of the larger BBs penetrated 350 pages at the same range. An old Super-X load of lead no. 2s passed through 428 sheets of the Register – still a far more effective load than either of the muzzleloaded assemblies. The smaller bismuth no. 2s gave a denser pattern than the steel BBs and had slightly greater penetration.

The goose hunt

For our first hunt of the season, Roger, Kevin and I ventured to two farm ponds in Hancock County, Georgia, where Bess had succeeded in previous years. I positioned myself in a gap between some tall trees thinking if the geese came from their usual direction they would fly to the pond through this opening in the tree line. Roger honked on his call, and in the gray light of the coming dawn, a flight of geese came in silently. They set their wings and passed directly over me. When the leading bird looked good, I swung ahead of his beak and pulled the trigger. Bess fired, but the recoil did not feel as stout as the test loads. The bird flew on. It was apparently unscathed, as not a single feather fell.

My shot caused the eight birds to disperse, and some flew near Roger who was standing under the eves of a boat shelter in the lower of the two ponds. He fired and soon had his first goose of the year. Later he told me that he was not calling anything in particular, and my shot surprised him. When he saw geese all around him, he grabbed his gun and shot. He also remarked that my load sounded a little soft.

Our next attempt at geese was on the same pair of ponds, but this time a pair of geese came over the dam and flew up the pond. I thought they were a little far for Bess, and I did not shoot. Roger bagged one of the pair as they passed within 15 feet of the end of the dock. In retrospect I think Bess could have made the shot. With two birds in line, I should have swung a bird length ahead of the first bird and fired. In better light I saw they were only about 35-yards out, and the shot would have been a reasonable one to attempt.

"Sorry about that Bess. That was my fault," I muttered. We saw no more geese. That pair was our last opportunity of the season.

Roger was shooting bismuth BBs loaded in 12-gauge cartridges, and I was very interested in how they performed. Shot striking the breast were spherical and intact, but one that hit a wingbone fragmented and left hard shards of metal in the meat. I had noted when testing the loads for penetration on book paper that some bismuth shot broke up on impact with the cardboard book cover and some of the penetrating fragments were quite sharp. When some lead no. 2s were shot for comparison, the lead shot deformed but did not leave splintery fragments.

Bismuth and small game

Intrigued by this aspect of shot performance and having no other opportunity to test bismuth shot on waterfowl, I asked Roger if he would like to try some small game hunting in February after goose season closed. He agreed and suggested a place where there would be opportunities for both squirrels and rabbits. This might also be an opportunity for Kevin to kill his first game.

*Author with Bess and squirrel.*

Bess had bagged a squirrel before with a .75-caliber round ball which had taken the rodent's head off very nicely. This load was somewhat much for a squirrel, but the target offered itself, squirrels were in season and the gun needed to be unloaded. As a consequence, Bess had got herself a squirrel.

It would be somewhat different to try for squirrels with a load of no. 2 bismuth. Checking to make sure, I found that that no. 2s were legal for small game in Georgia. I thought it best to take a close look at the regs as I normally used no. 4s or 5s in Bess for squirrels and rabbits. The coarser shot patterned better in the cylinder-bored barrel than no. 6s.

The first squirrel came from behind, climbed a tree, jumped to another and was descending when I fired. After the smoke cleared there was no squirrel on the ground. I saw him scamper, apparently uninjured up into a tree.

"Hummm, this loaded sounded a bit puny too," I thought. The next squirrel was feeding on the ground about 20-yards away. This time the loads caught the squirrel well, and it did not move from where it had been hit. The next squirrel at about 30 yards was taken with a no. 2 shot in the body and one through the head. One aspect of using coarser than usual shot was that I was getting either a clean miss or a kill.

In the meantime Roger and Kevin moved from where they started and were, from the amount of shooting doing well. I heard one shot from Kevin's 20-gauge and 10 or more from Roger's .22. (With one shotgun round and an embarrassing large number of .22s they had killed one squirrel.) Bess and I were two squirrels for three shots – not bad, I thought. The sun was well up now and it was time to start after our principal quarry – rabbits.

Hambone was let out of his box, and the four of us proceeded to hunt some thick tangles of knee-to-waist-high briers, broom sage and honeysuckle. Hambone started pushing through the briers with enthusiasm, working a bit of cover we had just walked through. I suspected the rabbits were sitting tight, and so they were. The first broke from cover, I apparently missed with Bess, but Roger anchored the rabbit with a load of 7½s from the full-choked barrel of his newly purchased Parker Trojan-its first kill. When the rabbit was cleaned, one no. 2 shot had struck its rear leg, but it was the swarm of 7½s that had killed it.

This was also Hambone's first flush of game before a gun. He liked it and continued to sniff out the rabbit trail even though the rabbit lay dead in front of him. The beagle was so intent on his work that he paid no attention to the sound of the shooting or its effect.

Later in the hunt a second rabbit swung around, and I took it with Bess at a range of about 15 yards. The load was still tight and mutilated the rabbit's hindquarters. For my purposes, however, the rabbit had caught a fair number of shot, and these would yield some interesting information when they were recovered.

Roger and I stomped a likely patch of knee-high briers about 15-yards square. We each got a rabbit from the tangle. In both cases they were sitting tight in the briers and could have easily been taken with a pistol. (One of my favorite ways to take late season rabbits after the leaves drop from the briers.)

Unfortunately, Kevin was having enough problems pushing through the brush to carry his Harrington & Richardson National Wild Turkey Federation Youth Model. He had fired the little 20-gauge shotgun with some light-recoiling reloads, but was still a bit fearful of the gun. For the present Kevin carried an empty gun when he and his father hunted. Under state law a child under the age of 14 may hunt with an adult provided the child in under close supervision at all times.

Hambone had a shot at the vet's the day before and was not feeling too well. That was the end of the hunt for him, and Hambone went back to the dog box. Kevin was fairly well done in too. This had been a tiring 2 hours pushing through the heavy cover. He had trudged manfully forward, but he was just about ready to call it quits. To have hunted much longer ran the risk of spoiling Kevin's enthusiasm for hunting altogether, so we agreed to call it a day.

Further load development

Considering my experiences with apparently underpowered initial shots from Bess, I decided further load development was necessary. On several occasions over the past 2 years, it appeared that the first shot fired from a clean barrel was softer recoiling than subsequent shots and had apparently delivered less energy to the target.

Having purchased on Oehler 35P chronograph, I now had a means for accurately measuring velocities. The first three shots indicated Bess' first round left a clean barrel at about 875 feet per second (fps), the second at 1,025 fps. and the third at 1,075 fps. Bess was cleaned as usual and two more series of three shots were fired. Most consistent pattern results were obtained when the velocity of the shot measured at 15 feet was in the range of 1,000 to 1,050 fps.

There were two potential solutions to promote more uniform performance between the first and subsequent shots. The first was to shoot a fouling shot and then reload. The second was to increase the initial load from 95 grains of FFg to 98 grains, which boosted the velocity towards the 1,000 fps. range and then cut back to 95 grains for subsequent shots. This loading change kept the followup shots from rising to 1,100 fps with a resulting decrease in pattern density.

Increasing the load for the first shot to 98 grains of FFg and decreasing the shot count from 101 to 87 no. 2 bismuth shot resulted in patterns in the 70-percent range when fired from a clean bore. The velocity of this load averaged about 900 fps. The second shot fired from a fouled bore with a reduced powder charge of 95 grains resulted in patterns that averaged in the 60-percent range with a velocity of about 1,000 fps. Firing two shots, completely cleaning the barrel and firing two more shots, cleaning the barrel again, etc. became somewhat laborious; however, three repetitions firmly established that the velocity differential was real.

Some people report having problems with plastic residue remaining in gun barrels when plastic wads are used with black powder. I clean dirty black powder barrels with warm water soaped up with Dawn dishwashing detergent followed by rinsing with clear water. Plastic adhering to the barrel walls comes off as soft stringy masses that are easily removed by the cloth cleaning patches.

Pattern testing

Several trends were noted when the loads were patterned. Bess threw better patterns with plastic wads, larger size shot, lighter powder charges and more cushioning between the powder charge and the shot. None of these are unexpected outcomes. An old shotgunning adage goes, "Little powder, more shot, kills far, kills dead." Shoulder-busting loads in a cylinder-bored muzzleloader may be macho, but usually result in patterns having hollow centers. Increasing the shot charge to a nominal 2 3/8 ounces of shot as measured in an antique shot measure only resulted in 27 or the 78 BBs striking in a 30-inch circle at 40 yards for a 35-percent pattern. Decreasing the shot weight to a nominal 1 3/8 ounces saw 34 of 52 BBs register on the target – a 65-percent pattern. Patterns with BBs were patchy with dense clots of shot striking some areas while other large parts of the target received no hits. Best patterns with this load were obtained with 93 grains of FFg from a fouled bore.

When the smaller no. 2 shot was used propelled by 95 grains of FFg, 54 out of 101 shot registered in a 30-inch circle when shot from a clean bore. Fired through a dirty bore the same powder charge gave 62-percent patterns. Although the percentage of no. 2s striking the target was less than the BBs, the more evenly distributed smaller shot caused me to prefer no. 2 bismuth shot over the BBs for birds the size of Georgia's giant Canadian geese.

Shot performance

*Bess at the pattern board testing bismuth shot loads.*

The no. 2 bismuth shot that had passed through soft tissue between the ribs remained intact, but shot that struck the tough leg bones of the rabbits fractured into two to eight angular pieces. The performance of the no. 2s was reminiscent of the initial batches of no. 5 bismuth shot that were offered in the first stages of shot development. Making the larger shot sizes has presented another series of technical problems. Some have been solved, and I am sure the performance of bismuth shot will continue to improve. Even as it stands, bismuth shot loads have considerably better killing potential on big birds like geese, cranes and swan than any steel-shot load can achieve even if it was, and is, inferior to present loads of HeviShot fired through cartridge or muzzleloading guns. Bismuth shot still has the advantage that it can be fired through tightly choked barrels without causing damage, whereas the non-deformable steel and tungsten-alloyed HeviShot should only be used in modified barrels. In addition HeviShot is very abrasive and must be used with a heavy plastic wad to keep from scouring the barrel.

Bess and I found out some things and learned our lesson. Next time we go after waterfowl we are going to use bismuth shot and 100 grains of FFg for our first shot and then cut back to 95 grains so that the bismuth leaves the barrel at a more uniform velocity. Out path to knowledge took some unusual twists, but doesn't a lady always come up with some surprises?

*Bismuth shot is available in both loaded shotgun shells and as loose shot. For those who do not want to use plastic wads to prevent barrel abrasion from steel or tungsten-containing shot, bismuth shot is ideal for loading with conventional wads. The shot that I used has a heavy graphite coating and leaves more fouling in the barrels. Lubricating the edges of the wads with a product like Thompson/Center's Bore Butter will help prevent carbon build-up and make the gun easier to reload.*

*Flight of tundra swan.*

## Chapter 11. Flintlock and percussion swan

The technological dilemma of modern muzzleloading for waterfowl is that out of a desire to return to a more sportsmanlike way of harvesting waterfowl we use slower-to-load single shot and double-barreled shotguns while nonetheless needing to employ the latest technology to cleanly kill our birds. Swan, the largest of North America's waterfowl, offers the chance to test the technological limits of guns and loads while providing one of the most exciting waterfowl hunting opportunities that exist.

American swan

Four species of swan are present in North America. There is an annual regulated harvest of the whistling (tundra) swan which is present in large numbers and breeds in Alaska and northern Canada. The trumpeter swan has a smaller range, but also migrates into the western U.S. This swan is completely protected. The whooper resides on a remote range in the Aleutian island and remains in the far north. The last swan is the imported European mute swan that can nearly monopolize waterfowl nesting and feeding habitats in areas where it has been introduced. Some states have requested permits to reduce numbers of mute swan in overpopulated areas, and it appears likely that limited hunts for mute swan will soon be allowed.

Swan are magnificent, and anyone can easily see how a pair of swan, perhaps with a pair of gray-feathered cyglets in tow, could add a tranquil touch to a city or private pond as they glide under and out of the weeping willow's green branches. Indeed, no one has a problem with a few swan, it is when several thousands of the huge birds become localized in small areas that they do damage to the local environment, consume most of the available feed due to the reach of their long necks and drive other waterfowl from their nesting territories.

Swan summer and nest in Alaska and northern Canada, and migrate diagonally across the continent to winter in the Southeast. They fly at altitudes as high as 5,000 feet and can make 1,000-mile hops between flights. They must raise their young in a hurry to take advantage of the short Summer season. The cygnets weigh 6 ounces when hatched, but have grown to about 12 pounds when ready to fly south 70-days later. Swans mostly feed on aquatic vegetation but will also eat waste corn and green sprouting vegetation in their wintering areas.

How big do swan get? An adult swan will weigh over 18 pounds, have a wingspan of in excess of 74-inches, a length of more than 50-inches with a beak that is 4-inches long and massive webbed feet equipped with very efficient claws. Even the largest of geese, which may weigh a little over 12-pounds, don't stand much of a chance going toe to toe with a swan.

Where to go

Any listing of hot duck-hunting spots in North America has to mention North Carolina's Lake Mattamuskeet as among the top destinations. The 40,000 acre natural lake, located in a productive agricultural district adjacent to Pamlico Sound, draws waterfowl by the tens of thousands. In modern times the lake is principally noted as the wintering ground for 25-30,000 tundra and a few mute swan, a variety

*Swan on a protected part of the Mattamuskeet Wildlife Refuge.*

of ducks and increasing numbers of Canadian and snow geese.

During most of the last century private clubs controlled the goose and duck hunting on the lake. An ambitious plan to drain the lake started in the early 1900s, and 13,000 acres of croplands were developed. High operating costs caused the development to fail, and the U.S. Government purchased the assets of the New Holland Corporation in 1934 for $312,000. Since then, the Wildlife Refuge has grown to 50,180 acres. Public access for hunting is now allowed from 16 permanent blinds on the south side of the lake which can accommodate nearly 1,100 hunters a year as well as an annual youth hunt.

"What we try to do," explained Biology Technician Katie Schill, "is to provide a quality hunting experience for a diversity of waterfowl. Just in the last couple of days hunters brought in swan, a snow goose, teal, gadwall, widgeon, wood duck, pintail, black duck, mallard and ruddy duck. Outside of sea ducks, almost every duck found in eastern North America at least occasionally visits Lake Mattamuskeet."

As if to underscore this point, a recent newspaper article posted at the refuge headquarters reported the presence of a few cackler geese, which are mallard-size versions of the Canadian goose. These uncommon migrants brought in bird watchers from as far away as Charleston, South Carolina, and Virginia.

Swan are taken by permit only with a limit of one per year. Each year a drawing is held in early October for between 3,000 and 5,000 permits. The easiest way to apply for a premit is when purchasing a regular hunting license by telephone in late Summer. Hunters will also need to file their HIP report and get a state Waterfowl Stamp at the same time. A Federal Waterfowl Stamp, available at local post offices, is also needed. Permit holders may take swan from the public blinds at Mattamuskeet as well as elsewhere in coastal North Carolina. Hunting is permitted in parts of the Eastern flyway because the ranges of the tundra and

*Guide Joey Simmons and Bill Krantz hold up a swan from Lake Mattamuskeet, NC.*

trumpterer swan do not overlap.

Applications for the permanent blinds on Lake Mattamuskeet must be received at the refuge by the end of the first week in October. The application consist of a name, address, date of birth and three hunt date preferences on a 3X5 index card. If not drawn for a blind, there is a chance of being drawn for a standby blind at 5:00 AM on each hunt date. The public blinds are hunted on Tuesday-Wednesday and Friday-Saturday of each week during the waterfowl season. There is a fee of $12.50 per person per day for the hunt that is collected the morning of the hunt. The person who draws a blind may bring up to two hunters with him.

One blind is available that is accessible by a wheelchair or walker. If this blind is needed a request should be included on the application. Most blinds require walking through water that may be from knee to waist deep. Waders and a wading staff are strongly recommended. The lake mud is sticky and it is easy to fall trying to pull a foot from the lakebed. Shooting hours end at noon, and a maximum of 30 shells per hunter are allowed.

For additional information write the Mattamuskeet National Wildlife Refuge, 38 Mattamuskeet Road, Swanquarter, North Carolina, 27885 or call (252) 926 4021.

A limited harvest of swan, also by permit, occurs in some Rocky Mountain states stretching from Montana to Utah where the ranges of the trumpeter and tundra swans do not often overlap. This range separation is important as the two species are indistinguishable in flight. The Canadian province of Manitoba has been donating its swan quota to South Dakota hunters, but is considering opening swan shooting in the province.

Guns and loads

Although I have cleanly killed swan with steel shot, this light-weight shot stinks as a waterfowl load fired from open-choked black-powder shotguns. The higher shot count does increase pattern density, but an all-to-often result is to plaster a bird, draw lots of feathers and have the duck fly off.

An inescapable conclusion is that modern muzzleloading waterfowlers need to use a higher-density shot along with protective plastic wads to stand a reasonable chance of cleanly taking a few geese and swan each year. In muzzleloading shotguns, bismuth shoot is a marked improvement over steel, and HeviShot is much better than steel, bismuth or even lead.

A fair question is, "How do you know?"

For the past decade I have been taking each year's new crop of replica muzzleloading shotguns to hunt ducks, and most especially swan, in coastal North Carolina. A typical week-long hunt will take me from Lake Mattamuskeet to Bodie Island and then down to Cape Hatteras. Each year I try for a different hunting experience and may shoot sea ducks one year and on another freelance for ducks on the sound.

*An Austin&Halleck 12-gauge shotgun with a North Carolina swan.*

Guns used have ranged from a replica flintlock .75-caliber (11-gauge) Indian Gun from Dixie Gun Works using 1¼ -ounce loads of steel no. 4s, to Knight Rifle's TK-2000 in-line shotguns which can throw up to 2¼ -ounces of HeviShot from its choked barrel.

What's a muzzleloading hunt like?

There is a thrill from dropping a passing duck, goose or swan with one blast of your black-powder smokepole that surpasses any other waterfowling experience. You can go to South America and shoot, shoot and shoot some more until you just have to quit. This is an exhausting, but interesting, experience.

However, shooting big numbers of anything pales in comparison to sitting in the blind with your black-powder shotgun stuffed with your custom-developed load. You wait to see if one of the approaching birds will come close enough, stand and track the bird with your long-barreled fowler and pull the hammer back. Although the shot is nearly instantaneous, time seems to slow to nearly a standstill. You visualize the feel the scraping of the rock on the steel or the fall of the hammer on the cap. You experience a jolt as the ignition sequence starts and the wad-column compresses. You keep tracking the bird as the shot starts moving down the long barrel and sense the release as the shot clears the gun.

Smoke, fire, wads and shot erupt out of the end of the barrel. In your mind's eye you can see the swarm of shot getting organized as it leaves the barrel. Errant and out of round shot leaving the swarm with the larger shot pushing ahead as the smaller pellets lag behind. The first shot hits the bird. It staggers and the remainder of the body of the shot charge strikes with devastating impact.

As the black smoke obscures your vision, you look under the dark cloud to see your snow-white swan falling from the sky. This is something more than bang, bang, bang and down comes a duck. It is one shot, one chance for success or failure. This experience elevates waterfowling to something more than just shooting a bag-full of birds.

There is certainly much more involvement in the entire process and a much larger personal stake in the ultimate outcome – the harvesting of a piece of game for the table. This experience yields a complex series of emotions such as pride in your accomplishment, regret over the death of such a magnificent fowl and admiration for the generations of waterfowlers before us who regularly used such guns.

A North Carolina Swan Hunt

From the helicopter the cygnets looked like three gray basketballs being escorted around a pond by their snow-white parents. Even from several hundred feet, the adults looked huge. This was my first glimpse of swan on their breeding grounds. In 1972 I had seen them while duck hunting in the Tarheel state of North Carolina and now they, like me, were in Alaska 3,000 miles away.

When I first hunted Lake Mattamuskeet, one could shoot geese and ducks, but there were no season on swan. I had swan over the "deaks," but they passed unmolested. My guide called them "sky carp," because the swan competed for the same food used by the geese and ducks his clients paid him to hunt. I was pleasantly surprised when as a newcomer, or Cheechako, in Alaska I saw hundreds of swan nesting on small ponds. I hunted waterfowl during the dozen years I lived in the state, but again, swan were not legal game at the time.

North Carolina began a limited harvest of swan in 1984. The North Carolina Wildlife Resources Commission along with the U.S. Fish and Wildlife Service agreed the population could sustain a 10 percent annual harvest. Permits, which may range between 3,000 and 5,000 a year depending on populations, may be issued by the state allowing the lucky hunters to harvest one of these magnificent birds apiece during the waterfowl season.

George Reiger, author of The Waterfowler's Quest (Lyons & Burford, 1989), was uncertain if swan could be the waterfowler's ultimate trophy. Reiger described making a poor shot at a bird at close range. He felt guilty about finishing the bird by beating its head against the frozen ground. He felt that this was a disrespectful way for such a magnificent fowl to die. Other hunters I interviewed who had killed swan also considered that their accomplishment somehow ranked less than a trophy experience. "Too easy" was their common complaint. I made the decision that if I were going to take a swan it would be with one of my muzzleloading smoothbores.

Even then, I had almost quit using cartridge guns. My preferred waterfowl gun was a flintlock 11-gauge Dixie Gun Works' Indian Gun. This is a shortened, browned cousin of the British Brown Bess musket used during the 1700s. "Bess," as I called her, had already shot dove, ducks and geese using steel shot and had also taken two deer with roundball loads. I thought that a swan, the waterfowler's equivalent of the big game hunter's elephant, would be an appropriate trophy for it to take.

There are flintlock fowlers with dainty locks, slim wrists and long barrels that have the sleek lines of a greyhound. Bess is more like a husky. It is built for strength, reliability and stamina rather than speed. With a 1-inch flint striking 1 inch of hardened steel, sparks are almost certain to fly into the pan. Reliability was important to Bess' military ancestors, and this trait is equally important to me as a waterfowler.

Having returned to Georgia to live, Mattamuskeet is in relatively easy reach, about a 14-hour drive. I tried to arrange a hunt in January of 1997, but because I omitted a sending in the special $5.00 application fee, I was not drawn for a permit. I had my guide selected, reservations arranged and deposit paid, but that hunt was regretfully scrubbed. With renewed determination I planned another hunt for January, 1998.

My usual partner was financially overextended by the purchase of some hunting land and felt that he could not swing another hunting trip. I needed another partner and found him in Tom Jones of Atlanta. The investment advisor and I met at an outdoor writer's conference and this unusual hunt appealed to him. We planned to go on a guided hunt on Lake Mattamuskeet for two days to shoot swan and ducks. This worked, except Tom did not get his swan permit for the same reason my application had been rejected the year before. He had not sent in his $5.00 fee. Good sport that he is, Tom said that he would go anyway.

We swapped driving and hunting tales on the long trip out. I told Tom about Bess' taking a Scotch double on geese two years ago and its exploits on other goose, duck and deer hunts. We arrived at the Mattamuskeet Inn and checked in with owner and fourth-generation guide Joey Simmons. He informed us that wake-up would be at 4:00 AM.

Joey was intrigued that I was going to attempt to take a swan with a flintlock. I told him I had developed bismuth loads for the gun. He said he recommended duck loads of 1¼-ounces of steel 4s to his clients. His experience was that the nearly yard-long neck and head were the vulnerable parts of the bird. He warned, "All of us can't pump enough steel shot into a swan to keep it from escaping back into the refuge if it is shot in the body."

So warned, I loaded Bess with 100 grains of FFg black powder, an over-powder card, 35 grains of Cream of Wheat, a MEC-122 pink plastic wad and 1¼-ounces of steel no. 4s. The wad was designed to be used in 3-inch, 12-gauge shells. It is slightly undersized for an 11 gauge and loads easily. The Cream of Wheat Filler in this load helps maintain a gas seal under the plastic wad and keeps the over-powder wad from jamming itself into the base cup of the plastic wad.

I had developed this load for duck and turkey hunting. I felt confident that pattern would be dense enough at 35 yards to be effective on swan.

Tom agreed to shoot backup using 3-inch Federal loads of tungsten no. 2s. If I crippled the swan he was to keep shooting until the bird fell. When using single-shot guns on large birds, I always try to have someone else with me in case my only shot is a non-fatal hit. The alternative is to take a second gun.

We flushed hundreds of ducks, geese and swan from the flooded corn when we went into the blinds before daylight. The predawn sky was filled with bright stars, and there was not a cloud in sight. The day before had been 70 degrees – very unusual January weather for North Carolina. These bluebird conditions did not foreshadow good duck hunting.

The only activity during the first part of the morning was that some hunters below us shot coot. By 10:00 AM we had only a single shot at a high flying duck. The guides were calling well, but the few ducks we saw would not work.

"Whuup, oooup, oooup, oooup," Joey called in a high-pitched voice to three swan in the distance. Responding to his mouth calling, the birds swung and turned toward the other blind where the swan decoys were deployed. "Whuup, oooup, oooup, oooup," and they set their wings. They rapidly lost altitude as they swung towards the decoys. We saw two swans hit and seconds later heard the reports from a fusillade of shots. With two birds down, that group had one more swan to take before their permits were filled.

In about half an hour more swan flew nearby. These also stooled to the decoys. The final hunter shot the lead bird as its feet touched the water. That group had limited out, and it was time to change blinds.

During the slow morning's shooting, Joey told us swan responded well to calling and decoys – particularly on sunny days. He used giant snow geese decoys with their wingtips painted white. Joey said if the "deaks" were placed in areas where the swan wanted to go, hunters had no trouble filling their tags. The most common problems he had were that hunters attempted to take the birds too far out and shot for the body rather than the head and neck.

"Use decoys, sit tight, take 'um close and shoot 'um in the lips," summarized his advice on swan hunting. "I can almost guarantee that if the hunter can half-way shoot, he will get his swan. I suppose what unnerves most hunters is that the birds are so big and we don't shoot until they are on top of us."

By the time Tom and I went into the other blind even the swan had stopped flying. We pulled out at 11:00 A.M. without firing a shot. Since I still needed a swan, I would shoot from the same blind that afternoon.

I checked Bess. I had fired one shot during the morning. When I reloaded I used 95 instead of 100 grains of FFg since I was now shooting through a fouled barrel. Experimentation had demonstrated that Bess was most effective when the loads were launched at about 1,000 fps. I cleaned the frizzen, flint and pan with alcohol, made sure the flint was tight in the cock and left the gun in the blind for the afternoon shoot. The last thing I wanted to do was to risk dunking it into the water on the muddy slogs from and to the blind.

123

After lunch we returned and soon had activity. It looked like this swan was going to be my bird. It was a single swan flying back to Lake Mattamuskeet from wherever it had been feeding. Joey called, and the swan set down outside of the decoys, too far to shoot. Meg, Joey's Lab, decided this was her bird, shot or not. She leaped off the dog shelf and was after it. The swan jumped off the water and flew away from the blind. Startled by the other group of hunters who were moving in their blind, the swan reversed directions and flew back towards us. It had a tail win and was in full flight. It looked like it would pass on the right side of our blind.

"Quick, move over here," Joey said. I climbed over Tom and Joey and took a ready position on the other end of the blind. I quickly checked the prime put the frizzen back down and waited.

On came the swan oaring through the air with its massive wings. If I thought swan were big before, this one looked gigantic.

"If you are going to take it, do it now," Joey said.

Cocking the massive flintlock as I rose, I put Bess to my shoulder and started tracking the bird. She felt good against my shoulder and cheek. The swing was smooth, but the barrel caught on a piece of brush that was helping to conceal that end of the blind. Lifting over it, I resumed my swing.

I pulled past the tail, past the body, past the neck and finally past the head. When the gun passed the head I pulled the trigger and smoke erupted from the gun's muzzle and pan and obscured my view.

The hunters in the other blind said that it looked like a column of smoke shot of our blind and enveloped the bird. The swan, apparently struck dead in the air, fell from the cloud like a ball of white paper. Meg, delighted that she had work to do, rushed towards the bird; but her efforts were unnecessary.

There was a resounding cheer from the other blind. They later said that they first thought that I must have had a misfire when the bird got close to our blind, and I did not shoot. Then they saw the smoke and the falling bird. Only after the swan hit the water did the booming report of Bess' shot reach them. They were impressed that Bess, even though a single-shot flintlock muzzleloader, was apparently as effective as their modern guns.

The swan had been hit from beak to feet by the pattern of no. 4s. One shot had penetrated the brain, four more in the neck, four struck the body including one that broke a wing and another cut the webbing between the toes. Joey said that neither he nor his father had ever heard of a hunter taking swan with a flintlock gun in two generations of guiding on the lake.

I was certainly pleased – one attempt, one shot, one swan dead. Bess had done well. I felt satisfied that Bess and I had taken a waterfowler's trophy in a sporting manner. Not bad for a pot-belled flintlock gun of antique pattern using steel shot.

The other end of the technological spectrum

After that first experience, I took swan with a variety of cap-lock percussion guns including a CVA single-barreled Trapper Shotgun which I cannot really recommend, a Thompson/Center Arms' Mountain Magnum single barrel and a Davide Pedersoli double barrel slug shotgun. With each of these I developed various loads and was ultimately successful. I liked the T/C Mountain Magnum 12-gauge after I had loaded up the hollow buttstock with sufficient lead shot and melted beeswax to give it a enough weight to be comfortable to shoot with a 1¼-ounce load of HeviShot and a charge of 90 grains of Hodgdon's new TripleSeven powder.

Modern in-line shotguns using 209-shotgun primers promised to be very effective as they used interchangeable chokes, and could take heavier charges of shot. Knight's TK 2000 stood alone in being able to belch out a full 2¼-ounces of shot. The down side is that sights or a scope had to be used with this super-heavy shot charge so that the charge could be directed to the point of aim. Although slow to aim, I did make a shot on a swan that patterned 21 HeviShot in the head-neck area at a full 40 yards as I teetered with one foot on the edge of blind's seat. The load knocked me back, the swan was killed and I was blooded.. For a very few shots taken from a stable position, the load was and would have been fine. If I ever had a chance to pass shoot sanhill cranes, this would be the gun and load I would use.

Austin & Halleck's new 12-gauge shotgun seemed to have considerable promise as an excellent shooting choked muzzleloader that could take an 1 3/8-ounce load of HeviShot in front of a charge of 100 grains of TripleSeven. In this gun I used a hard over-powder wad, a 12-gauge Wonder Wad, a shot cup for 1 3/8-ths ounce of lead shot with a piece of cut off 20-gauge wad in the bottom so that it would hold the same weight of the denser HeviShot and a thin over-shot card. I had accumulated a variety of screw-in chokes and picked out one that gave the best patters that also hit to the point of aim.

To give this lightweight gun more weight, I drilled a hole in the maple stock and filled it with lead shot. I also substituted the polymer ramrod with one made of steel to preserve the gun's excellent balance. I had used the gun on a quail hunt before I went on my swan hunt and killed seven of eight birds with it. From all appearances, it appeared that this gun was ready to take its swan.

Georgia's squirrel season starts in mid-August and extends through February providing an ample opportunity for testing the new gun and loads prior to using them on waterfowl. A load described above with no. 5 lead shot patterned well with a screw-in modified choke. Squirrel within 30-yards was most often cleanly killed with a single shot.

On my 2006 swan hunt, I and Paul Presley were hunkered down in the sparse cover of a drainage ditch. Guide Adam Jones had put out a series of white snow goose decoys and flags around us. Sitting in the ditch, we waited. An interesting aside was that Adam had been the guide in the other blind when I had taken my first swan with Bess eight years before. As Paul had never shot a swan, he had the first shot. His bird come in, and he empted the Mossberg 835 that I had lent him. We could see the bird laboring in flight and then fall into a distant field. Adam and Paul ran down to the road, jumped on a four-wheeler and went after the bird.

A few minutes later they returned with the bird. Fortunately, the white swan had been easy to spot when it fell in the huge, flat treeless fields.

In the meantime, more birds were coming. We all hunkered down and on they came. It looked like the shot would be ideal. The bird was straight over us at about 20 yards. I rose, pushed the safety off held slightly ahead of the huge head and pulled the trigger. Thunk! The striker fell on the 209 primer, but the primer did not fire. The swan continued its flight towards the sound behind us. Once we made sure that there were no other swan in sight, I tried again. Thunk. Thunk. This particular striker had only a very small protrusion on its face that could hit the primer. There were scratches and a tiny indentation on the face of the primer, but that was all. To say the least I was disgusted. I did have another back-up muzzleloader with me, but it was back in the hotel room 20-miles away.

Earlier I had intermediate problems getting the gun to shoot that I thought were caused by a harder cap used on Winchester 209 primers compared to the Remington primers that I started with. This was a part of the problem, but the real cause was that the actual pin on the face of the striker that struck the primer was too short. Later, I returned to Georgia, replaced the pin and used the same gun successfully on later quail and turkey hunts (Chapter 3).

We were in the field, the guide was hired, the swan were flying, and I took that year's swan with the Mossberg 835 and the steel-shot loads that Paul had purchased. The first shot dropped the swan like a stone, but it revived and I had to use subsequent shots to finish it. This was a less than satisfactory experience. I felt that my 1842 muzzleloading 11-gauge musket back in the room and the HeviShot load that I had prepared would have done a better job.

*If lessons were to be learned from this experience they were that all mechanical objects will someday fail and to keep your back-up gun more conveniently accessible when you hunt. Despite its failure on the swan hunt, the Austin & Halleck shotgun is a well balanced, good shooting and generally reliable gun that I later used on snow geese and with considerable success.*

*I chose to shoot this jake with a camera, rather than a gun.*

## Chapter 12. Turkey talking, hunting and shooting

In Mexico the wild turkey is known as a guajalote instead of the name pavo which is mostly applied to commercially-raised birds. I use to kid my wife Thresa that the reason for this was that the birds south of the border went "guaja, quaja, quaja" instead of our accustomed "gobble, gobble, gobble." This is not true. Although most turkeys  do gobble there is one, the ocellated turkey of Central America, that does not. Not only is this unusual fowl silent, it has a turquoise head, bright orange knobblies and a fan with eyes like a peacock.

In the U.S. we have huntable populations of Osceola, eastern, Rio Grande, and Merriam turkeys with a few reintroduced Gould's turkeys in southern Arizona. An extremely limited number of permits have been occasionally auctioned off for a Gould's turkey to help pay for reestablishing the U.S. population. The more accustomed way to get a Gould's is to arrange for a hunt in Mexico which has a larger population. A grand slam of turkeys is considered to be one each of the four more common species. Purest assert that this must be done in a single year, but unless you have a sponsoring organization or ample money, the time period is not important. Taking a slam with black-powder guns or other interesting hunting tools is an accomplishment, even if it might take several years to do it.

The first task is to locate a suitable population of turkeys of the sort you want to hunt, try to select the optimum time when the toms are most responsive to calling and then choose the precise area for the hunt.

Eastern wild turkeys

Historically the eastern wild turkey's range extended from the eastern seaboard to the Great Plains with the exception of a much smaller range of Osceola turkeys in south Florida. Easterns have the largest distribution and are often the most difficult to hunt. Sometimes a hunter will get lucky and bang one on opening day, but most often his bird will only come after eight or more attempts. Although I have occasionally ventured to Tennessee and Missouri, Georgia provides most of my hunting for this species. With a two-month-long season (mid-March through mid-May), a current limit of three toms and turkeys in my back yard I don't have much of a reason to go very far to get my eastern.

Each year I try to take my bird with a different muzzleloading shotgun or rifle. My most recent challenge was to use the same Austin & Halleck shotgun that had failed to fire when I had a swan over it to take a turkey. I had replaced the firing pin and used it successfully on February quail hunt, so the following spring was the first opportunity for it to redeem itself.

Now for my thirteenth attempt on very nearly the last week in the season, the Austin & Halleck smoothbore and I sallied forth. Today's hunt plan was to walk a circuitous trip down a pair of farm roads to get to my food plot without using a flashlight, put out a hen and jake decoy on the edge of a freshly plowed strip next to the woods and await developments. I had set up on this food plot several times before. Once, the tom had circled the decoys about 100- yards away, but would not approach any closer. A few days before there had been five toms that sounded off from the nearby oaks at dawn, but none would come in. I had only two weeks of season left, and now was the time, I hoped, that something would happen.

My approach had been successful. I got to my set-up point before daylight and put out the decoys without using my flashlight or disturbing any roosting birds. I had brought two cushions to sit on because this might be a very long wait. Daylight slowly came, but what little gobbling activity there was sounded like it was a mile away. Today, the turkeys were not calling very much. I took my turkey wing and did fly-down noises and a little hen cackle, but these activities elicited no response.

At nearly 7:30, I made a few calls with a push-rod box call, "Ahhhhh, Ahhhhh, Ahhhh, Ahhh. Ahhhh, Ahhh, Ahh, Ah."

This elicited a resounding gobble from the corner of the field some 150-yards away. Turning in that direction I saw two gobblers running towards the decoys. Although I was in deep shade and fairly well concealed by an overhanging branch, the lead tom stopped and started to turn. It took only an instant for me to place the bead on his head and pull the trigger. The tom went down flapping as his buddy sped off. I never did see the boss gobbler. I was very pleased after all this effort to have settled for a satellite tom. Even so, this was a very respectable bird with an 11-inch beard. It was unusual in that it had red waddles, a snouse and all the other attributes of a tom turkey; but no spurs. Both legs were completely slick without even a nub. This was a powerful bird and obviously competing for breeding rights, but it had, for a tom turkey, a serious handicap.

Turkey with an original 14-gauge musket

A 14 gauge? Standard U.S. shotgun gauges for which factory ammunition is commonly found include the .410, and the 28, 20, 16, 12 and 10 gauges. In Europe the big 4 and 8-gauge guns have limited use, and a few guns are still made for the smaller 24 and 32-gauges as well as the 9mm-shotshell. Notably absent is the 14 gauge which, while very popular during the muzzleloading era, was considered a redundant cartridge gauge as early as the 1880s.

Since the cartridge version of the 14 gauge had such limited use, why was the muzzleloading version so popular? One reason was that the 14 gauge is .69 caliber – the same as the French-supplied muskets of the Revolutionary War and the standard U.S. military caliber during much of the Pre-Civil War period. The issue musket with a charge of shot was very useful for foraging and also had obvious crossover uses in civilian life.

In an attempt to gain better accuracy than was available from the Brown Bess musket, the British military first adopted the Baker rifle, a flintlock, and then the percussion Brunswick rifle. This rifle was unusual in that it shot a belted ball with a raised ridge of lead that fit into the gun's two rifling grooves. These belts engaged the rifling and spun the ball to stabilize it for longer-range accuracy.

At one stage in the complex evolution of arming Nepalese troops, the Non-Commissioned Officers were issued Brunswick Rifles; however these were slower to load with a patched-belted ball than the issued smoothbore guns. The result was that the rate of fire of the entire unit was slowed while the NCOs struggled to get balls down their guns' barrels. This resulted in smoothbore versions of the Brunswick Rifle being made so that the NCOs could keep their distinctive-looking guns while keeping up the same rate of fire as the other members of their units.

*A real challenge is to rahabilitate guns like the 14-gauge smoothbore and this Brunswick rifle and use them to take game.*

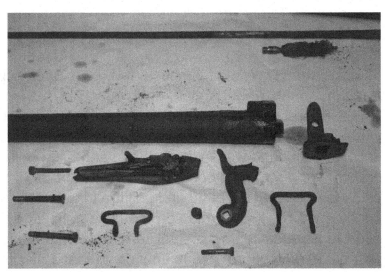

Both the rifled and smoothbore versions of the Brunswick design were made in England, Nepal and likely elswhere in India.

My Brunswick smoothbore has an iron barrel, a back- action lock, protective brass plates on the barrel keys, no brass patch box and matching Indian numerical script numbers on the barrel, stock, hammer and bayonet lug. The false breech and breech plug are hand forged. There are no British proofs or English-character markings anywhere on the gun. This Brunswick smoothbore showed signs of hard use, and was not up to the quality of British production.

The Nepalese Brunswick smoothbores have been imported by Atlanta Cutlery Co. (Atlanta Cutlery sells these guns strictly as collector's items – not to be fired. Although for the purpose of this article, I have proofed and shot my gun, these guns received very hard use and many are unsafe to shoot.) I was given one of these guns that was uncleaned with a non-functional lock. Once the gun was cleaned and reproofed, I was ready to see what a 14-gauge could do.

Although 14-gauge cartridges are very rare, 14-gauge card, fiber and over-shot wads are available from Dixie Gun Works. These were ordered and a bag of Remington 16-gauge plastic wads acquired from Cabela's. Plastic wads in smoothbore guns increase velocity, help prevent base wads from blowing through the shot string and improve patterns. They also raise operating pressures and leave a plastic residue in the barrel. The plastic washes out easily with soapy water, and the added pressure is helpful in allowing lesser charges of powder to be used and promoting cleaner combustion.

Wad cups on plastic wads are capable of expanding to fill an oversize bore if the difference in bore diameters is not extreme. This is witnessed in the now-common use of 12-gauge wads in "over bore" turkey guns which have 10-gauge barrels. Keeping this in mind, the use of a 16-gauge plastic wad in a 14-gauge barrel is not an outrageous practice. I do have the suspicion that paper wads sometimes jam in the bottom of plastic shot cups and may steer the shot charge off course. To prevent this outcome, I load Cream of Wheat between the over-powder card and the plastic wad to insure a clean separation of the wads.

The final load developed for the Brunswick smoothbore was 80 grains of GOEX FFg, a .125 over-powder wad, 20 grains of Cream of Wheat, a Remington 16-gauge plastic wad and 1 1/8-ounce of shot. I experimented with Knight's hard no. 5 lead shot, HeviShot no. 4s (actually 7s to 2s) and lead no. 8s. From previous experiences, I planned to use the HeviShot 4s on larger birds and waterfowl.

Patterns, as with any cylinder-bored gun, were nothing spectacular. The HeviShot patterned 78-83% at 30 yards which was certainly reasonable for pheasants and waterfowl. The lead 5s gave 60-70% patterns and the 8s had even looser patterns. The added density of HeviShot yields good kills and the mixed shot sizes may sometimes help in achieving a decisive result. The 16-gauge cushion wad's peddles were not thick enough to prevent the hard HeviShot from lightly scratching the barrel. This was obviously a load for limited use, if used at all. Squirrels are first up during the Georgia hunting season. The 14 gauge, with the considerable aid of my dog Demeter, brought in 11. I also used the gun to shoot pheasants, chukka and quail at the River Bend Sportsmen's Resort at Fingerville, South Carolina. After taking a total of 13 birds it was time to take the old war horse out turkey hunting.

Georgia's turkey season arrived almost immediately after my return from River Bend. The first morning I hunted near my house. I had hens stroll by my decoys, but no toms. That afternoon, I hunted the nearby Beaverdam Wildlife Management Area with friend Paul Presley. We were to hunt that afternoon and some on Easter morning. There were hens in the food plot at dark, but no toms. Although we went out Easter morning, it was too rainy to hunt.

The next Monday I was sitting on my food plot. I had arrived before dawn and had been sitting and calling a few times about every 20 minutes. This tactic had been suggested to me by friend and renowned turkey hunter Charles Elliot, the long-time writer and editor for Outdoor Life. Looking at the upper end of the field I saw two toms come in and start walking along the hedgerow. I called, but they paid no attention. Waiting until they approached a bit closer, I tried again.

This time they both spotted the decoys and approached. Occasionally the lead bird would go into a brief strut, but it was obvious that they wanted to get to that seductive hen as soon as possible and/or teach that jake some manners. I had already repositioned myself and by the time the leading turkey was in range I was ready to shoot. The gun bellowed, and my turkey was down. After the neck was picked I could see that there were 12 HeviShot hits in the neck, three more on non-vital areas and two lower in the breast.

With a full 10-inch beard and ¾-inch spurs this was a fitting trophy on which to end the Brunswick smoothbore's hunting career. The added pressure caused by a replacement mainspring was causing small slivers to separate from the already cracked stock beneath the lock. Although battered, abused and much-used by the time the gun came to me, it had demonstrated that it could still perform when called upon as it had in its youth.

After the Brunswick smoothbore had taken its turkey, I replaced the original non-functional parts and gave the smoothbore to Paul as a wall hanger along with a booklet containing several stories that I had written about the gun. It had done all I asked of it, and had earned an honorable retirement. Shooting old originals is always a chancy business, and while very satisfying, is best done with great care followed by a through cleaning and storage. (Hanging over an active fireplace or stove insert is about the worst storage possible.)

Osceola's, Florida's Fall and Spring hunts.

For hunters who like to season their activities with a little black-powder spice, Florida's Fall muzzleloading season offers the opportunity to take whitetail bucks, trophy hogs, bearded turkeys and an assortment of small game. Hunting may be done with muzzleloading rifles, pistols or shotguns providing the

*It took two years to bag this fine Osceola turkey.*

opportunity to use almost any muzzleloader you own. The general strategy is to hunt for turkeys all the time and take whatever else happens to walk by.

Florida Fish and Wildlife Commission's Eddie White sees growing interest in the muzzleloading season. "Six people I know bought their first muzzleloaders this year. Our hunters go after deer first, hogs second and will take a gobbler if they have a chance. Both the Eastern and Osceola turkeys are tough to hunt in the Fall. The toms don't respond to calling, and the best tactic is to ambush them on their travel paths."

I was invited to hunt private lands north and east of Lake Okeechobee. Although my outfitter had relocated to Idaho, his wife connected me with Steve Shaw who guides hunters on the citrus groves and cattle ranches that dominate the local economy.

"It should be no problem taking a hog. Deer are a maybe thing. Getting a Fall tom is tough, although we have plenty of turkeys," Shaw warned.

The land around Lake Okeechobee is flat, but better drained than in the more southern parts of the state. Some waste fruit is present in the groves during the fall, and this citrus provides excellent food for deer and hogs. People are working the groves all day, and the animals glean the fruit at night. Nearby pastures contain grassy bays which separate palmetto-choked wet lowlands used as bedding areas. Where oaks and pines shade out the undergrowth, clearer areas exist that are used by all species of wildlife. Favored foods for the deer and turkeys include acorns and palmetto berries while hogs happily add roots, tubers and grubs to their diets.

On my most recent hunt for a Fall Osceola turkey, I was in spitting distance of hens on numerous occasions, but could never get within shotgun range of the super-cautious toms. Each morning, daylight would find me in a blind or up a tree overlooking a pasture or game trail. The edges of pastures and the ridges of dry land between water bodies were favorite places for turkeys to feed. Numerous times I had hens come up to my blind, but the closest I got to toms was a look at a pair some 80-yards away. I moved in the tree stand. They spotted me and exited the area at a good trot.

Fall turkey hunting is a three-part process consisting of scouting, formulating a hunt strategy and execution. Scouting consists of glassing open areas and looking for sign to locate toms. Turkeys generally move all day in the Fall, although they stay put when the weather is extremely hot, wet or cold. Flocks of 20 or more toms may feed together in a freshly harvested cornfield or turkeys can be scattered in smaller groups of two or three toms scratching around for acorns. The toms may coincidentally follow flocks of hens, but most often avoid them. There are always exceptions, and I have seen occasional toms feeding quite happily among hens.

Sometimes it is possible to pattern turkeys. They may have an approximate time that they move into a field, use a particular path, work through a given bottleneck or visit a favorite dusting area.

The strategy for a particular hunt might be dispersing a flock and making gobbler yelps in an attempt to bring a bird back in, ambushing a turkey when it returns to a food plot or attempting to stalk close enough for a shot. Muzzleloading rifles are sometimes used by turkey stalkers (where legal), but trying to sneak up on a turkey is a low-percentage hunt with a muzzleloading shotgun.

Once a strategy has been selected the challenge is to stick with it. A hunter never knows then a turkey may choose to walk within range. I have tried putting out jake decoys, but these only attracted curious cows. A good plan is to find a spot that you have confidence in, blind up and wait – all day if necessary. Have confidence in your plan and be persistent. When the mosquitoes are out it is very difficult to stay still without a bug suite. Insect repellants work, but having a physical protective barrier is also important. The new ThermaCells provide the best protection now available. Sitting still also requires a comfortable seat and cushion.

During the course of the hunt, we hunted four different areas. One was a spot where the grassy bays necked down to an hour-glass shape. A cattle trail passed close to a palmetto thicket on one side of the bay. We saw hogs moving in the headlights when we came in the first morning, but nothing but cows came by my ground blind for the remainder of the day.

Thinking that this was still an excellent area, the second day I put my tree stand on a nearby pine. At mid-morning, a buck came out of the woods from the other side of the bay and headed in my direction. This was a thin-horned six-point "management" buck, which I took with the pistol. Later in the hunt I also shot a hog with the rifle. The closest that I came to taking an Osceola tom was when two came walking down the same path the deer walked, but this was the pair that spooked when they spotted me in the tree stand.

On one occasion mosquitoes were eating me alive even though I was wearing a bug suit. These were so bothersome that I could not sit any longer.

Spotting some squirrels in the palmetto palms, I used my Thompson/ Center Arms' Black Mountain Magnum 12-gauge to quickly bag four squirrels. This gun has interchangeable chokes that can produce tight patterns with charges of up to 1 5/8-th ounces of lead or non-toxic shot.

To hunt the Muzzleloading Season a resident needs an Annual Hunting License at $13, a Muzzleloading Gun Permit for $5.50 and a Turkey Permit for $5.50. All of these, along with fishing, are included in the Sportsman's License. Nonresidents must have a 10-day Hunting License at $26.50 along with the Muzzleloading Gun Permit at $5.50 and a $105 Nonresident Turkey Permit if they intend to try for a Fall gobbler. For the purpose of this season Florida is divided into southern, middle and northern zones. Osceola turkeys are only found in the southern and the lower part of the middle zone. Generally the muzzleloading gun season begins in mid-October in the South and mid-November in the north. The dates and durations may change, so check current regulations.

For the fall hunt I carried a Traditions Lightning .45-caliber muzzleloading rifle or a Thompson/Center Arms' 12-gauge Mountain Magnum shotgun or a Davide Pedersoli Bounty .50-caliber Flintlock pistol. For someone who is not a black-powder gun nut, a more reasonable approach is to use a scope-sighted rifle on everything.

Not being successful on my try for a Fall turkey, I eagerly accepted an opportunity to hunt a different area the following Spring. This time the hunt would be done using the typical Florida water taxi, the airboat.

My wife Thresa had a horrified look on her face when she asked, "How do you hunt turkeys from an airboat? Apparently she had an image of an airboat exploding out of a cloud of dust, smoke and feathers as a boatload of hunters shot their way through a flock of turkeys.

"Not the way you think," I replied. "All you use the airboat for is to get you to and from the hunting area."

"That's better," she responded. "I know how you love to turkey hunt, but I could not imagine how you could sneak up on them with a noisy airboat."

Turkeys can be some of the most aggravating animals to hunt that God ever gave breath to. There are many close encounters, but not many kills. Airboats provide a means of getting into areas where turkeys have not been hunted so heavily. They are particularly useful in areas where the higher parts of marshes and swamps hold good populations of birds that receive little hunting pressure. In Florida these areas of higher ground are often used for cattle grazing.

Eastern wild turkeys are tough birds to hunt anywhere, and swamp birds are harder still. For untold generations these turkeys have lived on isolated hummocks surrounded by water. They are hard to approach and are extremely cautious because of the higher density of alligators, bobcats and coyotes. In addition, the vegetation is often so thick that it is difficult to see a turkey more than a few feet away.

Tom turkeys in swamps still strut in the Spring, but the briers and swamp canes often abrade the breast feathers from their chests leaving naked skin. The perpetual dampness may also promote a fungal growth in their beards that first shows as a brown band across the beard and makes the beard so brittle that it breaks off.

Because Florida's semi-tropical vegetation can be so thick the best hunting areas are commonly those that have been recently burned and used for pasturing cattle. Strutting toms like to display in these clear areas and along pathways in open woodlands where the canopy has shaded out the rank understory vegetation. The hunt plan that friend and Florida native Dave Simpson developed was to use his airboat to hunt public lands. This area had been burned by a wildfire the previous year, and the turkeys were not only more visible they shared this area with one of the best populations of bob white quail that I had seen in decades.

Osceola turkeys don't gobble as loudly as easterns and shut up altogether when they are in areas that have been frequently hunted. A strutting tom was spotted, and I made several set-ups using calling and a jake decoy, but never managed to coax one of the birds close enough for a shot with the Thompson/Center Arms Mountain Magnum 12-gauge shotgun that I used. We made a good attempt, but could not get things to come together.

Simpson had an alternative plan. He had some wild game feeding stations near his house that were frequented by turkeys and deer. In Florida it is not legal to hunt over feeders, but it is permitted to set up 100 yards away from a feeding station that is maintained on a year-round basis. After several set ups, I managed to take a turkey with an attitude that we named Napoleon with the Mountain Magnum. This smaller, but super-aggressive, tom monopolized the food sources and drove not only other toms but also hens away from their feed.

On this hunt I used my favored waterfowl load of 1¼-ounces of HeviShot, 90 grains of Hodgdon's TripleSeven powder (the equivalent of about 100 grains of FFg), a 12-gauge Wonder Wad over the powder, a 1 5/8-ounce shot cup with a cut 20-gauge wad inside to reduce its capacity to 1¼-ounce of shot and a thin over-shot card. I used the easer-to-handle musket caps on this gun in preference to the smaller and weaker no. 11s. This load shot from a full-choke tube was very effective in killing the bird.

Texas Rios

As things turned out, my most recent Rio Grande turkey-hunting experiences was not with a muzzleloader, but with a crossbow. I present this hunt with the knowledge that if a turkey can be coaxed to within the 40-yard maximum range of a crossbow it certainly can be taken with a muzzleloader.

It did not take me long to accept Wade Nolan's offer to participate in Whitetail University's Texas turkey and hog hunt with Ten Point's new crossbows. I was particularly interested in the company's new-in-2006, 6-Point series "Slider," which featured adjustable limb settings enabling the user to have the option of

*A Rio Grande turkey and hog taken with a Ten Point Slider crossbow.*

shooting at 125, 150 or 175-pound draw weights. I had examined the crossbow at the Shot Show, but now I would get to shoot, and hopefully take game, with it too!

"Do turkeys gobble?" I asked Wade. "When and where do you want me?"

The when was in early April and the where was at the Herradura Ranch south of San Antonio. The ranch is located close to the Nueces River in the Texas brush country. This habitat is marginal ranching country, but does better at raising Rio Grande turkeys, wild hogs, deer, javelina and exotics. A prolonged drought had prevented the grass from greening up, but the mesquite, cat claw and prickly pear were doing well.

"We have to feed the game to keep it healthy," ranch manager John Beckett informed the group when we arrived. "Remember that everything in this country will stick, bite or eat you. Be careful. We have a good population of rattlesnakes, and it has been warm enough that you can expect to see them."

On arrival at the ranch, we sighted in the crossbows. The Slider impressed me as being lighter weight than the company's Elite models. This lesser weight made it easier to shoot from off-hand, but also somewhat less forgiving if the trigger pull was rushed. My crossbow mounted a multi-range scope, and I sighted in the mid-range crossbar to be dead on at 30 yards with Grim Reaper's Razortip mechanical broadheads.

Company Representative Jay Liechty Jr. recommended Reaper's 100 grain version with three 1-inch cutting blades (1 ¾-inch diameter total cut) for rapid kills on turkeys and another 100-grain point with a 1 3/8-inch cut diameter for the tough Texas hogs. I had previously experimented with a variety of turkey points. The problem was not hitting the turkey with an arrow, but keeping the bird from flying or running afterwards. My efforts had included blunted points, modified Judo points with and without "stoppers" on the shafts and wing-entangling strings. I was sometimes successful, but often failed because the altered arrow did not fly well or the trailing string caught on something and nosedived the point into the ground before it reached the bird. Grim Reaper's extra-large diameter mechanical point bulls-eyed the practice target, and promised to be a better solution.

Tucked beneath a drooping mesquite branch, I saw the tom silently move towards the feeder on the afternoon of the second day of the hunt. I raised the crossbow and pushed the safety off as the bird approached. The crossbow's 5-pound pull is smooth, but a bit long. I held low and continued the squeeze as the gobbler cut the distance to about 25 yards. The green plastic chair provided a steady shooting platform and the crosshair settled in to intersect the bird at the top of its leg. After the crossbow discharged, the turkey went down and flopped. I soon hefted the first Rio Grande turkey that I had taken in decades.

This was the most immediately immobilizing kill that I had ever made on an arrowed turkey. The point cut through the bird's backbone and had broken a wing. Three others on this hunt had similar results. Another did not take wind drift into account and cut feathers, but did not otherwise damage the bird.

Later that afternoon, hogs came in. I shot at the largest boar at 30 yards. The hog ran, but was hard hit. The 80-pound animal was recovered about 60-yards away. The stiff wind had drifted the arrow about 4 inches, and the hit caught the rear of the lungs half-way up the hog's body.

Advantages offered by the Slider include its adjustable draw that allows the pull weight to be set appropriate to the game being hunted and/or the strength of the hunter. I personally liked the Slider's lighter over-all weight and single safety. Other appealing aspects of this crossbow are that it retails for as little as $399 and will accept all of Ten Point's cocking aids and accessories.

Although not done in this instance, it is possible to take Rios by conventional decoying and calling techniques in the spring. This is how I would have preferred to have hunted, but when a sponsor is calling the shots, a writer has to go with the program. If you have hunted in the conventional fashion and can't get a tom to cooperate, last day set-ups over a Texas feeders can save a hunt.

Idaho Merriams

When bear hunting above Riggins, Idaho, I found a slate outcrop exposed in a road cut (Chapter 7). This was not the best slate that I had ever seen, but it had sufficient cleavage to yield thin enough splits to use as a turkey call. Taking a split and selecting a variety of dried branches from nearby fruit trees, I found that I could elicit reasonable-sounding turkey noises from my homemade equipment.

Also present was a good supply of Merriam turkeys, but unfortunately it was not turkey season. While it would have been very satisfying to have taken a turkey with this slate call on the same property, I wasn't invited back. However, I was invited back to Idaho by C.J. Buick, the CEO of Buck Knives to hunt near Kellogg. I tried for both turkeys and black bear. I did get a kill on an average-sized black bear with a crossbow. This 2010 video is on YouTube and my blog,

Turkey dance with feathers, chimes and cannon.

As any artillerist or turkey hunter will tell you, positioning is everything. If the set up is bad, cannon cannot be employed to maximum effect; and a hunter can have turkeys all around, but never close enough to shoot. There was no doubt there were turkeys somewhere in the swampy bottom below me. For more than a decade I had hunted the birds that roosted in the cypress trees on the creek. My task was to discover where along this mile of creek that they had chosen to spend the night.

Cannon are usually spoken of as being unlimbered, wheeled into place or dug in, but this was not the case with "Hostile," the miniature cannon that I carried in my daypack. Positioning it by hand in the upper part of a gully with vertical walls of red clay behind me and a rotten tree stump in front to catch the ball, I loaded up. Fifteen grains of FFg with a patched .36-caliber round ball went down the smoothbore tube. Carefully I aligned the cannon in its carriage and positioned the wedges to adjust for elevation.

It was time. I could see the tree tops clearly in the pre-dawn light. After priming the vent with a few grains of FFFFg, I lit the slow match, grasped it with metal forceps and blew up a firm red coal.

Ignition was instantaneous when I touched the coal to the priming powder. The little cannon fired with a sharp report which bounced back from the near vertical walls behind me and reverberated along the stream valley mimicking the sound of rolling thunder.

Success. Two groups of turkeys gobbled. One was a quarter mile to my right and the other off my property and across the creek to my left. Hostile had done its job, and I carefully replaced it in my pack. My late wife Thresa had a certain fondness for cannon and would not have been pleased if in the excitement of the hunt Hostile had been left behind.

Turkeys do "shock gobble" to loud noises such as slamming truck doors and thunder as well as to the more commonly used locater calls such as those that mimic owls, crows, wood peckers, geese, coyotes, predators, peacocks, etc. Individual flocks of turkeys that commonly roost near areas frequented by crows, geese or owls often become accustomed to these natural calls and seldom reply to the turkey hunter's store-bought imitations. Sometimes observations of a particular flock will suggest an inventive approach.

Kaolin mining plays a vital part in the economy of Central Georgia where I hunt. Mines and processing plants located in five counties happily coexist with an expanding population of deer, waterfowl and turkeys. Those who work for these mining companies may hunt on reclaimed lands which are often more productive turkey habitats than they were before mining. The downside is that mining typically begins at daylight and the woods are filled with industrial noises.

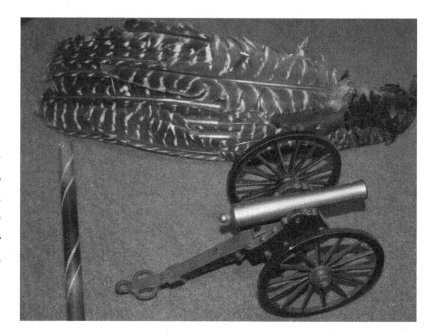

*Feathers, chimes and cannon are unusual turkey-hunting accessories that can sometimes be effective.*

One flock of turkeys I hunted happened to reside in several thousand acres adjacent to a kaolin processing plant. They paid no attention to the whirr of running conveyor belts and processing equipment as they went about the business of doing what turkeys do. During breeding season they strutted and carried on like all other turkeys. Well, almost. There was one thing that got to the gobblers - back-up bells. When a truck would back up the regular "ting-ting-ting-ting" of the back-up bells would elicit a strong gobble.

As it happened on our back porch was a set of wind chimes which also made "ting-ting-ting-ting" noises. After testing the tone of these chimes by striking each hanging tube with a steel tablespoon, I chose one that seemed to have the correct tone, timber and pitch. Some days later in the turkey woods, I had a chance to test my maybe turkey-locator-call to be. I did not think that Thresa would cotton too much to having one pipe of her wind chimes painted in camo colors while the others were polished aluminum, so I draped the chime in a piece of camo cloth.

"Well, here goes," I thought as I struck the chime squarely at its midpoint with a steel tablespoon. Keeping the rhythm, I struck it again at about half-second intervals. "Ting-ting-ting-ting" pause "ting-ting-ting-ting." A resounding gobble erupted from the creek to my left front. I have tried "turkey chimes" on other flocks. Birds without industrial noises in their experiences don't often respond, but I have consistent success with the flock by the plant

Any turkey hunter close enough to come within proper speaking distance of a turkey has heard the sounds of a flock flying down at dawn or flying up to roost at dark. If they have spent enough time in the woods they have probably also been "startled" by having turkeys flush from underfoot. If you think the flush of a covey of quail is unnerving, try 15 turkeys rising near simultaneously from the dry leaves of the forest floor on a Summer afternoon. "Startled" is a polite term fit for print, but does not come near close enough to adequately describing the experience.

Having come to the realization that turkeys make lots of noise when they fly, I reasoned that if I could simulate this noise I could convince a flock of roosting birds to fly to me instead of elsewhere. "What better to use," I conjectured, "than REAL turkey wings."

One negative is doing a turkey dance with a full set of turkey wings, even minus bird, is a challenge. They are just too big, too long and too cumbersome to carry by someone already encumbered with a turkey vest with multitudinous calls, chimes and cannon but also with all the gear it takes to keep a black-powder shotgun going plus turkey decoys and a blind. Unless I was planning to attempt to fly, an endeavor for which I am not particularly well structured, a full-size set of turkey wings was obviously an unacceptable additional burden.

I trimmed the wings at the final joint which still left more than a foot of black and white stripped feathers firmly attached along its 7-inch length. This was the wingtip of a big tom and the flattened ends of the well-drug feathers demonstrated that they were stout enough to stand abuse. I flapped tentatively and then more rapidly.

"Yes! This was the sound." The result was enhanced when I slapped my legs and beat the trunk of a nearby tree. I alternated flaps with pauses to simulate glides, and "cut loose" with flapping, tree banging and leaf rustling when the supposed turkey would have come to ground. The entire performance sounded like a hen flying from the roost tree and noisily landing in the forest.

When I first tried this technique of dancing, prancing and romancing these turkeys, I was glad that turkey hunting is mostly a solitary undertaking. Even to me my antics were ridiculous as I flapped the wings, pounded the bushes and rustled the leaves. "But what the heck, turkey hunting is suppose to be fun, isn't it?" What I was doing sure beat sitting behind a log going "yelp, yelp" every half hour.

To my surprise my antics worked too well. I didn't hear the first hen come in until she pitched down 12-feet away, then the second arrived, the third, fourth, fifth until I was surrounded by a flock of about thirty birds including three strutting gobblers. I COULD NOT MOVE. The instant I did I knew that they would fly.

Stretched out as I was standing on my tiptoes with arms extended and wingtips in each hand, I could not stay in that position for very long. My foot was already cramping and hot streamers of pain were running up my ankles through my calf muscles into my left thigh. My toes felt as if they were going to crumple.

I was dressed in full camo, and the birds had not spotted me yet. Ever so slowly I sank to stand flat footed to relieve some of the pressure on my toes. That helped some. Then I slowly drew the arms to my side. Bill Jordan's camouflage worked. The birds had still not seen me. My plan was to slowly sink to a sitting position, retrieve my gun and shoot one of the strutting toms.

Being well ballasted in the butt, it didn't come off quite that way. Like a ship listing to one side, I reached the point of no return and half-fell half-collapsed into an adjacent clump of greenbrier. Immediately thereafter, the turkeys were once more airborne and gone.  "Well, I can't say that I ever had a turkey hunting experience quite like that before. The next time I go turkey dancing, I will have to choreograph it to at least move me out of the briers," I thought as I gathered my stuff and took my freshly butt-pricked carcass home.

The next time you see someone out in the springtime woods, prancing about with a pair of turkey wings, banging on a chime and pulling a miniature cannon don't have him committed to a state institution.  He has a harmless affliction. He's just another turkey hunter after his bird. Smile, wave and pass quietly by. I will do the same.

*Shooting Bouncing Bounty yields interesting quantities of smoke.*

## *Chapter 13. Bouncing bounty*

Outrageous appearances sometimes translate into positive functions, and this was the case with a long-barreled flintlock pistol that I came to know as "Bouncing Bounty." The gun had no known historical antecedent, and I would not hazard a guess why Davide Pedersoli chose to make .45 and .50-caliber rifled flintlock pistols with 16-inch barrels. The basic design utilized the same stock and fittings of the company's Kentucky flintlock to which was attached a long barrel and a brass fore-end piece to provide a more esthetically pleasing end cap than just attaching a barrel thimble under the front sight.

From a production point of view, the gun had some merit because it provided what was hoped to be an interesting variation of an existing design without the expense of producing a new stock, hardware etc. If one were going to play pirate, the long barrel would provide sufficient length to stick through a sash, but the length of the barrel and the gun's weight would almost preclude it being shot with one hand. To link this gun with any sort of bounty hunter, as Pedersoli did, is even more fantastic. Some Arabic smoothbore pistols had similar-length barrels, but these were large caliber and had almost paper-thin barrels to make them more manageable.

I was attracted to the Bounty's design because this gun appeared to offer the promise of providing enough barrel length to burn a sufficiently heavy charge of black powder to pass Georgia's then-existing requirement that handguns used for big-game hunting must develop 500 foot pounds of muzzle energy at 100 yards. To meet this objective not only must a large charge of powder be poured

144

down the barrel, there must be sufficient barrel length and bullet weight to provide reasonable combustion. Otherwise, much of the powder would burn outside of the barrel and do nothing more useful for the shooter than providing large amounts of choking black smoke.

Another potentially interesting aspect of this pistol was that it was rifled with a twist of 1:17¾-inches which meant that the barrel would stabilize an elongate bullet and not be limited to a patched round ball. Since I already owned a variety of .50-caliber muzzleloaders and had easy access to different-style bullets, I elected to purchase the then new .50-caliber version of the gun rather than the .45. As it turned out using the larger, heavier bullets somewhat hampered my quest to get the highest possible velocity out of the gun, but things ultimately worked out.

By this time Thresa was fairly use to be bringing home some unusual looking guns, and Bounty certainly fitted into this category. If I were going to use this pistol as a primary hunting handgun, I could carry it in the reverse-carry-thumb-hooked-into-the-belt method that I had developed (Chapter 4), but if it were going to be used as a back-up gun some sort of holster would be required.

Casting about, I did have an old camo shirt with a bad rip that would potentially provide a pre-sewn component. I cut the sleeve, folded the edges and attached a belt loop to make a holster. Having the pockets left over, I sewed one to the outside of the holster to provide an attached pouch for extra flints and other accessories. That accomplished, I now had something that I could carry with me up a tree stand without getting too much in the way.

Some time was also taken to smooth up the action and trigger pull. Shooting flint is difficult enough, much less fighting a bad trigger. With a little personal attention flintlock trigger pulls can be much improved.

Working on the trigger pull required disassembly and careful stoning of the parts as well as fitting a yoke made of a section of deer antler on top of the trigger bar to take up the slack between it and the sear. I reduced the thickness of the antler until the hammer would stand at full cock with the barrel tang and trigger plate screws fully down in their seats. Ultimately, I achieved a crisp two-pound pull. Now that the gun had been cleaned and prepped it was time to take it to the range to see if I could develop some useful hinting loads that would meet the state's requirements.

Taming Bouncing Bounty

Twisting and writhing in my hand like a smoke belching junior dragon, the Bounty pistol left my grasp, did a flip and bounced off the top of my head. It this gun was going to be used to shoot game rather than as a black powder propelled club, I was going to have to do something about that recoil.

Load development had proceeded at a cautious pace. Even though the pistol had a .50-caliber, 16-inch barrel that promised to give the gun big game killing potential, the recommended load was between 20 and 30 grains of FFg

*Bounty's holster was the sleeve of an old hunting shirt lined with deer leather*

black powder and a patched round ball. Clearly, Pedersoli and I had different uses in mind for their outsize flintlock. At first I increased the charge in 10-grain increments. The 40, 50, 60 and 70-grain thresholds were passed, and there were no indications of excessive pressures gauged by the difficulty of withdrawing the threaded clean-out screw – my self-contained crusher gauge.

Switching to 295-grain, .50-caliber CVA PowerBelt bullets, I again tried 70 grains of GOEX FFg. Pressure indications remained normal, but recoil was stout. Charges were now increased in 5-grain increments. At 90 grains my chronograph indicated that I was getting where I wanted to be. This load was developing 1,060 fps. and 736 ft.lbs. of muzzle energy.

After consulting Lyman's ballistic tables for similar bullets, I felt confident that this sleek protected point Aerotip bullet would meet Georgia's 500 ft.lbs. of energy at 100 yards. There were still no indications of excessive pressures as I disassembled the gun and cleaned the lock, barrel and vent screw between shots, but there was one small problem.

I could not hold onto the gun. Even with lesser loads it had left my grasp, and I found myself catching the pistol by the cock or some other inconvenient part. When the pistol clobbered me atop the head, it was obvious that something needed to be done. Putting sticky tape on the grips might have helped, but I didn't want to do that. Checkering might have helped, but I did not have that skill.

What the gun needed was a heavier barrel. I considered casting some lead barrel weights and attaching them to the barrel using the screws provided for the gun's rear ramrod pipe. This would be possible as would be having some steel weights machined. Then the solution came to me.

Saddlebags. Yes! A bag of lead shot taped to near the end of the barrel behind the front sight.

Elegant? No. Workable? Yes.

This approach had the advantages of not costing me anything, allowing weight variability, and the saddlebags could be removed without disfiguring the pistol. I already had a shirt pocket left over from my homemade holster, and the other one would do nicely for a saddlebag. I put two pounds of shot into the

*Saddlebags provided the means of taiming Bounty's recoil from heavy charges and Power Belt's 295-grain-bullet*

pocket, rolled it up and taped it onto the barrel. It worked fine.

"Saddlebags?" Thresa asked with an incredulous tone in her voice. "You put saddlebags on a gun. Whatever for?" I assured my wife that that my leather saddlebags were not now draped across the barrel of the pistol. With some further explanation, she hesitantly agreed that there was a sort of logic to my thought process. She was more concerned that I was going to blow this gun up with an overload.

That thought had also occurred to me. Thresa was somewhat comforted when I explained that the barrel had been proofed to the same pressure as Pedersoli's rifles, with a black powder proof of 620 kilograms per square centimeter (8,800 lbs. per square inch), as shown by identical proof marks on both rifle and pistol barrels. In addition the breeching and touchold vents were exactly the same on the pistol and a similarly-sized rifle barrel used on the company's Kentucky rifle. As a cost-saving expedient, Pedersoli had used identical breeches, barrels and vent hole systems on both guns. It was logical to assume that the guns could be loaded to the same level, despite the disparity in the maker's recommended loads.

Notwithstanding, a very cautious approach was prudent, and this was the reason for my progressive testing with heavier powder charges and bullets. Anyone using this data needs to be similarly cautious, and does so at their own risk; although these loads were safe and effective in my gun. It should be noted that these loads were developed using GEOEX FFg black powder and that finer granulations or other powders may generate dangerously high pressures. These heavy loads should not be attempted with saboted bullets or any other bullet than the copper clad 295-grain BlackBelt or PowerBelt projectiles that I used.

Bounty's rifling twist of one turn in 17 inches stabilizes two types of bullets: low velocity round ball loads and higher velocity elongate bullets. Round balls lose accuracy suffered when powder charges exceed 50 grains because the patches are destroyed, but elongate bullets become more stable. Poor accuracy with round balls at the velocities needed for a humane hunting load argue against using the lead spheres for hunting big game.

To make sighting easier under low-light conditions, I enlarged the narrow rear sight notch to a wider "V" shape. With my hunting load, the gun shot to the point of aim at 25 yards and about 3-inches high at 50. Sighting in a flintlock pistol is always a balancing act of determining what effects on accuracy are caused by ignition problems, which encourages a downward-pulling flinch, and what effects are caused by changes in powder charges, bullet weights and the like.

Cleaning the barrel and lock between shots and retouching the flint helped minimize ignition problems. The added barrel weight and two-handed hold also aided accuracy. When everything went right I achieved 3-inch groups at 50-yards. This was acceptable for deer hunting, but I preferred to take my game at half that distance.

The hunt

Florida's black-powder hunting season instantly appealed to me as it offered the opportunity to take a buck deer with 5 inches of horn, a hog that stood 15-inches high at the shoulder, an Osceola gobbler and small game during the same week. The strategy is to hunt all the time for the Fall gobbler and take whatever else might walk by. Thus Bounty, in its newly fashioned camo holster could go along and be brought out when necessary.

In the vicinity of Lake Okeechobee there are a large number of cattle ranches. The cattle frequent relatively open grassy bays between the palmetto-choked swampy lowlands. Cattle travel along the edges of these bays as do hogs, deer and turkeys. I spotted a pair of toms working the edge of one bay a previous day from my climbing stand and reoccupied it in hopes they might return. At about 10:00 A.M., I noticed a 6-point deer come out of the brush on the other side of the bay about 200-yards away. The buck was looking for company as it crossed to my side of the open area. When it stepped behind a clump of palmettos, I readied my pistol and found my grunt call. I gave a grunt on the call. The buck stopped, and then slowly walked towards me instead of in the opposite direction.

If the deer stayed on the path he would pass about 20-yards away – an ideal range for the pistol. I silently cocked Bounty, checked the prime and waited. The deer plodded on. I feared that if the buck reached the point where I had walked, it might pick up my scent. The buck briefly hesitated behind another palmetto clump and put its head down to nibble on some vegetation. I decided to try for the animal when I had a clear shot at its shoulder.

I braced the pistol on the stand. When the wide 6-pointer stepped clear of the palmettos, I took aim. When I pulled the trigger the sight picture on the right shoulder looked good. The trigger dropped the hammer cleanly, and flint struck steel. The gun fired instantaneously. Through the smoke, I could see the deer swerve, run to the other side of the bay and collapse. It raised its head once, and died.

Bouncing Bounty and the load that I developed for it had done everything that I might reasonably expect of it. The PowerBelt bullet penetrated the deer. It expanded on entrance and sent bone and bullet fragments through both lungs, into the heart and busted ribs on the way out. Because of the shot angle, the bullet entered the deer through the shoulder on the near side and exited below the mid-line of the chest cavity on the far side.

Because the PowerBelt bullets must upset to expand their pure lead cores to fill the rifling, they require a minimal pressure to work well. This operational threshold appears to be about 85 grains of FFg black powder. An indication that they are working correctly is that the skirts will separate and be found 10-to-15 yards in front of the gun muzzle and be well expanded.

Later in the hunt, I saw several much better deer. Nonetheless, I was very pleased with my "management buck" as it was "big enough to be respectable, but not so large as to inspire envy" on what turned out to be a reduced price hunt. Bouncing Bounty had "bounced" its deer, instead of my head, and taken a reasonable buck.

*I had some criticism regarding my development of hunting-level loads for this pistol. Even though I had indications from the proof marks that my loads were safe, I proceeded very cautiously and would suggest that others do the same. Every Pedersoli barrel undergoes proof testing, but this does not apply to all muzzleloading barrels. A balance must be maintained between ignition sources, powder charges, granulations, types of powders, bullet design and bullet weight. Changes in any of these components can adversely increase pressures.*

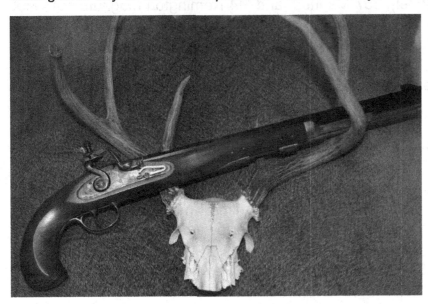

**Bouncing Bounty with the skull plate of its Florida deer**

*Bunk house at the Nail Ranch. The antler arch and longhorn cow skull say that this is unmistakably Texas*

## Chapter 14. Texas hog hunt

Thompson/Center Arms' first gun was the Contender single-shot pistol, and although I have owned, shot and hunted with T/C's handguns, muzzleloaders and cartridge guns since the late 1960s, I have always had a soft spot in my heart for T/C's pistols. Interchangeable barrels have always been a part of T/C's designs. After I purchased no. 1618 while I lived in Fairbanks, Alaska, I systematically accumulated .22 LR, .22 Jet, .357 Magnum and .44 Remington Magnum - .44 Hot Shot barrels to go along with the gun. For those who don't remember, the .22 Jet is the .357 Magnum pistol case necked down to .22 caliber that was introduced in a Smith and Wesson revolver and the Hot Shot barrel used a special .44 Magnum case with a plastic capsule loaded with birdshot and shot through a screw-on choke. With the choke removed it would also shoot solid-bullet .44 Magnum and .44 Special loads.

Because of its 10-inch barrel lengths and weight, the pistol was not legal for NRA competitions, but I enjoyed shooting it free-pistol style with the various calibers. Over the years I shot some ground squirrels and grouse with the pistol, but as handgun hunting was in its infancy at this time I never took any big game with no. 1618. My interest drifted more and more towards muzzleloaders as did Thompson/Center's.

By the early 1980s T/C had introduced its Hawken Rifle in both flint and percussion versions, and it seemed that each year brought another addition to their line. These even included the Patriot .45 caliber target pistol with double-set triggers that I also purchased and shot in competition. Although all of T/C's guns to this date vaguely resembled historic firearms they were not replicas. They were older patterns redesigned to take advantage of more modern manufacturing techniques, such as investment casting, and new materials. T/C built up an enviable, and justifiable, reputation of making solid, reliable hunting guns.

An unusual looking pair of guns, even for T/C, was the Scout series. Available in both muzzleloading pistol and rifle versions, these vaguely resembled the 1873 Colt Peacemaker and Model 1894 Winchester in profiles, but utilized the same receiver and action mechanisms along with the interchangeable barrels common to many T/C designs. As might be anticipated, I had a hanker for the pistol version. The opportunity arose to purchase a used gun with a .50-caliber barrel in Macon, Georgia, and I was quick to take advantage of it.

With its plow-handle grip the Scout felt good and gave the feeling of being very responsive. As this was an early in-line design, it used a no. 11 cap for ignition and ported the rear of the barrel so that it vented through the side of the frame.

Blackpowder handgun hunters are a small subset of an only slightly larger group of handgun hunters. When a fire destroyed a portion of Thompson/Center's facilities and the tooling for rifle and pistol versions of the Scout, there was no incentive to continue production. As described in Chapter 4, I did take a Cumberland Island, Georgia, deer with the gun using a load of 85 grains of FFg and a 370-grain Thompson/Center .50-caliber MaxiBall during the coldest winter in 80 years.

Thompson/Center wanted to take the Contender concept to the next operational level and designed a stronger-framed gun which became the Encore. Like the Contender it featured interchangeable barrels and stocks, but the stronger frame allowed this gun to be chambered in standard cartridges like the .30'06 whereas the Contender was limited to relatively low pressure pistol and rifle rounds which maxed out with the .30-30 and .45-70 Government. The larger frame

*Shooting the Encore 209X50 muzzleloading pistol at the Nail Ranch*

allowed the gun to also be made in muzzleloading rifle and pistol versions as well as being offered in a wide variety of centerfire rifle cartridges including a .416 on special order.

While I much liked the operational and appearance factors associated with the pistol version of the Encore, I felt that the rifle and shotgun versions of the gun were esthetically challenged. Although T/C never assumed that sales for such a gun would be large, the Encore was offered as a 209X50 muzzleloader in both rifle and pistol versions. Both used the 209 primer, and the pistol sported a 15-inch barrel – a length sufficient to burn a reasonable amount of powder.

These upgrades permitted the gun to use the then new Hodgdon Pyrodex pellets and the more compact TrippleSeven pellets that followed. This combination of components and pistol enabled the gun to utilize the equivalent of a charge of 100 grains of FFg black powder and the same .370-grain MaxiBall that I had employed in the Scout. This was more powerful that than the loads that many hunters used to kill deer with their muzzleloading rifles. Although I had taken a Georgia beaver out of a friend's pond with the Encore, its first opportunity to shoot big game was in Texas.

A hunt with Thompson/Center on the Nail Ranch

I had known many people at Thompson/Center Arms over the years, and when I was invited to hunt with designer Ken French and Gregg Ritz, who later became Thompson/Centers COO, I leapt at the opportunity. In 2002, when the hunt took place, I had already spent considerable time working with the muzzleloading version of the Encore pistol and the FireStorm, a flintlock muzzleloading rifle that could use Pyrodex pellets. The last gave me considerable trouble. The flintlock rifle was accurate enough, its problem was with functional reliability. I experimented with several different loading methods, including using black powder priming pellets that I made, ahead of the Pyrodex pellets, but the problem always came down to poor lock design.

Although T/C's coil spring lock worked fine as a percussion gun, it was only a sometime performer as a flintlock in either the Hawken or FireStorm design. I had to use new, or freshly touched-up, flints for almost every shot, clean the lock and frizzen with alcohol between shots and strengthen the mainspring by adding some washers to the guide rod to coax the gun to work. Just by the laws of chance, every company that makes a series of innovative products will ultimately shoot a blank, and the FireStorms in either flint or percussion versions proved to be Thompson/Center's. When everything was absolutely perfect the gun could be coaxed to fire, but other flintlocks, such as those made by Davide Pedersoli, were more reliable performers.

Neither Gregg nor Ken were overjoyed at my opinion of the FireStorm. Because I had already cleaned up the lock on the gun I had and was somewhat accustomed to it I brought the gun I had been loaned along with the 209X50

Encore pistol. I didn't make any points with Gregg or Ken when I informed them that I loved the Encore, but had serious reservations about the FireStorm. Gregg informed me, "This is just part of the challenge of shooting a flintlock."

Indeed, shooting flintlock guns is more of a challenge, but a tuned flintlock with a quality lock will perform very well even under some rather adverse conditions. Sorry about that Gregg, but locks of indifferent quality yield a gun that performs poorly, and no hunter needs to be saddled with such a temperamental gun.

At the range a series of targets was set up to try the guns. Gregg and Ken had brought a target divided into numerous quadrents and multi-colored squares which were fine for sighting in scope-sighted rifles, but not very useful for an iron-sighted flintlock. I requested something that I could see and Ken found a 4-inch square of cardboard that he posted at 50 yards.

I whiped the barrel of my FireStorm and loaded it with two Pyrodex Pellets a .50-caliber Wonder Wad and a 370-grain MaxiBall and settled down at the bench. I had the gun sighted in to hit 2-inches high at 50 yards. Aiming an appropriate amount below my target square, I squeezed the trigger. The gun fired promptly and the bullet drilled the center of the square. As usual when the gun was perfectly prepared and shot under perfect conditions, it functioned. (On a later hunt in Kansas, I had shot the gun at 100 yards at a paper plate. Because of the range and stiff crosswind I had to hold 4-inches high and aim 6-inches left to compensate. On the second attempt I got the gun to spark, and the shot hit within 2-inches of the center of the plate – an excellent shot considering that I was using iron sights and fighting a crosswind.)

Ken wanted me to repeat the shot, but I declined. The shot had looked and felt good when I pulled the trigger, which amply demonstrated to me that the gun was still sighted in. I also felt little confidence that I could coax the gun to fire a second time without re-cleaning and drying the lock and barrel. Considering that we could take hogs, deer or coyotes on a ranch that had an abundance of game, I hoped that my jinx with the FireStorm could be broken.

Shooting the Encore pistol presented no surprises. With iron sights I could put the same load that I used in the rifle within a 3-inch group at 50 yards. This is not spectacular shooting and only generated the remark from Ken that, "That's a heavy load to use in that pistol." The pistol did develop considerable smoke and recoil. At home most of my shooting had been from a sitting position using a two-handed hold while applying forward pressure with the left hand and pulling back with the right. This tensed the muscles and provided stability to the long handgun. Shooting from a bench felt somewhat awkward, but I got the job done. Now I was ready to hunt.

Each of the writers and editors on the hunt was given a separate vehicle and guide and assigned a hunt area on the 56,000-acre ranch. Brian Cope and I would have two days to hunt and take whatever game presented itself. The usual day was divided between a morning and afternoon hunt that began and ended with chuck wagon-style meals.

Texas hunting cowboy style traditionally consisted of riding out on horses to a section of the ranch known to have game of the sort desired. The animals were spotted from horseback and stalked on foot until in range of the iron-sighted lever-action rifles that most cowboys carried.

The same hunting style is still in vogue, except that pickup trucks have replaced horses. Roads that run among stock tanks, pastures and holding pens traverse large ranches like the Nail. Main roads are passable in all weather, but side "tracks" become too slimy to navigate with just a touch of rain. (I knew this from firsthand experience. Brian and I had already had a three-mile slither, slide and slop when we were caught in a brief thunderstorm).

Brian and I attempted several set-ups with the Firestorm. I had two opportunities with the FireStorm. I shot at and missed one animal by passing the ball over its back on a steep downhill shot. On my second opportunity, I was shooting from a solid rest at a doe about 50-yards away. Brian was watching with binoculars. He saw blood splatter splatter from the hit. Apparently this was a high-lung shot, and two hours of searching the thick Texas brush failed to recover the animal. At least I got the gun to shoot twice under hunting conditions, but that was as much of an accomplishment that I could claim for the FireStorm.

I hate to lose game, and I have reanalyzed this shot many times. First, I should have aimed lower on the chest, but in my lack of confidence in the gun I aimed at the middle of the chest and hit higher in the body cavity and produced a non-optimum hit. Secondly, a saboted expanding bullet might have produced more damage on this all-soft-tissue shot. I have no doubt that the MaxiBall just punched a .50-caliber hole through the animal. Third, it would have been nice to have had a tracking dog available. Brian and I did as good a job as we could on the dry, rocky ground; but I personally know of three dogs that could have done better — unfortunately, they were 1,000 miles away (Chapter 4).

Hogs

Hunting wild hogs in Texas has evolved into three different sports. One is to hunt hogs with dogs. This is exciting but had the drawback of having to shoot, or capture, whatever hog the dogs have caught. Another method, which does allow selectivity, is to stake out trails to watering and feeding areas where a good hog has been seen and ambush it when it appears. The third method, the one we chose, was the truck-mounted spot-and-stalk approach.

My impression of the boar that we spotted was that it was big, black, had an evil disposition and smelled bad, even at a distance of 30 yards. As I approached on foot, it was hooking a younger boar that had the nerve to approach a sow which had attracted the older boar's immediate interest. I could see tusks protruding above the big hog's lower lip. As I fingered my single-shot muzzleloading pistol, I began to have some reservations about my selection of firearms.

154

Raising the 4½-pound pistol with both hands, I pushed on the forend and pulled on the grip as I pointed the gun at the boar – a  stance that I have found provides the best off-hand stability for the big single shot.

"This time at least, I can see my target clearly," I thought. I had already missed a boar earlier that morning. A sow had alerted that hog, and it was trotting away as I fired. The poor light and moving target caused me to miss – or so I told myself. With handguns of all sorts it is not unusual for me to average a 50 percent kill rate on small game. Bigger guns, longer barrels, better sights and using rests increase this percentage; but any handgun hunter is going to miss game from time to time. I had experienced my miss. Now it was time to kill something.

I had done my preparations with the Encore pistol. I was well aware that "Big hogs take a lot of killing." For this hunt I chose T/C's 370-grain MaxiBall bullet (for maximum penetration) powered by two 50-grain Pyrodex pellets. This combination necessitates loading a .50-caliber Wonder Wad under the MaxiBall to provide a better gas seal. Omitting the wad resulted in a loss of 300 fps of velocity, and I felt that I might need all I could get from this load.

Fired from the Encore's 15-inch barrel, my load developed 1,022 fps of velocity and 858 foot-pounds of muzzle energy. At 100 yards, the MaxiBall still retains 537 foot-pounds of energy – similar to the .44 Magnum. The significant difference between my hog load and the 240-grain 44 Magnum was that the heavy MaxiBall slug drops 15 inches at 100 yards. By contrast, the .44 Magnum drops only 2 or 3 inches at that range. It was obvious that my optimum shot with the iron-sighted pistol would have to be at my 50-yard zero point or closer.

Would putting a scope on the pistol have resulted in increased performance capabilities? I had a scope on the Encore pistol's .30'06 cartridge barrel which aided considerably in making shots at 100 yards. For the muzzleloading version of the Encore, the scope was too slow to use for close-range shots, bulked up the gun and was generally unnecessary as I could still see will enough to effectively

*Dragging out the Nail Ranch boar took four men to hump it out of the pasture and onto the truck. Photo by Dr. George E. Dvorchak*

employ iron sights. Although this might not always be the case, it was at the time.

With the hog that close and in front of me, I felt that I did not have time to employ the Ashley Outdoors Steady Stix II that I carried. By the time I sat down, deployed the bipod and aimed, that hog could have been gone. Psychologically, with game in front of me and moving away, I could not bring myself to find a place among the cactus to sit down, deploy the bipod, aim and fire. I knew the gun and I had every confidence of making a good shot. I would shoot from off-hand, and I would shoot quickly.

With an opportunity to redeem myself at hand, I had another troubling thought. I had taken a shot 6 hours ago and used a speed loader to reload. I was sure that my load was correct, but there was a potential problem with water of combustion from the previous shot contaminating the pellets. Consequently, there was the possibility of getting only a pop from the 209 primer – the loudest sound in the world of muzzleloading hunting.

There was another reason that we needed to get on with the task of killing that hog. We were still in bright sun, but there was lightning from dark rain clouds generated by a rapidly approaching thunderstorm a few miles away. If we were going to get that hog and get out before the roads turned to mush, we needed to load that hog and make tracks.

Lining up the sights to shoot the hog, I was grateful for the long sight radius allowed by the Encore's 15-inch barrel. I was going to try for a quartering shot that would enter behind the rib cage and range forward to the front shoulder on the opposite side. The shot had to be good because it would take some time to reload.

Take a breath and hold it. Align the sights. Squeeze the trigger. Align the sights. Squeeze the trigger. Align. Bang! The big pistol recoiled back in my hands. There was enough wind from the approaching storm to sweep the smoke away, and I could see the boar and the other hogs run through the brush.

"You got him! He's down." Brian said. "Reload and we will walk up together."

Brian had good reason to be cautious about approaching hogs. He had been hooked by a boar once and had the scars on his leg to prove it. He had no desire to repeat the experience.

As I hurriedly put another charge in the Encore, I thought about the fact that muzzleloading pistols take more time to reload than rifles. Pistols must be wedged between your legs and held upright by your feet while the powder and bullet are loaded. If the bullet is a tight fit, the contortions of reloading can get quite complex. I was happy that I was using the easily loaded MaxiBall, instead of a saboted bullet, which is much more difficult to push down a dirty barrel. When I had finished reloading, I stood and looked in the direction in which the hogs had gone.

"I thought I saw him flopping on the other side of that tree, but I don't see anything now," Brian said.

Either the hog was dead and down, or it had run. If it had run, it would be difficult to find. Hogs leave little if any blood. Their loose hides slip over wounds and seal them.

Now that Brian, who had been standing at the ready with his .270-Winchester rifle in case the boar charged, and I were ready, we took a few steps. There was no sign of the big hog. However, after we crested a slight rise, we found him about 25-yards away from where he had been shot. From the look of things, he had run, collapsed and died within a few seconds. Nevertheless we made sure he was dead before taking photos.

With considerable difficulty we moved the hog for the pictures. It was obvious that we were not going to be able to load it without help. Fortunately another group of hunters happened by to give us a hand. Grabbing a leg each, we moved the boar a foot at the time until we could boost him into the truck bed. We all made it out to the graveled road just in time before the rain started pelting the dry soil.

Examining the hog back at the ranch, we were able to find the bullet's entrance hole near the rear rib cage. There was no exit so it was still inside the hog. After locating the bullet with a metal detector, I cut through the two-inch-thick gristle plate on the left shoulder and found the bullet. It had expanded to about .75 caliber, penetrated 26 inches and passed through both lungs. The 370-grain bullet retained 95.2 percent of its mass – excellent performance on the heavy animal.

The MaxiBall and Pyrodex load had given a quick, one-shot kill. This surprised some of the guides, because handgun hunters using cartridge guns often take several shots to finish a hog. Lightly constructed bullets can expend much of their energy penetrating the hog's gristle-plate-protected shoulder, failing to penetrate deeply enough to be immediately fatal.

I later used the same pistol and load to take warthog, impala and to finish off a blue wildebeest in Africa. Its reaction performance had been nearly identical. On the wildebeest, the only other animal from which a bullet was recovered, the slug penetrated 27-inches including chopping through a portion of the spine. Within 50 yards I would not be hesitant to use it on the smaller species of plains game, but would draw the line with zebra and greater kudu. With broadside shots these animals can be killed, particularly with water hole sits, but the slug will likely remain in the animal making tracking more difficult.

One problem that I noted in Africa was that if the gun were carried loaded (but umprimed) in a bouncing holster the slug would tend to creep down the barrel during the course of a day's activities. It only takes a few seconds to check the barrel and reseat the bullet, but this is a wise precaution. The harder-to-load saboted bullets usually grip the bore tighter and do not give this problem, although I have had relatively loose-fitting bullets fall from the sabots.

*Much of the material in this story was first published as "Black Powder Boar, Texas Style" in Safari Club's magazine Spetember, 2003.*

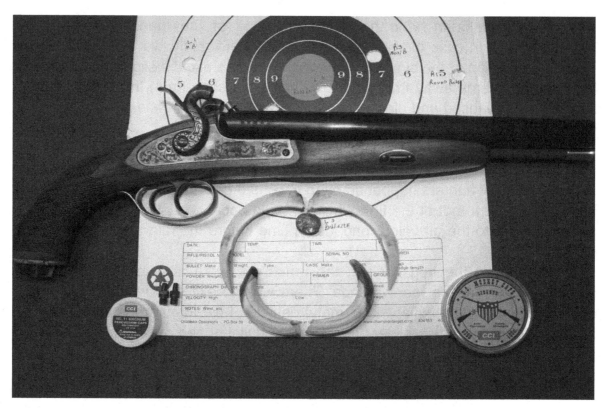

*The Davide Pedersoli .50 caliber Howdah Hunter with its sight-in target, hog teeth and percussion cap options.*

## *Chapter 15. Howdah hunting*

It was the first evening sit of a two-day hunt, and my mind was asking, "Do you want to take this boar or wait for a bigger hog?" The "Boss Boar" in this bunch of pigs was by far the largest animal and looked like it would weigh about 150 pounds. This boar offered both a good-size target for the .50-caliber Howdah Hunter and the potential for yielding some good-eating wild pork.

The double-barreled pistol that I had in the tower stand represented those carried in howdahs as a last-ditch defense against tigers. The fearless cats would sometimes claw their way up the sides or trunk of an elephant to kill hunters occupying the lightweight structure on the elephant's back. My location in a tripod stand 20-yards away from the feeding pigs was the best substitute that I could arrange at Texas' San Saba Ranch. The pigs had come in cautiously, and several times the largest hog had stopped feeding and looked directly at the stand. I had added fresh branches for concealment, but needed to remain nearly motionless to avoid detection.

Early Spaniards had released wild hogs everywhere they settled in North America to provide fresh meat for passing ships and colonists. The descents of these animals, and later escapees, proliferated in North America to the extent that millions of wild hogs are present in the Southern States, Texas and California. Some of these animals may weigh over 1,000 pounds. Each year several 400-to-

600-pound hogs are taken in the Southeastern states.

Baiting with corn was used frequently by the early settlers to coax hogs and other big game to within the sure-kill range of their crossbows, matchlocks and flintlock smoothbores. Although the percussion Howdah pistol had no direct North American antecedents, it was representative of muzzleloading handguns with two barrels and only front sights. These pistols were meant to be employed at ranges of a few yards against potentially dangerous animal and human adversaries.

The Davide Pedersoli Howdah Hunter

Physically, the Howdah Hunter is a large double-barreled holster pistol that is not a replica of any particular gun. It is made in the Pedersoli factory in Gordon, Italy, utilizing locks and other components already made for the company's double-barreled shotguns and rifles. The pistol is offered with two .50-caliber rifled barrels, the version I had, or with 20-gauge smoothbore barrels or with one rifled and one smoothbore barrel. All of the guns are 18½-inches long and weigh between 4½ to 5 pounds. A leather holster is sold as an accessory.

Pedersoli's recommended charge of 25-grains of FFg and a patched round ball is insufficient for big game hunting. Conversations with Pierangelo Pedersoli and the editors of Italian hunting magazines repeatedly elicited the statement that hunting with handguns is illegal in Italy. Despite the pistol's name, it was apparently inconceivable to these editors that anyone would want to take game with muzzleloading pistols when many more effective tools were available. I took it as a point of honor to demonstrate that the Howdah Hunter could, and would, hunt.

I had confidence that this gun with its shotgun-breeching and robust components could safety handle much stouter loads than the recommended charge. My challenge was to develop loads that would yield the 500 ft.lbs. of muzzle energy necessary to reliably kill deer-size game from the gun's 11¼-inch barrels.

*Howdah hunter disassembled showing the gun's relatively short twin barrels*

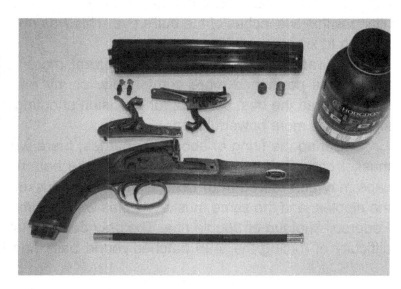

### Table 1. Velocities and energies

| Bullet .50 caliber | Weight gr. | Charge FFg granulation | Velocity fps. | Energy ft./lbs |
|---|---|---|---|---|
| Round Ball | 177 gr. | 60 gr. TripleSeven | 1247 | 611 |
| Ball-Et | 270 gr. | 60 gr. TripleSeven | 1088 | 710 |
| Maxi Ball | 370 gr. | 60 gr. TripleSeven | 1022 | 853 |

Load development

In order to provide a stronger kick-off to the combustion process, I changed the nipples from no. 11 size to the musket cap size. I also selected Hodgdon's FFg Triple Seven black-powder-substitute powder to take advantage of this power's 10 percent energy increase over equivalent volumes of black powder. In order to raise operating pressures, I also tried 270 and 370-grain bullets. Whatever combination of components I chose, it was vital that both barrels shot to about the same point of aim at 20 yards – even if I had to load different components in each barrel.

Heavier and lighter bullets not only shoot to different points of aim vertically, they will also show horizontal displacements. I slowly worked up to a charge of 60-grains of FFg Triple Seven using a 147-grain round ball, Buffalo Bullet's 270-grain Ball-Et and a 370–grain Thompson/Center MaxiBall. I discovered that the right barrel shot the round ball 6-inches to the right, the Ball-Et struck closer to the bull and the MaxiBall was closest. With the left barrel, the Maxi shot 6-inches left of the bull, but the same powder charge using the Ball-Et was closer to the center with one hitting the red bull, although two other shots were low. I attributed the low hits to my arms tiring from supporting the gun, even though I was using both hands. Later shooting sessions confirmed that these loads were workable with each hitting within two inches of the bull's eye. This was not precision shooting, but good enough to kill game at 20 yards.

It was easier to shoot the left barrel more accurately because the rear trigger was positioned more comfortably for my relatively short fingers. The left barrel offered the best potential for precision shooting while the right one offered a significantly more powerful load.

During the firing of about 20 charges, there were no failures to fire and the musket caps worked well without altering the hammers. These ¼ X 28 threaded caps may be ordered from Dixie Gun Works. Musket caps are easier to place on the nipples, and the same musket nipples will also improve the performance of any Pedersoli shotgun or double rifle. The only detrimental aspect of the pistol was the difficulty of forcing the .490 patched round balls and lubricated bullets down the bore. I quickly abandoned using the wooden ramrod and employed a large T-handled aluminum ramrod for bullet seating and barrel cleaning.

These loads are somewhat comparable to the .45-70-300 that was a favorite 19th century deer cartridge, and the Maxi Ball produces equivalent energies to some .44 Remington Magnum pistol loads. Even though velocities were limited by the short barrel, I had every expectation of these loads being adequate for hogs.

Because of the pistol's 5-pound weight, recoil was noticeable, but manageable. The effective range of the rifled barrels is limited by having only a fixed front bead sight and comparatively short barrels. I am accustomed to shooting smoothbores that only have front (or no) sights. Although those who have never shot such guns wonder how they can be shot with any degree of accuracy, I can make repeated hits within the six-inch kill zone of deer-size game at 20 yards. For accurate shooting it is imperative that the pistol be held the same for each shot, that the amount of bead showing above the rib is identical and that the bead is exactly centered in the swamped barrel rib. With aimed shots I was confident that the Howdah Hunter could kill close-range game animals.

This gun cannot be expected to give accurate results with a jab-at-the-target-and-yank-the-trigger kind of shooting. It takes a deliberate shooting style to produce good results with pistols of this type. The more primitive the sights the better the trigger pull must be for best results. (An inexperienced duelist was likely a dead duck when up against a man who knew his pistols whether the guns had sights or not.)

The hunt continues

Earlier that morning I had put extra corn under the feeder. After getting my partner settled in another stand, I returned to mine at about 3:00 PM. About 30-minutes before dark, about a dozen hogs come in. Most of these hogs were small and colored shades of black, red and grizzled white. Because of their cautious nature, I was thankful that I had taken the precaution of wearing a face mask.

Making the decision that this hog was big enough, I started raising the pistol up to the firing rail. Once its barrel was resting on the rail and pointed out of the blind, I silently cocked the right barrel by pulling back the hammer, holding it, releasing the trigger and allowing the sear to positively engage in the full-cock stop of the tumbler. I held my hand under the hammer and wiggled it slightly to insure that it was fully caught in the "fire position" on the sear.

It had taken about 2 minutes to elevate and cock the gun. In about another 2 minutes I had it pointed down at the hogs. I waited until the boar positioned itself away from the other hogs and offered a broad-side shot. I wanted to take a spine shot to drop the animal. I put the bead in the front-quarter of the animal and raised it slightly. Then I had the long trigger pull to contend with. As this was a loaner gun, I had not polished the lock parts as I usually would.

I held my breath while sighting, squeezing the trigger and watching the other hogs. When the hammer fell everything looked as nearly right as I could make it. With the shot, white smoke erupted from the barrel. The hog was down in its tracks, but still moving – typical of a spine shot. Waiting until it was suitably aligned I cocked the other barrel and delivered a shot in the neck. Within a few seconds the hog was dead.

The pistol had done well and both shots hit very near where they were aimed. The first shot passed under the spine, but close enough to disrupt it. The MaxiBall traveled downward and laterally through the left lung and broke a 2-inch hole in the ribs as it exited. The other shot had penetrated the spine, broken the off-side front leg and was found imbedded under the skin. This bullet had expanded to about .75-caliber. The first shot was fatal, but with a second charge in the other barrel, there was no need for the animal to suffer. Both barrels had performed well.

When skinned, this hog was found to be between two and three years old and very lean. The usual layer of fat under the skin was absent. Almost a foot-square of hair was missing from the right side of the hog at the shoulder. This animal may have had an injury which prevented it from developing more fully. I boned out the animal and cut the meat for roasts and made sausage from the ground meat. When handled the meat was unusually sticky indicating the animal's lack of fat.

Conclusions

The Howdah Hunter is an appropriate pistol to finish off game animals, as a primary hunting pistol to use within 20 yards and a fine gun to shoot with reduced loads just for fun. Howdah pistols were never common in the 18th and 19th Centuries, and this reproduction is an opportunity to own one. Using this gun recaptures a bit of the Howdah Hunter's historic times when death by fang and claw might be only inches away and a powerful double-barreled pistol was considered good insurance.

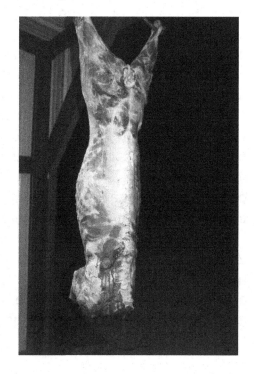

*The skinned carcass revealed an unusually lean hog with the large, trimmed-out, exit wound caused by the 370- grain Thompson/Center MaxiBall.*

## Chapter 16. Hunting Italian style

As the line of hunters slowly proceeded up the forested slopes of Mount Prati Alti that towered over Lake Montedoglio, I did not have time to consider the historic, cultural and scenic attributes of my surroundings. I was hunting the European wild boar, and fresh rootings told me that the hog was not far away.

This part of the hunt was being done the old-fashioned way as recent rains provided ideal stalking conditions. The rocks and trees were overgrown with moss and grasses reminding me of mountain creeks that I have hunted in Alaska and the Rocky Mountain states, but in Italy they did not have nasties like devil's club and stinging nettles.

Spread apart at about 40-yard intervals, our host Pierangelo Pedersoli anchored the left part of the line. Aurelio Boninsegni, the owner of the 200-hectare La Conca agricultural preserve was beside me and ballistician Alberto Riccadonna and editor Emanele Tabasso were to the right.

I had hunted hogs many times in the U.S. and sometimes on my own property, but this was the first time I had hunted the European wild boar in its native habitat. The footing on the moss-covered boulders was treacherous. I was looking for a safe place to make my next step when a noise from ahead and a glimpse of something big and black informed me that the boar was on the move and very close.

As I wanted a European hunting experience, the gun I carried was particularly appropriate. It was a Davide Pedersoli .54-caliber early -American Jaeger rifle whose Germanic antecedents had been designed for this type of work. Pedersoli was carrying a 12-gauge double slug-shotgun, Riccadonna used his own Pedersoli double Kodiak rifle and Tabasso had Pedersoli's new Hawken rifle.

True to the Jaeger style, my rifle was a relatively short barreled large-caliber gun intended to deliver a heavy ball into large game animals, particularly wild boars. Often these were .75-caliber, but the Pedersoli version was .54(-caliber and its 27½-inch barrel was rifled to stabilize a Thompson/Center Arms 430-grain MaxiBall. This gun was introduced into the United States by Dixie Gun Works, and was one of the late Butch Winter's favorite muzzleloaders. He liked it because of its quick handling and easy shooting characteristics.

Jaegers were historically produced in both flintlock and percussion versions. Although I would have happily shot either, my gun was fired by a no. 11 percussion cap and stoked with 106 grains of Swiss FFg black powder. I had fired the gun only twice. The first shot was off-hand and the bullet hit an inch or so above the bull at about 40 yards. When the shot broke I was aiming 3 inches to the left. The second shot, with a closer hold, confirmed that that the gun was shooting to the right. I also fired two shots with a Fair over-under rifle-shotgun combination gun that I might use the next day.

My favorite style of rifle for off-hand shooting has always been the set-triggered Hawken design. The forward-weighted barrel aids in steady off-hand holding that is nearly impossible with broom-straw weight tubes. Smaller-diameter barrels make guns lighter to carry, but I must shoot from a rest to make consistent shots beyond 30 yards with feather-weight barrels. I have made off-hand killing shots at a walking boar at 85 yards with one of my Hawken rifles and used another to hit a 1-by-2-inch kill zone on an alligator's brain at 30 yards. The Jaeger I was using and the Hawken rifle that Tabasso carried exhibited the excellent off-hand shooting characteristics of their designs.

"Enough shooting," our host said. "It is time to hunt."

Hunting Italian Style

I was in distinguished company. Marco Ramanzini, Danilo Liboi and Tabasso have editorial responsibilities for the magazines Diana, Sentieri di Cacca and Cacca a Palla while Pierangelo Pedersoli and Luca Rizini are presidents of the gun-making companies, Davide Pedersoli and Fair. My responsibility as an outdoor writer was to take the Pedersoli Jaeger and a Fair rifle-shotgun combination gun and cleanly kill a game animal with each of them. I had only seen these guns a few hours before and fired only a shot or two with each of them.

Another task was that Pierangelo Pedersoli was attempting to convince the Italian government that muzzleloading guns were effective on game and that it would be advantageous to have special seasons for these guns. He had invited me and the other writers to help publicize muzzleloading hunting. For me this hunt was more about shooting well than taking trophy animals.

This was very much a two-way interchange. Just as these Italian editors and writers were interested to learn about my American exploits with muzzleloaders, I wanted to hear about European hunting. The basic difference was that in Europe, hunting is more of a group experience, whereas in the U.S. it is commonly a solitary undertaking, even though game drives with hunters and standers are practiced in some parts of the U.S.

"Often," Ramanzini explained, "these will be quite large affairs. There may be 40 dogs used to move the game and perhaps 50 people participating in the hunt. Large tracts of land are driven at one time. It is not unusual for a hunting club to take 200 to 400 boars a year, as well as much other game. This is a cooperative effort. The hunter who kills gets the trophy, but all share in the meat.

"At each kill honor is paid to the animal by placing a broken branch into its mouth as a 'last meal,' and very often a ceremony with horn playing, banqueting and toasting is done at the conclusion of the hunt."

It came as something of a shock when I told them that the only aspect of European hunting traditions that was practiced in the United States was blooding the face of a young hunter when he took his first big-game animal. Some more pensive hunters might spend a few seconds over the animal reflecting on the hunt, but mostly it was gut and drag to get the animal back to camp as soon as possible.

*The hunting party in "civilian dress." From L. to R. Danilo Liboi, Luca Rizini, Pierangelo Pedersoli, Marco Ramazini, Alberto Riccadonna, Emanele Tabasso and the author.*

*Danilo Liboi(L.) and Marco Ramanzini (R) shown in different, but typical Central European hunting garb. They do not shoot in formal clothes as the English sometimes do.*

When asked why this was so, I replied, "Remember that America was settled by those who were escaping wars, famine and religious persecutions. Things were so terrible at home that they risked their lives to cross the Atlantic and settle in what was often a hostile environment. These were not the titled nobility of Europe, but people who needed to feed their families. Many European traditions were left behind in favor of what a man could accomplish with his own hands as fast as possible. For most Americans, even though they might belong to clubs, big game hunting is still a solitary undertaking with one man taking one animal per trip.

"Native Americans, with cultures tens of thousands of years, did have complex hunting traditions; but Europeans in the New World largely left their hunting traditions behind."

On the trip from Gardon in the Val du Trompia through Bresca, Verona, Florence and down the Apennine Mountains to the la Conca reserve near the historic city of Sansepoicro, Pierangelo Pedersoli talked non-stop for over an hour about Italy's complex hunting and gun laws. Both are very closely controlled by a series of restrictive licenses that govern gun ownership for target shooters, collectors, hunters and self defense. Hunters are licensed, for example, to hunt only within their provinces. With the exception of hunting on shooting preserves, they must relinquish their hunting licenses in their home provinces to obtain one in another. They may also only buy and possess ammunition for guns they have on license.

Non-Italian hunters may not hunt on public hunting areas, but are restricted to hunting on shooting preserves. La Conca specializes in agriturismo (agricultural tourism) and maintains four former home sites where tourist may experience something of rural life while living in modern comfort, including swimming pools. These farms had been abandoned, and Boninseqni rebuilt the old farmhouses using wood that he cut and milled on the property. Vallorsaia, where we stayed, once kept cows on the ground floor, the second floor was used for living quarters and the third for drying vegetables and fruits. The address was Paradiso 15, and for me the game animals and settings lived up to the billing as a hunter's paradise.

The hunt continues

Getting ready for a possible shot, I cocked the hammer and set the trigger – carefully holding my trigger finger outside of the trigger guard. Although only 25-yards away, the boar was moving away at a trot and twisting this way and that on its path. This was a going-away shot that was partly obscured by intervening rocks and trees. Perhaps smelling one of the other hunters, he hesitated in a clearing across the creek, briefly offering a shot at 40 yards. I quickly put the sights on the animal and touched the set trigger.

Smoke from the gun obscured the result. I heard crashing noises, and Boninseqni said, "Bravo. Multo bravo." The 175-pound boar was down and dead. When the bullet was recovered it had expanded to .75 caliber and exhibited a perfect mushroom. It had passed through both lungs and the heart. I was very grateful that my quick, off-hand shot had struck the animal well. Pierangelo had a shot at a running hog and missed, but others of our group took a fallow deer stag,

*Aurelio Boninsegni in his buckskins holding the Jaeger rifle as he poses with the boar that the author shot.*

a doe and two mouflon. It had been a good day, and we returned for supper.

We were served in typical Italian style at a long table that now sat where the cow stalls were located. Amid ancient beams, rocks and boards; we were had several courses starting with a pasta dish, then salad, meats, dessert and coffee accompanied by local wines. Particularly memorable were wild boar backstraps and homemade Italian lasagna. Some of the cooking was done in a wood-fired furno (outside stone oven) by Luca, one of Boninsegni's two sons. The main part of the meal had been prepared by Boninseqni's wife and daughters. Another son, Davide, assisted in the hunting operations and cleaned the game. The entire operation was a family business with everyone working very hard to make it succeed.

Pierangelo Pedersoli took a gold-metal class mouflon at 80 yards using his 12-gauge slug-shotgun. I was not surprised that his smoothbored gun did so well. I also own one and have used it to take deer in the U.S. as well as a blue wildebeest, guinea fowl and other birds in Africa. At home I often load one barrel with a round ball for deer and another with shot for small game.

These hunts are expensive. To a base fee for housing and meals trophy fees are added for each animal. The mouflon goes for 200 to 2,000 Euros, fallow deer from 250 to 1,500 Euros and boars for 10 Euros a kilogram. My boar, for example, would have cost about $1,200. Seasons vary, but everything is open during the last half of October.

Gunmaking in the Val du Trompia

The historic gunmaking city of Gordone is located in the steep mountain

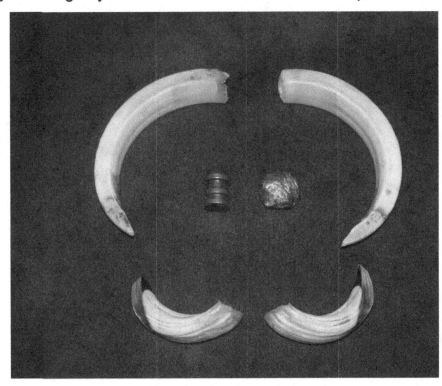

*The boar's teeth and the fired slug that was recovered from the animal beside an unfired .54-caliber MaxiBall.*

### Table 3. The guns

| Type | Maker | Barrel/Caliber | Length | Weight | Features |
|------|-------|----------------|--------|--------|----------|
| Jaeger | Pedersoli | Single .54 | 43.5 in. | 8.25 lbs. | Set triggers |
| Hawken | Pedersoli | Single .54 | 48.5 in. | 10 lbs. | Set triggers |
| Kodiak | Pedersoli | Double .54 | 45.25 in. | 9.3 lbs. | Double triggers |
| Slug Shotgun | Pedersoli | Double 12 ga | 45 in. | 6.25 lbs. | Double triggers |

valley of the Mella River about a 30-minute drive north of Bresca in the Tuscan province of Bresca. The presence of iron ore, wood for gunstocks and waterpower resulted in the establishment of iron foundries and gun-making activities in the 1400s. Fine examples of these early efforts can be seen in the Luigi Marzoli Museo delle Armi in the Castello in Bresca. This fortress also houses the Museo del Risorgimento where arms are exhibited from the revolution that led to the establishment of the modern Italian state in the 1840s.

Arms making in the narrow confines of the valley has its advantages and disadvantages. Perhaps nowhere else in is located so many arms-making companies and related activities. These include a proof house, engraving shops, a 100-year old gun-making school and suppliers of goods and services. The valley is so small that there is no railroad service, and the access road through the historic town is sometimes choked with traffic. There is no room for factory expansions except by adding more stories to existing structures. The valley is also subjected to periodic flooding making it prudent to put multi-million-dollar machinery on upper floors with resultant increases in building and gun-construction costs.

*Davide Pedersoli factory with the steep hills of the Val du Trompia rising in the background.*

*CNC machine milling barrel*

Despite, and perhaps because of, these constraints companies like Beretta and smaller firms like Davide Pedersoli and Fair have modernized to produce very-high-quality arms from the best materials using modern techniques. Computer-controlled CNC machines enable a variety of guns to be made on the same machines, requiring only changes of computer programs to switch from one model to another. This saves considerable space over the former practice of having separate production lines for each gun. Because of the lack of space, Italian gunmakers in Gordone were among the first to adopt this new technology. Some 700,000 guns a year are made in this small valley.

The firms of Davide Pedersoli and Fair are typical of companies that passed from fathers to progressive generations of sons and daughters. The present generation of Pedersolis includes Pierangelo Pedersoli and his sons Stefano and Paula. Stefano takes an active part in the business while Paula is still in school, and shares his father's hunting interests. I have shot Pedersoli's replica guns for decades, and met the family at numerous Shot Shows. This connection led to my being invited for the hunt and factory visit.

Making high-quality replicas of historic firearms for shooters, reinactors and hunters has given Davide Pedersoli a world-wide market. Although the firm's largest volume of sales are in the U.S., there is also keen interest in his guns in Europe, Russia and South Africa. Unlike in the U.S. where hunting muzzleloaders may be of advanced designs, muzzleloaders used in other countries are usually restricted to traditional patterns or are regulated as cartridge arms. Pedersoli guns regularly sweep both U.S. and international muzzleloading shooting events and are increasingly winning black-powder cartridge competitions.

*Pierangelo Pedersoli in the American cowboy hunting costume that he prefers*

Decorative possibilities offered by Pedersoli include gold inlays and engraving. Once the base guns have been produced, the possibilities of using local craftsmen to make unique examples of the gunmaker's art are limited only by the client's desires.

Wood, steel, brass and nowadays high-strength aluminum alloys are components of modern Italian firearms. At Pedersoli these are produced in house, as are the barrels. Good gunstock wood is becoming increasingly scarce, and Pedersoli gets most of his from North America. Planks are sawn and made into blanks which are later milled into finished stocks. During assembly the final inletting is done with hand tools.

Machining operations inside the computer-controlled CNC machines consist of the machine selecting a particular tool, verifying that it is not broken, performing a particular operation, replacing the tool, choosing another, performing another

*If the wife objects to visiting Brescia, an overnight in Venice might make amends.*

operation, replacing the tool, choosing another and so on until the machining operations are completed. In this manner frames, action parts and other components are milled to a very high degree of precision and sorted into individual boxes for assembly.

Pedersoli rifles all of his barrels in house. Each barrel is rifled, broached and straightened to insure maximum smoothness and accuracy. Guns undergo a rigorous final inspection prior to shipment to insure that they are up to quality standards.

All told I had a good hunt, a fine visit and shot some excellent guns. Brescia and Gardone are off the popular tourist routes, but for gun enthusiasts these are places that are well worth visiting. Most gun makers have in-house showrooms, and it is often possible to special-order guns to fit individual requirements. If you must convince a spouse to include Bresca on your Italian trip, Venice is only a 2-hour train ride away.

*Different countries have different hunting traditions and even within a country individual hunts vary from host to host. If lucky enough to be invited, or go on your own, pay close attention to your host's insturctions. Honor the customs of the local hunting community within the bounds of safety and reason.*

*The steep country around Riggins, Idaho, holds many bear, elk and much other game.*

## Chapter 17. Bear at the apex

The Winchester-branded XP-150 bolt-action in-line muzzleloading rifle had impressed me as being among the best of the bolt-action muzzleloaders, so I eagerly anticipated the opportunity to see if Black Powder Incorporated (BPI's) new Apex pivoting-block single-shot muzzleloading rifle was up to the same standards. It did not take much convincing to have me on the plane to hunt Idaho's black bears when company founder Michael McMichael offered me a chance to use the new gun along with an experimental low-friction PowerBelt Platinum High-Performance bullet.

I knew the Salmon River country through the writings of the late Elmer Keith. The hunt area near Riggins was described as being in the Idaho rain shadow, semi-arid and steep. It certainly did not look like the thickly vegetated environment where I bear hunted in eastern Canada and even less like the bear-infested swamps of southern Georgia. I had only two days to hunt. I wondered if first, there were any bears; and, if so, what they could find to eat? There were rocks, trees and some pastures; but very few patches of irrigated croplands next to the river. McMichael said there were plenty of black bears feeding in orchards. He added that I would probably have no difficulty in getting my bear, even on a very short hunt. My mind conjured up parallel rows of apple trees with me sitting on a

*Trees heavy with plums attracted bears for miles that came into the abandoned orchards to gather an easy meal.*

wooden fruit crate waiting for a bruin to come and feed. Arguing against this notion was his warning that the country was steep, and I would need to bring a good pair of boots.

Arriving in Boise, McMichael and I passed unseen. He was leaving for an African hunt while I was being met by Dan Hall. The plan was that I was to have a brief factory tour and then be driven to the hunting area about two hours to the north. The factory tour completed, we were soon on our way. Dan mentioned that the previous day one of the hunters had seen 14 bears, but had not shot at any of them. "Humm," I thought, "as I wondered why not? Surely out of 14 bears, he would have had an opportunity to take at least one reasonable-sized bear."

Asking Dan for more details, he explained, "In the 1860s there was a boom town about 15 miles further back in the mountains. The miners needed food, and a number of people homesteaded in these valleys and raised stock, crops and fruit to supply the miners. The valley that we will be hunting was too steep for

*Making PowerBelt bullets at the Idaho factory.*

crops so the early settlers planted plums, pears and a few apples. The plums went wild and now grow on all but the steepest slopes. The bears feed on this fruit."

Already in camp were two editors who worked on different National Rifle Association publications. One, Jeff Johnson, is an editor with The American Hunter and was holding out for a trophy-size bruin. A fellow NRA magazine editor had gone out with McMichael the previous day. They had attempted to stalk bear, but the dry conditions and fickle winds had thwarted their efforts. Everyone had been seeing bears, and the prospects appeared favorable that I would at least have a better than average opportunity to take a reasonable bear.

### The Apex rifle

The Apex uses a pivoting-block muzzleloading action operated by a downward pull on the trigger guard. Thompson/Center Arms was the first company to introduce this general operational style with their Omega rifle. This action functions much like the one typically used in the Ballard single-shot rifle action in that a light-weight breech swings down from a fixed barrel to expose a chamber for a cartridge. In case of the muzzleloaders this chamber now takes a 209 shotgun primer, rather than the long black-powder cartridges typically used in the Ballards.

Pressures generated by the powder charge are contained by a long breech plug, so the block does not have to be very strong to control the relatively small amount of gasses that might leak around the primer. More importantly, the block had to be easily removable so that black-powder fouling could be scrubbed from the action, although this was demonstrated to be less important than I had previously assumed.

It is not unusual for writers on industry-sponsored hunts to be loaned sample guns that have been on the trade-show circuit or even guns that had been previously used by other writers. The Apex that I was handed was not only used, but it appeared to have been never, or seldom, cleaned. The breech was so crud-incrusted that it was nearly as black as the stock and barrel. I was frankly surprised that the gun would still shoot. After Dan passed a couple of patches down the barrel, we fired a couple of sight-in shots at a nearby barrow pit. From a rest the gun shot fairly well, but I found the barrel somewhat light for off-hand shooting, particularly when as the Weaver scope added additional weight above the action. I have this same complaint about many modern cartridge rifles. Reducing the amount of steel contained in a barrel is certainly a way to cut weight, but it makes many rifles hard to shoot accurately from anything but rock-steady rests.

For me, for this gun on this day it looked like 50 yards was about the tops for an accurate off-hand shot. I would have felt much more at home with any of the older Hawken-style muzzleloaders for close-range shooting. The gun was also sighted in for 3-inches high at 100 yards which would put the bullet at the point of aim at 150 yards with the 100-grain charge of Hodgdon's Triple Seven

*The Winchester-branded Apex Rifle shown here with the 100-grain charge of Hodgdon's Triple Seven pellets, Platinum PowerBelt bullet and a 209 primer*

pellets. Patches were run down the barrel after every couple of shots to help improve the grouping qualities of the saboted bullets. The rifle functioned well, and the stock felt good in the hands. I only wish that it had a little more weight up front. I sometimes install solid steel ramrods to improve the off-hand shooting qualities of light-barreled muzzleloaders, but I did not have that option in Idaho.

Like PowerBelt's AeroTip, the new bullet features the a polymer base skirt (actually black and ribbed on production bullets), 270-grain copper-plated lead bullet and a green (now black) plastic plug in a large hollow point. The difference is that the copper has been given a molecular rearrangement so that it is now platinum colored, rather than the customary copper yellow. "To be sure," Dan explained, "it is still copper, but the process makes the bullet slicker. This makes it easier to load and gives it a slightly higher velocity due to decreased barrel friction. This is not a molybdenum or silver coating or anything like that."

As is the case with the copper-plated .50-caliber 295-grain PowerBelt bullet which have been used by millions of hunters for over a decade, the new 270-grain bullet may also be used with a 150-grain powder charge. A significant advantage of the Platinum AeroTip is that it has a better ballistic coefficient (.220 vs. .186) and develops more energy and has a slightly flatter trajectory at all ranges.

The platinum bullets were attractive, but would they kill bears? We were to do our best the next morning. Hall and I started out on a 4-wheeler as soon as it was light enough to see. The plan was to spot a bear from either the road or from a ridge-top view point and then stalk it until we were close enough for a shot. We did spy one small bear that day, but I elected to hold out for a larger one. One thing that impressed me was that the lower slopes near the creek bottoms and a good-ways up the ridges was covered in wild fruit trees that were heavily laden with ripening plumbs. The yellow plumbs were particularly plentiful and delicious. Every pile of bear droppings that we saw was full of fruit seeds. This certainly answered my "What do these bears eat?" question.

The editor who had seen 14 bear the day before chose to set overlooking the upper part of an adjacent drainage. He saw and stalked a nice bear and took him with a single shot. The bear was down a steep slope and it took three people to help drag it out to the point where it could be loaded on a 4-wheeler.

One of the places Dan and I had tried the day before was a small drainage with a flowing stream and a switchback road that ultimately led to some ridge-top glassing points. On the second day, I elected to sit on a point overlooking a small meadow at the junction of three tributary creeks. Plumb trees were growing in and above these creek bottoms, and I felt sure that sooner or later, I would hear a bear breaking branches and be able to stalk him or take one as it crossed the open ground at the creek junction.

In preparation for a long sit, I took a cushion, the rifle, some reloads, my rangefinder and lunch. Events transpired a bit faster than I anticipated. Walking up the road to my stake-out location, we heard branches breaking above us. From our walk up the ridge top the day before, I knew the switchback above us would bring us nearer the bear and perhaps provide us with a shot. We proceeded up the road to the apex of the switchback and as quietly as possible walked up the road towards the noise.

"There he is. Shoot." Dan exclaimed. The bear was above us and about 40-yards away. He turned slightly and started moving uphill. I aimed at the shoulder and pulled the trigger. At the shot the bear ran. As I reloaded, Dan went to the site. "There's lots of blood. It's a good hit," Hall shouted. "Come on up, and we'll trail him."

About 20 minutes later Dan found the bear and finished it off with a shot from a Marlin .45-70 lever-action rifle. It was a 200-pound bear, somewhat larger than the Idaho average, with a fine black coat and a distinctive white "V" under the neck. To preserve this distinctive marking, I decided that we would skin it for a head mount, rather than a rug. That afternoon the bear was skinned and later

*The author with his Idaho bear and the Apex rifle.*

*Platinum PowerBelt bullet fragments recovered from the author's bear. I suspect that the bullet struck a branch first and then hit the bear judging from the size of the entrance hole. Although the bear needed a follow-up shot, the hit would have been lethal.*

that night I trimmed the fat from the bear and cut the meat to freeze for the flight home. The previous bear that I had taken in Canada has been fine eating, and I thought that this fruit-fed bear would certainly do as well.

The bullet had struck the bear back of the front shoulder and raked diagonally through the bear coming to rest against the large leg bone of the off-side leg. The bullet may have struck a small limb before hitting the bear as the entrance wound showed a large puffed area of flesh and fat. The bullet was recovered in two pieces.

As I was to leave the next day, that afternoon the bear was skinned, quartered and hung in the cooler. I had wrapping paper, tape and a cooler with me. My plan was to return to the cooler after supper to butcher, wrap and freeze the bear to get it ready for its trip back to Georgia. Working by the barn's lights, I also made up several packages of bear fat for rendering. The fat would be used for making biscuits and baking.

Jeff had also been hunting two days, but had not seen a big enough bear. While my bear at about 200 pounds was a bit larger that Idaho's 165-pound weight of an average black bear, Jeff was holding out for a 300-pounder. He had been on a long road trip which had by this time included a successful bowhunt for antelope near Forsyth, Montana, and a trout-fishing excursion near Dillon. After he arrived at camp we had a chance to dine on some delicious antelope backstraps that were made even better by being cooked over an open fire by the side of a rushing stream.

With about three decades separating us, Jeff and I were an interesting contrast. He still had the relatively youthful stamina and drive that I had also possessed when I was in my late 30s. I could hold my own on level ground and tromp up to the top of these steep ridges once, but a bad hip prevented me from doing the over the ridges and across the valleys kind of traverses of my younger days that Jeff was eager, and able, to attempt. The years had taught me patience, and I had come to learn that patience will often trump speed.

In the meantime, Jeff was much enjoying his adventure. He, like I, had seen mule deer, whitetail deer, elk, turkeys and quail in this game-rich country. Bear had been attracted from miles around by the ripening fruit, and he had also seen a number of them. After five days of hunting, he spotted the bear he wanted at a range of 173 yards. He took a steady position and the bullet hit the bear. After some scary moments trailing the wounded bear through thick brush and looking for it in a dark cave, he relocated the bear and finished it with a second shot.

A few days later he was back at his desk in Wapples Mill, Virginia, with the bitter-sweet job of editing stories about other peoples hunts, while nourishing warm memories of campfires and a 2,000 mile road trip through some of the best hunting and fishing country in North America.

When to make a change

Technological advances most often come in incremental steps with many fewer "aha ha" moments along the way when someone offers something that is different enough to change the sport. Introduction of the in-line rifle and Pyrodex pellets were such moments in muzzleloading's recent past. Each improvement offers more convenience, simplifies operations and sometimes enhanced ballistic performance. Instead of trying out every new gun model and variation as I do, most hunters buy new guns or change their loads when it can be demonstrated that the new guns/loads offer significantly improved performance on game.

My suggestion is to make a muzzleloading checkup every few years. Look at the new guns, powders and bullets and see if they offer any significant advances in utility and performance that you want, or need, to take. The same gun and load that you have used for decades will do fine, but maybe you want to retrograde and look at some of the older back-powder technologies or perhaps you need a gun that will mount a scope to enable you to make better hits on game. Or maybe even do some of both and purchase a flintlock for close-range hunting and a drop-barrel in-line for packing off on a distant hunt where light weight, portability and reliability may be the most important factors.

Don't be fearful of trying different things. They will all work if you take the time to learn how to use them effectively. Working and hunting with the new guns will be great fun. Find what new, or old, technologies interest you, get the guns and go for it.

*Although shopped around, this story never found favor with editors. Parts of it were incorporated into materials used in Crossbow Hunting (Stackpole, 2006) and into the 2010 issue of "Gun Digest." I returned to Idaho in 2010 and took a similar-sized Fall black bear with a Parker Tornado crossbow. Two videos related to my bear hunts are on YouTube at http://www.youtube.com/watch?v=GSbemqFJTjQ&layer_token=36b7a68defdca363 and http://www.youtube.com/watch?v=YkFYpUarYsQ.*

*Big Toothy, a Georgia alligator taken with a Ruger Old Army muzzleloading revolver.*

## *Chapter 18. Black powder alligators*

Big Toothy is looking at me as I write this. When last in life I was pushing a 7-inch Bowie knife behind its head to cut its spine and finally kill the 10-foot reptile. It had been hit with two crossbow arrows, harpooned, taped, shot with a black-powder revolver, drug up on shore with a gaff made from a cotton hook after an hour-long fight and knifed behind the head. Least one think this was overkill, it still took 15 minutes before it stopped thrashing long enough for the three of us to load it into the boat. These big alligators are tough.

Found all the way from the Texas coast to North Carolina, the American alligator is one of the most primitive, but effective, predators in the southern swamps. It is not the least bit afraid of taking on anything smaller than it is, including man.

Alligators routinely feed on fish, turtles, beaver and otter and will also lie at the edges of water holes to grab deer, hogs, cows and horses when they come to water. When an easier meal may not be had, or when they feel like it, they will also eat other gators. These are truly equal-opportunity feeders. If it moves in or near the water they will try for it. Florida, which has about 14,000,000 people and 14,000,000 alligators, usually has several alligator attacks every year with some having fatal consequences.

Once considered endangered and protected, alligator populations have rebounded to the extent that hunting seasons are held in Texas, Louisiana, Alabama, Georgia, South Carolina, Arkansas and Florida. Mississippi started a restricted alligator season in 2005 on the Pearl River and on private lands in three counties surrounding the state capitol at Jackson. These permits were only available to state residents.

Because alligators sink when shot, all states require that sport hunters only shoot the animal after first attaching a snare, hook, harpoon or other restraint to it. This is certainly a reasonable approach as I have lost a gator that was shot, apparently dead, but either escaped or was drug off by a larger one. As I later discovered, even alligators with their brains blown to mush may revive and move enough to escape.

Each state has a little different approach to the details of dispatching an alligator. Some like Mississippi and Florida require sport hunters to use a bang stick, while Georgia will permit the animal to be dispatched by a pistol. After I was finally drawn for a permit, I chose a muzzleloading revolver because this handgun developed sufficient energy to do the job without destroying the skull or sending unwanted bullet or bone fragments through the boat's hull or into us.

Rifle

That instant I faced the possibility that I was no longer the hunter, but the hunted. A 13-foot alligator had surfaced 7 yards to the right of the table-top-sized patch of landing I was standing on. I had one alligator dead in the water on my left and there were two more 10-foot gators nearby. I definitely had more alligators that I needed.

My empty muzzleloader, a .50-caliber Traditions Magnum Hawken, offered little comfort in its present condition as an 8¾-pound club. This side-lock gun is unique as it is one of the few designed to function with Pyrodex pellets, although it needs a musket cap to guarantee prompt ignition. As I fumbled for my speed loader, the lines of the Charge of the Light Brigade ran through my mind – except now it was "gators to the left of them, gators to the right of them", and so on.

The big alligator probably weighed 800 pounds and, if he was so inclined, could be on me in less than a second. Don't assume that Florida alligators are tame. Nearly 150 attacks on people have occurred since records were kept in the 1940s.

I was supposed to take only one alligator and not shoot any over 11-feet long (although I doubt that the big alligator cared very much about my agreement with the outfitter). The one I just shot appeared to be dead. The other two had disappeared, but the 13-footer was very still, as if trying to decide whether he was hungry or nor.

Florida alligators can be hunted in two ways, but only one allows the use of firearms. The usual Florida alligator hunt consists of entering the annual drawing for a limited number of tags, which are allocated for specific geographic areas. If a tag is drawn, a Florida resident pays $250 ($1,000 for non-residents) for a license that allows him or her to take one (sometimes more) during a weeklong hunt in

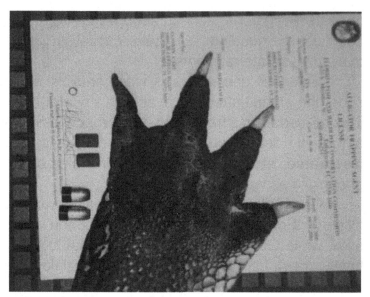

*Florida Trapping Agent license enables a hunter to take alligators with a variety of firearms.*

September. Successful applicants are allowed to hunt at night on public and private waters. Only bows, crossbows and hand-held harpoons may be used to attach one or more lines to an alligator. It is then pulled to the boat and killed with a bang stick loaded with a .357 or .44 Magnum pistol cartridge.

Because of the use of expensive air boats, specialized bow-hunting rigs, and the scouting needed to find trophy-sized alligators (nine feet long and larger), the cost of a guided alligator hunt is often more than $1,000, plus additional charges for skinning and processing the meat.

As Florida has an alligator population of over 10,000,000 animals, some must be killed each year to keep their numbers under control. Besides permitting sport hunting, the state also licenses trappers to take alligators from private lands, process the meat for sale and sell the hides. This commerce is closely controlled by state wildlife officials, who conduct an alligator count and issue tags for each property. A trapper may hunt his lease all year and shoot alligators with firearms but must restrict his activities to daylight hours.

Each licensed trapper is allowed to employ agents, and these agents may also use firearms. Trappers like Carl Godwin can offer gun hunts for alligators where his hunters (officially state-licensed trapper's agents) may take alligators with rifles, pistols and muzzleloaders. This idea appealed to me immediately, since I hunt almost exclusively with muzzleloading guns. We struck a deal: I could take a 9-to-11-foot alligator for a set price and he could retain the meat and hide.

Godwin's hunts range from $2,000 for an 8-to-9-foot gator, to $5,200 for an alligator more than 12-feet long. This includes a 3-day hunt, the use of an air boat or other equipment, preparation of the meat and skinning the alligator.

During our pre-hunt conversations, Godwin said that he has killed more than 1,000 alligators with rifles ranging from the .22 Hornet to the .25'06. The one he uses most of the time is a .222 Remington Magnum. "It's not so much what you use; it's being able to put a bullet in exactly the right spot that counts," he explained. "Most people don't have any idea where their rifles shoot at 20 to 50

*The author with his gaff pole and gun with the alligator he took from a narrow grass-choked peninsula which extended far out into the lake.*

yards. The worst hunter I had showed up with a big magnum rifle and missed seven gators. He never came close. Shoot what you can shoot well, sight it in at 25 yards, and you will get your gator."

I was thinking about all this as I retrieved my Rightnour speed loader and rotated a charged chamber over the muzzle. I heard the satisfying "plop, plop" of two 50-grain Pyrodex pellets dropping down the barrel and felt resistance as I started the 348-grain, copper-clad BlackBelt (now PowerBelt) bullet. After ramming the bullet home, I was most of the way towards being an armed hunter once again.

My outsized gator, which had been watching all this intently, sank beneath the surface. It would either explode from the water in a fury of spray, gaping mouth and teeth or swim away. Alligators don't waste time jaw-popping like hogs and bears. It's just charge, open, chomp and go.

It had taken four half-day hunts to locate the alligator I shot. We had seen between 12 and 20 alligators a day that were more than 4-feet long, getting one large enough, close enough and in a position to shoot was the problem. I had Ashley ring sights on the rifle that lined up fast and gave an excellent sight picture, but I had not anticipated the difficulty of seeing the dark, knobby lumps housing the alligator's eyes on the black water.

I passed up a shot at an 11-foot alligator at 100 yards. I figured that the probable results of this shot would be to make a splash near the alligator. Then we stood a good chance of spending the remainder of the day looking for a gator that was not hit. Another time, only the knobs of the eyes and nostrils were exposed at 40 yards, and these were partly covered in pond weeds. By the time I was sure I was seeing an alligator and not cypress knees, the gator had sunk beneath the surface.

Even with their eyes at water level, the alligators could obviously see

Godwin and me approaching 100-yards away. They would go into the water or swim away as we got closer. We knew from tracks that there were two 10-foot alligators in one section of a canal, but I could never get more than a glimpse of them. These alligators knew that they were being hunted.

Once we crept up on a 7-foot gator in a canal. I already had the hammer of my muzzleloader cocked, but when I set the triggers, he heard the metallic click and instantly disappeared into a nearby culvert, or "gator hotel," as my guide called them. These alligators were not like the overfed, blimp-like specimens that I had seen at Okefenokee Swamp Park on my way to Okeechobee. Not only were these wild gators "lean and hungry," they could hear, smell and see very well.

After looking for a suitable alligator for the better part of 2 days, I now had more gators that I really wanted on the stock pond that we were hunting. While I was putting a musket cap on my rifle, Godwin drove up. I shouted, "Visible gator. Dead in the water!" By the time he arrived with his alligator-retrieving gear, I was gratified to see that the 13-footer had resurfaced about 75-yards away – a much more comfortable distance.

With some alligator sticking above the water for a target, Godwin had no problem getting the four-pronged grapple hook into the animal and pulling it in with his deep-sea fishing rig. Once close to shore, he hooked the gator with a gaff, and we both pulled it up on land. The big reptile, about 300 pounds worth, was loaded onto the back of his pickup with a barrel hoist, and we took it to back to his cooler to start the processing.

Only after we had the alligator safely loaded did I have time to think about the shot. I was standing in armpit-tall grass when I saw the alligator. The closest one was the appropriate size, but it was facing me and offered a very poor shot angle. Fortunately, it began to turn so that a bullet could pass under his eye to the brain. The alligator's back started to disappear beneath the surface, and I had to shoot quickly. The heavy lead bullet completely penetrated the gator's skull, about 7 inches, and killed the animal instantly. The combination of a heavy rifle and set triggers enabled me to make a 25-yard, off-hand shot and put the bullet where it needed to go.

Black-powder alligator hunting in Florida was certainly an interesting experience. The

*The author with the Traditions Magnum Hawken rifle and his Florida alligator*

potential exists for taking large alligators from private lands leased by state-licensed trappers. Trophy alligators taken with muzzleloaders are a new category in Safari Club International's listing of this species. Mine was the first one sent in and the 9-foot 11-inch alligator was awarded a bronze metal.

I can verify that there is at least one 13-foot alligator in Florida that would look good in anyone's trophy room. A bow hunter tried to take him, but could never get close enough. Perhaps a black-powder hunter can.

Pistol

For the past 4 years Georgia residents have joined hunters in Gulf Coast states in having an annual alligator hunt. This regulation change was taken to permit hunters to help in controlling the state's expanding population of over 250,000 gators. As soon as I and friends, Roger Kicklighter and Ed Foster, heard that applications were being accepted, we started applying for the quota hunts. The third year we were finally drawn. We were going to have our chance to go hand to jaw with one of this continent's most deadly and hard-to-kill animals.

After Georgia's first two successful hunts, the numbers of permits had been expanded to 500, the length of the hunt increased to 4 weeks and the size of the hunt areas more than doubled. Since applicants must apply for one of eight zones, the first step in the process was to select our area.

Georgia's alligators are found along the coast, through the Okefenokee Swamp, in Lake Seminole in extreme southwestern Georgia and extend north to the Fall Line cities of Columbus, Macon and Augusta. Populations are highest in coastal areas. The best opportunity for a big alligator is to hunt an area that had been previously closed. I selected Zone 7 that included the lower Altamaha River because I knew from previous duck hunts, that this area still supported a thriving population despite two previous years of hunting pressure. Although we all applied for the same zone, Ed drew his second choice which was the adjacent hunt unit to the south.

This meant that we had two parts of the state to scout before we finalized our plans. Unlike other states with longer histories of gator hunting, Georgia has few alligator guides and much hunting is done on a freelance basis. I had already purchased a 15-footX54-inch aluminum boat and 40-hp. motor that would be needed to navigate Georgia's coastal rivers. Our approach would be that one person would run the boat and another handle the lines attached to the alligator while the third fought the big reptile. We needed to scout the area together while simultaneously learning to do the tasks necessary to kill and recover a 10-foot alligator.

Each hunt would have a designated shooter. His responsibilities would be to shoot the alligator with a crossbow, harpoon it, shoot it with a pistol, wrap its mouth with electrical tape and finish it by severing its spine with a knife.

A pre-hunt orientation by members of the State Wildlife Resources Division explained why these steps were needed. Knifing the alligator is necessary because alligators, even with their walnut-size brains shot to mush, have a nasty habit of reviving once they have been pulled into the boat. The attachment of lines is required before shooting to help insure that shot alligators will actually be harvested.

All the officers emphasized that most of the action would take place within inches of the boat, and that alligator hunting was among the most adrenalin-charged hunts that may be experienced. They remarked that no other type of hunting puts the game and hunter in such close proximity for perhaps an hour or more with an animal with lightning-fast reflexes and bone-crushing jaws. They stressed the need for careful preparation, safely handling the hunting instruments and properly tagging the alligator.

In preparing for the hunt, I rigged a 150-pound draw weight Horton Hawk crossbow with fiberglass fishing arrows, Muzzy Gator-Getter points and 600-pound lines. These shortened arrows were shot from tubs, rather than from reels attached to the crossbow. This arrangement allowed a second arrow to be fired very quickly as there was no need to re-spool line back onto a reel. Using a chain-saw file, I also cut the half-moon notch in the rear of the arrow that Horton, Barnett and some other crossbows require to prevent the string from jumping the arrow. I sighted-in the crossbow's iron sights (preferred over scopes or red-dot sights for night hunting) to hit the point of aim at 5-yards and drop 6-inches at 10. All of us had a chance to practice with the crossbow prior to the hunt.

I also worked up a load for the Ruger Old Army. For those not accustomed to shooting black-powder revolvers, these guns employ relatively mild charges of powder (23-40 grains, depending on the gun) and no. 11 percussion caps to propel a series of lubricated round balls. Most commonly available in .44-caliber, they use a slightly oversize round ball which is covered with a dab of lubricant to prevent "flashovers" when all of the chambers fire simultaneously. I chose the Ruger because of its excellent adjustable sights which allowed the gun to be zeroed for a shot that I expected to be at 5-yards or closer and chose a stainless version to better resist corrosion in the salt-water environment.

My choice of the Ruger Old Army was deliberate. More powerful handguns might destroy a sizeable portion of the skull while also spraying bullet and bone fragments into the hull since most alligators are killed beside the boat. I chose a load of 40-grains of Hodgdon's Triple Seven powder, a .457 Hornady lead ball weighing 144.5-grains and CVA's Grease Patch over the balls. This load generated 920- fps. and 271.6-ft./lbs. of muzzle energy. To eliminate the possibility of grease working past the ball and spoiling the powder, I did not apply the lubricant until I was ready to shoot.

As with all single-action revolvers only five of the six chambers were loaded and the hammer rested on an uncapped nipple. As a safety precaution and to further protect the gun, I planned to keep the pistol in its plastic shipping box until it was time for it to be deployed, rather than hang it in a holster which might be

*Out first "chicken gator" that was taken by Roger Kicklighter and the tools that I used kill mine the following week.*

caught up on a line or restrict my movements in the confines of a small boat.

Our scouting trip took place on a weekend prior to the hunt. After talking with the area's Game Management Officer, we selected an island with abandoned rice paddies for our first attempt. Our reconnaissance was not only to locate alligators, but to also learn the waters around the island. Georgia's 12-foot tides dictated that we launch at near high tide. We would also need a smaller boat that we could haul over the exterior dike to access the island's interior canals. This meant we would have to use two boats and two vehicles.

We also scouted two locations in Foster's area. This weekend trip gave everyone a chance to operate the boat. By the time the first hunt day arrived, Roger had rigged two harpoons, Ed had made a gator gaff out of a cotton hook and I had the crossbow and a Ruger Old Army percussion revolver ready to take an alligator.

After arriving at the launch area, we put both boats into the water and started across the river towing the smaller boat. I noticed a clear approach to the island and made for it. Kicklighter and Foster took the smaller boat and hunted with a harpoon while I sat on the dike with the crossbow. After 2 hours the boat returned. They could not get close enough for a harpoon throw, and the battery for the electric motor had been exhausted.

Kicklighter said he would paddle me around to give me a chance with the crossbow. I missed a shot at a smaller gator and we swapped positions. Kicklighter took a 6-footer, and I assisted as he crossbow shot, pistol shot and knifed the reptile. We skinned and salvaged the meat from that alligator the next day. This was smaller than the 9-to-12-foot alligator that we were looking for, but after all the trouble we had gone through we were determined to leave with a gator in the boat.

The following weekend we attempted to get Foster's alligator from one of the tidal creeks that we had scouted in his area. Although we hunted for 12-hours that night, the one big alligator that we saw sank just before Foster could shoot. Completely bushed, we crashed for 5 hours in a motel.

189

On our way back home, we decided to look at another part of my hunt area that we could possibly work using only one boat. We saw nothing in the salt marsh. Rounding a corner as we approached a small island, I spotted a large alligator pulled up on the bank. We motored by the basking gator and, as previously agreed, paddled silently back. Fortunately, the tide was running with us.

Sensing our approach, the alligator rose on its legs and turned towards the water. I fired as he started to move. The arrow imbedded itself in the rear leg. The gator plunged under the boat and carried the line, tub and attached float into the water. (Floats are used because a rolling alligator can wind up the line and swamp the boat.) Foster gently pulled the alligator towards the surface, and I made two unsuccessful attempts to plant the harpoon in the animal's back. I reloaded the crossbow and put another arrow through the alligator's chest the next time Foster pulled it up.

I sensed that the alligator badly wanted to bite something. Rather than have the old bull gator take a hunk out of the boat or one of us, I jammed the straw end of the broom into its mouth.

"Whomp!" The broom had its desired effect, and the gator's jaws snapped shut expelling water and straw between its inch-long teeth. I had ample opportunity to examine his dentition as he was less than two feet from my hand. His work on the broom also enabled me to appreciate the power exerted by his 20-inch jaws.

Holding the broom with my left hand, I attempted to move his head so that I could plant a bullet from the Ruger Old Army revolver into its brain. He did not take kindly to this treatment. Again, he chomped the broom and ejected another half-gallon of muddy marsh water from its mouth.

To this point, the alligator had been hit with two crossbow arrows and one was imbedded deeply into its side. Although obviously bothered by the proceedings, his actions demonstrated that we had done little more than provoke the animal.

*"There he is," I say as I point out an alligator that we surprised that was sunning itself on a small island in the coastal marsh. Photo by Ed Foster.*

190

*An off-hand shot at the gator's head put a bullet into its brain and stunned it sufficiently so that I could wrap its mouth with electrical tape and we could tow it back to shore. Photo by Roger Kicklighter*

Now that we could raise the front part of the alligator, I plunged the harpoon head into its neck. Although hampered by lines attached by two crossbow arrows and a rope, it was not seriously injured. At this stage we were a half-hour into the fight, and we would have to exhaust the alligator before I could safely put a pistol bullet into its brain.

Ultimately, the gator started to pull the boat into the marsh and raised its head. This allowed me to take a safe shot with the pistol. The bullet stunned the animal. I quickly pulled the boat to the alligator and put five wraps of electrical tape around its deadly jaws. Using the boat motor, Kicklighter towed the gator back into the channel.

Approaching the shore, I tugged the still squirming reptile up on the bank with the gaff and finished it by plunging the blade of the Buck Bowie knife up to the hilt behind the gator's head. Even so, it was 15-minutes before the alligator quit thrashing long enough for us to heave the 10 ft. 1-inch, 300-pound animal into the boat.

*Any alligator is not considered "killed" until its spine has been cut by a strong blade forced between the spine and the skull.*

We made another trip for Foster's gator, but although he had shots, he was unsuccessful. Even so, we had all participated in one of the most exciting hunts available to American hunters.

If drawn for the hunt, the Georgia alligator license was $50 for resident and nonresidents in 2005 to which would be added the cost of an appropriate hunting license. This alligator license permits the applicant to take one gator with a minimum length of 4 feet. A successful applicant may have helpers, who can assist but cannot take alligators themselves; but each helper must also have hunting and alligator licenses. More complete information is available in a booklet, Guide to Alligator Hunting in Georgia, published by the Georgia Department of Natural Resources and also available online.

Alligator applications are available in June and must be returned by July 31. The 4-week hunt starts in early September and extends into October. Applications and information are available at www.gohuntgeorgia.com or by calling (770) 761-3044. If rejected on the first try, resubmit the next year to advance to a higher priority. No money is required to submit an application.

Alligator hunting has become more popular as additional states have added sport-hunting seasons. Some of my articles on alligator hunting have appeared in Dixie Gun Works' 2002 "Blackpowder Annual, Fur-Fish-Game (August, 2006) and in Georgia Sportsman (July, 2008) among other publications. A blog entry "Alligator Hunting and Eating" is found at www.hoveysmith.wordpress.com.

*Gate of the Triple U Ranch, about 20 miles west of Pierre, South Dakota.*

## Chapter 19. A South Dakota buffalo

Nineteenth century images of tens of thousands of buffalo being pursued by Indians on horseback or by white hunters with their long-range black-powder rifles will forever color the American hunter's view of buffalo hunting. These images are periodically reinforced by movies such as Dances with Wolves and Wyatt Earp which depicted classic buffalo hunts.

Gone are the vast herds of yesteryear. Yet, buffalo are part of the success story of modern conservation, and herds have been rescued from the brink of extinction. There are now thriving buffalo populations in many western states, although the majority of these buffalo are on private ranches. There are a few hunting opportunities for free-ranging buffalo on public lands in the Henry Mountains of Utah, in Alaska and sometimes on a mix of public and private land adjacent to Yellowstone National Park.

Today's hunting is nothing like the old hunts where the animals were shot until the hunter ran out of ammunition or lost the desire to kill. The plains are now crisscrossed by interstates and dissected by feeder roads and fences. Many of these features were designed to facilitate raising and transporting stock, and now this stock includes buffalo as well as cows and sheep. Some ranches raise buffalo to supplement their income with hunters' fees helping many of them avoid foreclosure while providing a hint of what buffalo hunting was once like.

Why hunt ranched buffalo?

Motivations that drive individual hunters to take any species of game are complex. On one level buffalo hunting is a spiritual experience – particularly for someone who is part Native American. It is a direct link to a lifestyle and ancestors who are now long gone. This sharing of experiences in this place in modern times connects back and forward to link a distant past to the present.

Times long gone also draw those who wish to recapture the spirit of the early white trappers who first saw the plains with their seemingly endless herds of game. These hearty individuals shot an occasional buffalo, but had neither space nor time to deal with the heavy hides, and always had to keep an eye out for Indian war parties who resented this intrusion onto their lands. Today's buckskinners with their antique-pattern rifles hunt buffalo so that they can personally experience what was part of this nation's progress to a modern state.

Buffalo are also hunted because they are the largest land animal native to the Americas. This alone is a reason for a passionate hunter to take a real piece of Americana. No collection of North American game animals would be complete without a buffalo. To have hunted in the U.S., and to not have hunted buffalo, would have been to those like Grand Duke Alexis (the future Russian Czar) almost like not to have hunted at all.

Strong influences of the historic past, adventure, risk taking, confidence building and accomplishing something that relatively few in modern times will do are all reasons that compel today's hunters to kill a buffalo. For some, more practical considerations dominate and a buffalo represents, as it always has, a good portion of a family's meat supply.

Personal reasons

My motivations for shooting a buffalo were, in part, technically driven, because I was seeking first-hand information for this book. The historical aspects of the hunt and the chance to take the animal from its native habitat also had considerable appeal. At 1-month short of 65, it was also time for me to confront my buffalo.

I determined to drive from Georgia to the hunting area and transport the trophy to my Taxidermist, Tim Hill, in Missouri. Since this was likely to be my one, and only, buffalo I wanted a trophy animal. Price was also important. The best opportunity that I could find was to book through Table Mountain Outfitters at the Triple U Ranch in South Dakota, about 30 miles west of Pierre. This ranch offered trophy and meat hunts for the same $1,700 price.

This hunt would be the climax of a 20-day trip which would include cooking a wild game meal at the Columbia Café in Shreveport, Louisiana; a spear hunt for wild hogs at San Saba, Texas; and a prairie chicken hunt at Atkinson, Nebraska. Hunting tools included spears, a crossbow for a fellow outdoor writer to try, two muzzleloading shotguns and the Austin & Halleck .50-caliber muzzleloading rifle that I planned to use on the buffalo. I had worked up a load of 150-grains of TripleSeven powder and a PowerBelt 444-grain bullet and sighted the rifle in at 50-yards for the close range neck shot that was required.

Unusually warm late November weather greeted me in South Dakota. There had been a dusting of snow and a little of the white stuff still held on in shaded areas. I found visiting pheasant hunters complaining of dry conditions. The drought had the advantage of making overland travel possible, because with a little rain the unprotected soils would very quickly turn into axle-deep mud.

My hunt was to begin on the 21st, but I was to accompany Jon Schiller and Roy Bain on their hunts the day before to insure that I had adequate photography. When I arrived at the ranch they had already sighted in their rifles. Both would use Bain's .50-caliber Thompson/Center Encore .209X50 muzzleloading rifle with 150-grains of powder and a Thompson/Center saboted ShockWave bullet with a bonded core designed for deep penetration.

We hunters were welcomed, but were only an incidental part of everyday life at the ranch. Ongoing activities including attempts to find a veterinarian to do pregnancy testing on some cows that were to be sold because the lack of grass would not enable them to be carried-over through the Winter. Others were engaged in moving cattle from one pasture to another.

Guide B.J. Humble questioned Schiller and Bain about the buffalo they wanted. They replied that they were looking for nice display heads with good capes. Schiller opted for a darker-colored animal while Bain was looking for one with a lighter-colored cape. After driving a mile or so from the ranch, a small group of 15 animals was spotted. These were glassed and Humble said that there were a couple in that group that might do, but it was early and we would look some more.

Cresting a rise we saw about 200 animals scattered towards the horizon. We could see at least a mile and buffalo were scattered in groups of various sizes feeding or just standing. There appeared to be no inclination for the herd to move except to go from one clump of grass to another. There were no trees to break the slopes and only buffalo trails indented the prairie. With blue skies and scattered white fluffy clouds this was the view that all of us had hoped to see, and from all appearances we felt fulfilled by the experience.

Leaving the large herd we drove to where we could examine another detached group. "That first group still looks the best," Humble said.

"Can we stalk them on foot," Schiller asked?

"We can get closer with the truck, but they will likely move off if we try on foot. There is no cover, but you can try if you like."

As predicted, the stalk was unsuccessful, and the group returned to the truck. Approaching the group from another direction, Humble drove the truck to within 100 yards of the standing animals. Schiller got out of the truck, used the hood as a rest and aimed at the designated animal. The first shot hit low on the neck. The animals milled around, but did not run. Schiller reloaded and tried again.

*Roy Bain with his muzzleloaded buffalo. This is a handsome animal, but smaller than the old bull that the author was seeking.*

This time the shot hit the spine and the buffalo was down. A point-blank shot with the guide's 7mm-Remington Magnum finished it. This buffalo was taken back to the ranch; we ate and then returned for Bain's buffalo.

Bain took his animal from what was apparently the same group. He tried a head-on shot at the brain, but the big buffalo only shook its head. He reloaded, waited until the animal offered a side shot and then finished it with a neck shot. Humble remarked that he had once recovered a bullet from a .45-70 that was stuck in the front of a buffalo's head that he was skinning. "It takes a tough bullet to penetrate the brain on a head shot," he remarked.

Asked what he thought of the experience, Schiller answered, "It was really more like buffalo shooting than buffalo hunting."

"Frankly," I replied, "that is what buffalo killing has always been. You can see how easy it was to nearly exterminate them. A hunter takes one out of a group and the rest just stand there waiting to be shot."

One-shot buffalo hunt

On the following day my turn came to take my buffalo. On my sighting -in trip at the shooting bench I was more than a little aggravated with the Austin & Halleck .50-caliber in-line that I had chosen for my once-in-a-lifetime hunt. I could not get the gun to shoot despite reassembling and readjusting the position of the striker on the bolt several times, changing bolt assemblies and even making a 2-hour trip to town and back for another bolt. The firing pin would strike the 209 primer and indent it, but would not fire the primer

The gun had performed perfectly 15-days before when I sighted it in with the load I planned to use on the buffalo. This gun's shotgun equivalent had also done well 2-days previously when I had shot pheasant in Nebraska. A year before I

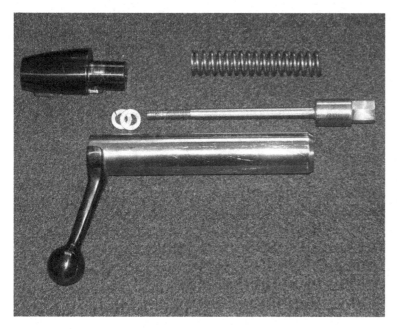

*Dissembled bolt assembly of the Austin & Halleck rifle. The author had difficulties with both the rifle and shotgun caused by weak mainsprings and, in one case, a short firing pin.*

had missed my chance at a North Carolina swan with the same shotgun, when it also refused to fire due to a defective firing pin and/or weakened bolt spring.

Whatever happened on this hunt, I was not going to stand there on the South Dakota prairie with a trophy buffalo in front of me holding a gun that might, or might not, shoot.

"It is time to put the toys away, and get out a real gun," I remarked to my guide B.J. Humble who looked rather puzzled as I went to the truck· and pulled out another gun case. I am sure that he wondered if I did not consider a .50-caliber gun that was loaded with 150-grains of Hodgdon's Triple Seven powder and a .444-grain PowerBelt bullet to be a real gun, what was?

Among the hunting tools that I had brought on this trip was a replica 12-gauge flintlock fowler made by Italian maker Davide Pedersoli. This replica was patterned after a 1790s gun made by Mortimer in England. His fowlers were among the most advanced and elegant of the period. When I first used the gun a decade back, I had trouble working up an effective shot load for it; but had recently discovered that it performed very well with HeviShot and plastic wads. I had also worked up a patched round ball load (.680 round ball, lubricated canvas patch and 120-grains of black powder). This load shot to the point of aim when the stock was firmly cheeked and the gun aimed by sighting down the barrel and lining up the brass bead on the target.

Earlier in the season, I had taken a deer at 47-yards with this load and also used it on the last evening of the Texas spear hunt to take a wild hog at 20 yards. The round ball completely penetrated both animals. I had also squirrel hunted with this gun and used a shot load to take a dozen bushytails with as many shots. In preparation for this trip I had brought shot, black powder, priming power, a few round balls and wads with the idea of using the fowler on game birds and to take a hog. This gun had proven that it would perform. Using nominal 12-gauge round balls on big game was not new to me as I had employed a similar load to take a blue wildebeest in South Africa (Chapter 8).

Nebraska unfortunately produced only one desperation shot at a fleeting prairie chicken and one pheasant for the Austin & Halleck shotgun, and there was no opportunity to use the flint fowler. I had one round ball remaining for the smoothbore, and I had put it in my truck with the idea of using it to provide a second rapid follow-up shot if it was necessary. When hunting with single-shot muzzleloaders, I always like to have a second loaded gun at the ready in case it is needed.

The Triple U Ranch

Most people have seen the Triple U ranch, although they did not know it at the time. This ranch was where many of the western segments of the Kevin Costner movie Dances with Wolves was filmed. The remains of part of the Ft. Sedgwick set are located not far from the ranch headquarters. This large ranch has 8-miles of highway frontage and is located west of Pierre, South Dakota.

Owned by Kaye Ingle and Shari Amiotte, the Triple U is operated as a combination cattle and buffalo ranch. To provide extra income, hunters are allowed to take either trophy or meat buffalo on day-long hunts. With the trophy bulls the hunter keeps the hide, head and horns; whereas the meat hunters shoot yearling buffalo for their freezers. The buffalo are skinned, inspected by a federal inspector and processed on the property. Because the meat is to be sold, no chest cavity shots may be taken. The buffalo must be taken with either head or neck shots, with spine shots being preferred. Should meat be damaged, the hunter is charged extra for the carcass.

*The Ft. Stedwick set from the Costner movie is located a few hundred yards from the Triple U ranch headquarters.*

A guide accompanies the hunter to help him choose an appropriate buffalo, as any buffalo looks huge to first-time hunters. Usually a 4-year old buffalo has the best combination of horns and hides for those who want attractive wall mounts. Older animals may be larger but very often have heavily broomed horns and may have rubbed and scared hides. Shots are usually taken at 100 yards and less and cartridge rifles having the power of a .30'06 or greater are preferred.

My hunt can be said to have started when I drove to the ranch and spotted four buffalo bedded down on a small bench above a creek about 4 miles from the ranch's gate. Looking at the largest of these, I thought that this was the sort of buffalo I was looking for. It was a large animal with slight brooms on both horns, but with very heavy bases.

They were still in the same area when I made my trip back to town, and I told Humble about them. He said that someone else had seen these buffalo, and that he thought that this group contained the old animal that I was looking for – one of the largest on the ranch.

After putting away the Austin & Halleck, I found myself asking, "When is a flintlock smoothbore better than an in-line muzzleloader?" The answer was, "When the flintlock shoots and the in-line does not."

Several miles of road and overland travel ultimately found us overlooking the valley and the buffalo. Humble examined the group and concurred that this one contained the old buffalo that I had seen.

I had loaded Mortimer before we left the shooting bench and opened the frizzen and put the hammer down on the empty pan. (The only way to safely transport a loaded flintlock). Now picking it up again, I checked it over. The lock was firmly screwed into the stock. The flint was sharp, properly aligned and firmly held in the cock. All that was needed was to get within 30 yards.

Getting out of the truck, I primed the gun and we approached the group. If Schiller and Bain's buffalo were big, this one was huge. We slowly inched up on the group. "Is this close enough?" Humble whispered. "It looks like they are going to run." Compared to deer, they certainly "looked" close enough, and I cocked the hammer and lined up the front sight bead in the middle of the buffalo's neck.

With the shot the buffalos repositioned themselves and started moving down into the creek valley. "You hit the neck all right, but I think it was low." Humble said. "We are going to have to chase this bunch."

By the time we returned to the vehicle, the buffalo had crossed the creek and gone up the other side. Humble had given me his scope-sighted Model 700-Remington in 7mm-Remington Magnum to finish it off. After going up the creek we found a crossing and ultimately took a position overlooking the buffalos' travel path.

"Second from the rear," Humble said.

I braced the rifle on the hood of the truck, found the walking animal in the unfamiliar rifle's scope and shot. Again the bullet hit the neck, but the animal continued. The buffalo changed their gaits from a walk into a run, and we moved

*The author with his trophy-size buffalo shot with, but not killed by a Davide Pedersoli 12-gauge flintlock fowler. With hard lead balls and a lung shot, this gun would have worked, but it would likely have taken multiple shots to kill this massive animal quickly.*

the vehicle to get ahead of them again.

"It's your turn this time," I told Humble. With good reason the ranch has a two-shot policy. If the hunter fails to kill the buffalo with two hits, the guide finishes it. The buffalo stopped and fell to a single shot from the guide's rifle.

Epilogue

In retrospect, if I had known that I was going to take my buffalo with the smoothbore, I would have used hard-cast lead bullets. The ball recovered from the neck had expanded to 7/8ths of an inch in diameter, but failed to penetrate the neck. Increasing the powder charge to 150-grains of GOEX FFg might have also flattened the trajectory. Judging from the scars on the bullet it had not hit bone, but remained in soft tissue without cutting the jugular vein which is carried well below the spine. It also appears that the shot was taken at 50, rather than at 30-yards, which might have lead to less precise aiming and a lower trajectory.

Once home, the Austin & Halleck rifle bolt was again reassembled, two washers put around the striker to increase the working pressure of the spring, and the rifle restored to full serviceability. For whatever reason, the bolt spring had apparently lost sufficient strength between the sighting in and its attempted use that it failed to fire the primer.

Austin & Halleck discontinued operations on October 1, 2006. I think that the poor functional reliability of their guns contributed to their demise along with a failure to keep up with emerging trends towards simpler to operate in-line muzzleloaders. Other than the firing pin and weak spring problems, the guns are excellent performers. If you own one, buy some ¼-inch lock washers to fit over the firing pin and provide more tension to the mainspring and, if necessary, have a machinist drill the old firing pin and install a new one of hardened steel in the striker. These two corrections will keep these attractive and otherwise excellent guns shooting for decades.

From my later experiences with the 444-grain PowerBelt bullet in Africa, I believe that I would opt for their steel-pointed 530-grain bullet for another attempt at these huge animals. This bullet worked well on a Cape buffalo (Chapter 20) and would likely provide pass-through performance with lung shots on a bison.

*The primary purpose of this bison hunt was to gather material for this book. Although the story was submitted to Blackpowder Hunting, the magazine ceased publication before it could be published.*

*This group of Cape buffalo present problems for a hunter because he dares not risk shooting this fine trophy for fear the others might charge or in the mix of tracks that he will not recover the animal he shot.*

## Chapter 20. Cape buffalo in the long green

Big, black, tough, intimidating and dangerous are words that are commonly used to describe the Cape buffalo. Of Africa's big five, the buffalo is most accessible, and most affordable, for visiting hunters. Typically, these animals are priced at about $15,000 and sold with a minimum 7-day hunt package. Ideally, the outfitter would like for you to get your buffalo early, and then, since you are already in Africa, shoot some other plains game so they can pocket a little extra change from the hunt.

Collecting animal heads was never a strong need of mine, so shooting more antelope did not appeal to me. I told my professional hunter Earnst Dyason that if I saw a huge warthog or a bush pig those would be possibilities. More unusual, was the fact that this was big-bird hunting season in Georgia. As I would be in Africa rather than at home hunting wild turkeys, it seemed appropriate that I should also hunt Africa's "real big chicken." Although Earnst and Marita, the owners of Spear Safari, had lived in South Africa all of their lives and had ostriches on their family lands, neither of their families had shot one in living memory.

I had hunted with the Dyasons before taking five species of plains game with a black-powder rifle, smoothbore and pistol (Chapter 8). He E-mailed me that he had a good deal on a big buffalo and could offer me a discount price on a hunt. A good-paying consulting contract came my way a few months later. I had the money, I was healthy enough to do the hunt, I had the time and most significantly I had a gun that needed to kill a Cape buffalo. With much of the hunting season already booked (mid-Summer), he said that he could get me in early, and we arranged for a hunt the first week in April.

It was time for Rex, a Traditions over/under .50-caliber double-barreled rifle, to prove its metal in Africa. Over the decades Traditions has briefly imported many black-powder guns from Europe. Sometimes these have only been offered for a season or two. The instant I saw this 12-pound gun, I was thinking "poor man's African double rifle." Although it did offer two shots, there were many handier guns to use for deer hunting. However, the gun's weight would be useful for soaking up the recoil of powerful loads that would be suitable for Africa's dangerous game.

Preparations

Converging happenings strengthen the possibility that Rex and me would go to Africa. Michael McMichael, of PowerBelt bullets, had developed a 530-grain steel pointed bullet with a pure lead midsection and plastic skirt for use on buffalo and elephant. However, because of poor demand for such a specialized projectile, production had been discontinued. I had a sample bullet, but needed more for sighting in and testing. Dudley McGarity, the CEO of BPI, the holding company that now owns PowerBelt, had some of these bullets that he was saving for an African hunt. He was willing to give me a packet. Nate Treadaway of CVA (another of BPI's companies) provided me with another package, so I now had 30 bullets for the rifle.

Hodgdon Powder Company also introduced a new pelletized black-powder substitute powder, IMR WhiteHot that I had successfully used in other guns. My hunt with a reasonably new gun, powder and bullet would provide sufficient reasons for me to undertake the hunt and "new" materials to write about. I could have shot the same buffalo with a .458 Winchester or .375 Holland & Holland, but so have thousands of others. Using Rex and the new components would give readers a new approach to an African buffalo hunt. I did my initial sighting in with PowerBelt's 444-grain solids and made fine adjustments with the now-irreplaceable steel-tipped projectiles.

Ultimately, I sighted in Rex's fixed lower barrel to shoot the 530-grain bullets to the point of aim at 30-yards when powered by a 150-grain black-powder equivalent charge of three WhiteHot pellets. This load developed 1,316 fps. and 2,038 ft.lbs. of muzzle energy. The 444-grain bullet with the same powder charge had a velocity of 1,505 fps. and yielded 2,234 ft.lbs. These were consistent loads that shot accurately out of the heavy rifle. A problem was that the gun unpredictably doubled with these loads. On Rex the front trigger fires the lower barrel. I suspect that the unusually heavy recoil from the 530-grain load was causing my trigger finger to slip back and slap the rear trigger with sufficient force to fire the upper barrel. The way professionals shoot heavy-caliber double guns is to fire the rear trigger first and then let recoil move the finger to the front trigger. This approach did not work for Rex, because the top barrel patterned 3-inches higher than the lower barrel. If I shot buffalo, or anything else, I wanted to shoot my most accurate barrel first. A skilled gunsmith could have changed the order of firing, but I did not want to risk any alterations to the gun.

The lower barrel shot the 444-grain bullets 3-inches high at 30 yards and the upper barrel shot this bullet 7-inches high at the same distance. At 100 yards the bullets were still rising. The 444-grain bullet at 100 yards hit 7-inches high from the lower barrel and the upper one hit 15-inches high. I did not waste any of the 530-grain bullets plinking at 100 yards. This buffalo was a large target and was going to be taken at 50 yards or closer with the lower barrel. I was not going to try to keep this confusing set of trajectory figures in my head when faced with a dangerous animal.

I purposefully chose to use the lower barrel where I would aim the bullet where it needed to go and pull the trigger. The other barrel would be there for a back-up shot. In effect what I was holding was not a double gun, but two single-barreled guns on the same frame that could be fired as rapidly as I could open the gun and load a 209 primer. I had a loading tool in hand that would enable me to swipe a primer into the action almost as fast as I could open and close the gun.

Because the first shot at the buffalo would be from a clean barrel, I wiped the barrel between shots in hopes of getting a more consistent result. On the range I purposefully kept my cleaning and loading materials well away from the firing bench. This walk from the bench to the porch of my house and back again allowed sufficient time for the gun to cool. The Kales scope that I used has the potential of being able to sight in the barrels to different points of aim. This would have required turning one of four scope turrets to a preset stop. I had shot this scope enough to know that it worked fine on the range, but I did not trust myself to make delicate sight adjustments when facing more than a ton of charging black fury. If such a circumstance arose, it would mean putting the gun on the target and pulling the trigger with no time for "fiddling around."

Getting there

As I had done before, I made up and labeled "Cartridges for Muzzleloading Guns," which were sealed and placed in a metal box (required by South African law) for transport to South Africa in my luggage. As I was also taking an Austin & Halleck muzzleloading shotgun, I padded this box with plastic shotgun wads and also stored a bag and a bottle of shot in the same container. This ammunition was declared on the firearm import permit (SAPS 520) and put in my check-in luggage. I took only one carry-on bag, a briefcase and had my gun case and suitcase as check-in bags. As now required the suitcase was unlocked, and after being inspected the gun case was locked. I incorrectly assumed that the South Africans would like their metal ammo box locked, and locked it when I put it in my suitcase. With only two checked bags, I did not have to worry about additional baggage charges.

Arriving 4-hours before my departure I checked in and went to my gate at the Atlanta airport. When standing in the check-in-line I heard a page for me, and spoke to the ticket agent. Something was wrong with my luggage, they said. A security agent collected me and I was taken back to the main terminal where I was met by six officials from various agencies. By the time I arrived, I correctly surmised that they wanted me to open the locked ammo box. The box had been put into a mobile bomb-proof safe. It seemed that a dog had smelled powder residue in an empty power horn that I had packed in my luggage. They had then X-rayed the bag and seen the metal box that contained some very dense materials (my shot) and became suspicious that that box might contain a bomb.

I opened the box, and the contents were inspected and passed. I was assured that I and my bag would make it on my flight. Following a car ride on the tarmac back to my loading gate, I made my flight and my bag, now sealed with U.S. inspection tape and tags, did too. I had unexpectedly provided the TSA officials with an unexpected security test, and I am pleased to say that they handled a potential problem situation very efficiently and politely.

They appreciated that I was a hunter who had gone through all of the steps to leave the U.S. with properly declared hunting equipment and had no unauthorized materials in his check-in luggage; but because I had possibly misinterpreted another country's regulations, I had locked my ammo box when I should not have. Had they been able to open the box, the entire situations might have been avoided. Next time I will know better.

So as not to potentially lose 18-hours of work during my flight and the time I would spend on an overnight stay in a Johannesburg hotel until I could fly out the next day to Phalaborwa , I took some work with me. This was a manuscript of Backyard deer hunting: Converting deer to dinner for pennies per pound   (Author House, 2009) to work on. During my long waits I was able to make another editing pass through the book and place the photographs in their approximate positions in the manuscript.

The hunt

Many of South Africa's regional airports are interesting places. Phalaborwa is noted for having animal sculptures in life-like poses positioned between the terminal and that runway. A giraffe is eternally drinking while a leopard and a troop of baboons are about to engage in their eternal conflict. Earnst met me at the airport. On the 80-mile trip back to camp, Earnst explained that he had built a new camp. The sleeping quarters included a roofed-over tent on concrete foundations attached to a permanent part of the structure containing a bathroom. I had run tent

*Phalaborwa Airport provides a unique welcome for visitors with its wild game statuary.*

camps in Alaska, and Earnst's efforts far surpassed anything I had ever seen. Not only is he a very capable Professional Hunter, but he is also a gifted designer.

One thing that was markedly different on this hunt was that the last time I was there it was the first week in May. Now I was starting my hunt a month earlier on April 1. Recent rains, and often daily showers, had turned the brown and dry Winter vegetation that I had seen into a lush green landscape. Pools and puddles of water were everywhere. Many of the dry watercourses that I had seen were flowing. It was not uncommon to be standing in waist to shoulder-high grass and shrubs.

Earnst warned, "The area where we are going to be hunting is even thicker that where you hunted the last time. There are a lot of buffalo. The problem is going to be finding a lone bull, a "dogga boy" that we will be able to successfully

*This early April hunt provided unusually thick cover and high grass as continuing rains provided ample water for the vegetation.*

hunt. It is very rare that a buffalo will fall dead at the shot. They are very tough animals. Almost always, we have to track them. If he is in a herd with others, that becomes very difficult, if not impossible. It may take us some time to find you a good bull, but if you are patient, they are certainly there."

Earnst's statements proved to be prophetic. We saw, stalked and photographed herds containing over a hundred buffalo on our first and following days, but none of the animals offered a suitable shot opportunity. Once we closed in on a smaller group of about 15 animals. Although we could see bits and pieces of different buffalo all around us, there was apparently not a trophy-sized bull in this group of cows and calves. When leaving the property one morning, the tracks of a solo bull were spotted crossing the road. "This one is alone," Earnst remarked. "We will come back and try for him this afternoon. He may be the one we are after."

He was. When we returned John, the tracker, found that he had crossed the road again since we had driven out. Getting out of the vehicle we started to trail the animal. The buffalo was apparently walking in a seemingly random pattern, feeding as he went. The nearly constant ground cover showed clear evidence of the passing animal with chewed-off and broken vegetation as well as his large hoof prints in the soft soil. Perhaps a mile from where we started, Earnst spotted the feeding buffalo.

We were within 20-yards of the animal, but the intervening brush prevented a clear shot. There was a slightly clearer area in the direction that he was feeding, and we all stood and waited. Previously, I had asked if Earnst wanted me to attempt a neck shot, but he said, "No. The spine is very deep in the neck and offers only a 2-inch target. I want you to shoot it low in the chest – through the lungs."

While we stood and waited I made sure that my scope caps were off and my trigger finger was poised to pull the front trigger. It was only minutes, but it seemed much longer before he stepped into the opening. Earnst nodded. I put the gun to my shoulder, found the crosshairs, aimed as far down on the shoulder as I could see and pulled the trigger. By the time I had opened the gun to put in another primer, the buffalo had turned and run in the direction he was facing. I fully expected to hear the crash of a heavy animal going down and a death bellow, but neither event occurred.

It was soon apparent that we had a wounded buffalo in heavy cover. John said that he had seen it dragging its leg as it ran. It had been hit hard by the 530-grain bullet and taken over 2,000 ft.lbs. of energy, but it was still mobile and on its feet. At the site where it was shot there was a small amount of blood, but none of it was frothy pink which would indicate a hit through the lungs. The shoot looked good, and I was wondering if the bullet had made it into the chest cavity.

Before proceeding I carefully reloaded my lower barrel. The buffalo would bed down about every 300 yards and get up again as we approached. We all could see the beds, but there was very little blood. Each of us hoped to see bucketfuls, but there were only a few scattered drops – not good. This tense trailing process continued for about 2 miles. We all knew that wounded buffalo in cover were notorious for circling back and coming at a group of hunters from the side or even from behind. Not helping the general situation was that it was getting late, and darkness falls very quickly in southern Africa. We needed to get that buffalo killed, and soon.

"Hovey, if I have a chance at that buffalo I need to take it. All we are likely to see is a bit of animal running away. We need to get another bullet into it. Do you want me to shoot it?" Earnst asked.

With darkness approaching and a wounded buffalo in thick cover that could come at any time from any direction, I had no problem giving Earnst permission to shoot. This was not the time to play around with niceties like moving me into position and so on. That buffalo needed to be killed. Soon.

There was a crash ahead followed by a two fast shots from Earnst's Model-70 Winchester that was chambered for the 458 Lott. Earnst had tried a shot at the animal's head, but it had dropped as he pulled the trigger. When the buffalo ran, he had shot again; but apparently missed both times.

He reloaded, and we proceeded as before. John and Earnst were in front, I was behind them. If anything, the situation was even more tense than it was before. The heat seemed to be pressing down on me. More slow trailing, perhaps another 500 yards. Unseen ahead of me was a crashing noise. John came running by me. There was a shot. Then silence. I walked up and only when I was 2-yards from Earnst could I see the buffalo apparently dead on the ground. Earnst said, "Give it a finisher." I did, and the buffalo remained immobile. Rex, Earnst and I, had killed our buffalo.

"That was close," Earnst said. "What is that – 5 yards, 7 yards? I was very lucky to get that bullet in its brain."

When the animal was butchered, the PowerBelt bullet was found to have

*The author and PH Earnst Dyason with what is rightly considered their Cape buffalo after what had been a very close call.*

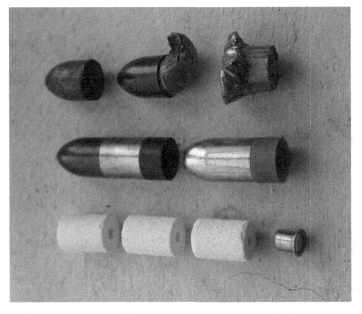

*Bullets recovered from the Cape buffalo and ostrich. The steel points of the bullet remained undeformed, but the lead mid-section separated as a secondary slug as it traveled through the body. The 444-grain lead slug mushroomed within the body of the ostrich.*

penetrated the near-side leg, gone through the ribs, cut the bottom of the spine, through the ribs on the opposite side and broke the off-side leg. Although the bullet had entered the chest cavity, it was 2-inches too high to damage the animal's lungs. Asked what he though about the load's bullet's performance Earnst said that this was exactly what he would expect from a heavy caliber dangerous-game bullet. The bullet had performed well, but the hit was not low enough to be effective. "If we had sufficient daylight, I could have waited and I suspect that the animal would have died or been very much weakened from your shot. I did not want to take the chance of the scavengers getting it, if we had left it overnight," Earnst concluded.

For my part I now know something about how to hunt and shoot buffalo. April, in the tall green, is not the time to do it. I found myself looking at every other buffalo that I saw and thinking, "I should have shot mine there." I had my buffalo hunt, and I had done my best at taking the shot that was offered. Next time I will know better.

Hunting Africa's real big chicken

American turkey hunters, and me too, get excited about taking a 23-pound tom. Considering that I was after something more like a 123-pounder complete with 3½-inch claws, a telescoping neck nearly 4-feet long and a tendency to run like a race horse, my quest for a wild bull ostrich was certainly different from any other fowl that I have ever shot.

It does a considerable disservice to call the ostrich a "chicken" of any sort. First off, it does not have the typical three-toed foot of most ground-dwelling fowl. It does have wings, but these are about the size of turkey wings – altogether insufficient for supporting such a large bird in flight. In addition, the wing tips and joint support small claws which are an apparent hold-over from the archaeopteryx,

*Ostrich in open country on a game farm. The author's hunt was nothing like this.*

its remote reptilian ancestor.

Whereas the tom turkey changes its head colors to indicate its indication to breed, the ostrich carries a barber pole of red bands around its legs when it is in the mood.

Because ostriches are running birds, rather than flying ones, they have little need for heavy breast muscles. They expend their developmental energy building huge legs and thighs to enable it to run for miles at high speed. Its head, unlike that of most birds, in unadorned with a gray color containing wide-set eyes and more nearly resembles a knobby stick than anything else. This coloration makes it hard for potential predators to pick it out of a brushy landscape – us too, as we were to find out.

With a modern scope-sighted rifle, ostrich hunting can be as simple or as difficult as you wish it to be. In arid country were the animals live in the open, wild ostriches are not often willing to permit humans to approach them. In fact, they become aggressive during breeding season and will attack, and kill, unarmed men. In open country often the only shots that are offered are at ranges of 200-yards or so, which is no problem with a modern hunting rifle.

When using a range-limited black-powder gun in brushy cover, the usual approach is to attempt to stalk them. This process is made difficult by the animal's excellent vision and extra-long neck. The close cover provided by the small trees and high grass aided in concealing both the hunter and the hunted. Hunting under these conditions made our efforts much more nearly an even contest. Although I could have made a shot at 100 yards with the .444-grain bullet and load of 150 grains of powder, Earnst wanted to get me and my strange gun within 50 yards if possible.

Our first encounter with the ostrich was on Earnst's brother-in-law's farm where we found a family group of three. There is an adult bull, a hen and an immature male. Compared to the bull with its white plumes, the females were dull grey. The young male had just begun to grow its distinctive white plumes. The hen, being the wariest of the group, took off the instant she saw the vehicle. The teen-aged ostrich equivalent apparently thought that this was probably a good idea and followed the hen. We never saw them again. The trophy male had apparently been conditioned to stay in the close company of cows, perhaps thinking that they offered protection. In fact they did, as I was not about to shoot an ostrich near the bovines for fear of a pass-through shot might hit an unseen cow in this thick cover. We made two attempts to stalk this ostrich, but he eluded us.

Earnst said that we would try another part of the large property and see if we could find another one. There we spotted a bull ostrich standing in a road cut about 400-yards away. We approached to within about 125 yards with the vehicle before it bolted into the adjacent thorn and grassy thicket. Trying a different tactic we drove past him, parked the vehicle and attempted to stalk him through the cover. The bird was able to make better progress through the brush than we could, and by the time we reached the next road junction he was already well ahead of us. Again we tried to loop around through the brush and perhaps get ahead of him on the road. This was akin to the naval maneuver of "crossing the T" where the commander would seek to cross his enemy's battle line so that his entire battle group could deliver broadsides down the enemy's line of ships, but the enemy was prevented from returning fire with more than a few guns.

It was if the ostrich was up on his naval tactics too, and he again outdistanced us. By the time we arrived at the road junction he was running down the track away from us. Earnst who is a quarter-century younger than me, has longer legs and could probably run marathons if he was inclined, very quickly outdistanced me. This spotting and chasing might have continued almost indefinitely had not the ostrich made a tactical error.

*Thick brushy cover provided a challenging hunt for both locating an ostrich and approaching it close enough for a shot with a limited-range black-powder rifle.*

*The author with an adult bull ostrich which had taken 2,000 ft./lbs. of energy from a 444-grain bullet and stayed on its feet.*

When running away he spotted our truck. This caused him to reverse directions and start running up the road towards us – apparently unable to keep in mind that there might be two sources of danger.

"Get ready," Earnst said.

I raised my gun, made sure my finger was on the front trigger and waited for the bird to approach. It was time for Rex to deliver its broadside. The bull ostrich was running at a fast trot. When he broke into my field of view he was about 30-yards away. I put the crosshairs low on the chest and pulled the trigger sending the 444-grain PowerBelt bullet on its way. Sped along by the equivalent of a 150-grain charge of FFg this load generated over 2,000-ft./lbs. of muzzle energy. The ostrich took the hit, stayed on its feet, reversed directions and moved away from us, although at a slower pace.

Using a speed loader I rapidly reloaded the lower barrel and we continued the pursuit. The next time we saw the ostrich he was moving through the brush off the road. I raised the gun, took a quick aim and fired. Click. I had pulled the rear trigger and attempted to shoot the unprimed upper barrel. Repositioning my trigger finger, I waited for another shot opportunity and tried again. This time the bullet raked the ostrich from low rear to front quarter, and the bird went down. I recall that Teddy Roosevelt and his son Kermit had considerable trouble trying to kill these birds with their then-new .30'06 Springfield rifles. I could now appreciate why their full jacketed bullets had little effect on the huge birds.

I had now taken, Africa's "real big chicken," but it had been a different experience than either Earnst or I had anticipated.

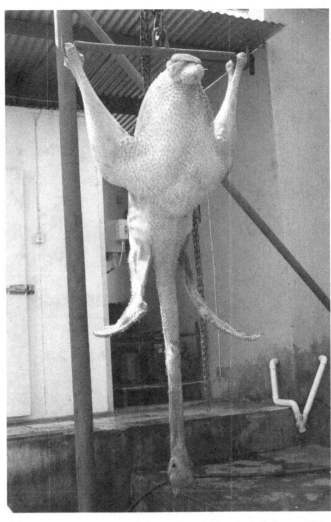

*Cleaning the ostrich was something that the Professional Hunter or author had never experienced.*

When the bird was plucked and cleaned, it was found that both of the .440-grain bullets were still in the ostrich. Although of large caliber and heavy weight, these bullets would have been ineffectual on Cape buffalo. They would have likely never made it through the shoulder into the chest cavity. I had been warned about this by PowerBelt's Michael McMichael. He had tried this bullet in Africa, but found it suitable only for soft-skinned animals.

Before I departed the Limpopo province, we ate some of the ostrich meat, which was excellent. It was interesting, in that some of the meat, although it was cooked exactly the same way was very tender, while another bite from the opposite end of the same steak was a tad chewy; but still excellent. On a following hunt in the Karoo Basin in the Eastern Cape Province, I saw herds of commercially raised ostriches. These birds would come to vehicles, like cows coming for food, and were quite unlike the wild birds that I hunted.

*Material in this chapter is largely from a story, "Death in the long green" first published in the February, 2010, issue of Safari Magazine. That ostrich is likely the largest fowl that I will ever shoot. I enjoyed the experience as a unique hunt with an interesting rifle.*

*From top, Browning ExtraLite Winchester 1886 in .47-70, Ruger Vaquero in .44-Remington Magnum, Traditions 1873 muzzleloading revolver and CVA "Confederate" revolver in .44 caliber.*

## Chapter 21. Game with black-powder cartridge guns

"Almost muzzleloaders" was a potential title for this chapter as several of the first cartridge guns used by military units around the world were designed to use components from existing muzzleloading rifles. One of the first to be adopted was the Snider conversion of the .577-Enfield rifle. The muzzleloading version had been used in both the British service and in large numbers by both sides in the American Civil War. The Snider conversion consisted of a laterally rotating breech block with an offset firing pin that enabled the gun to shoot the new metallic cartridges.

Cartridges, even those using foils and metallic components, were nothing new. For hundreds of years paper cartridges carried in cartridges boxes had been employed by the world's armies. What we now know as metallic cartridges had predecessors where a cartridge case which was reloaded with powder and ball but the center of the case was left with a hole to allow the flame from the percussion cap to ignite the powder charge. It was not much of an advance in technology to attach a primer and make a metallic cartridge.

Rimfire cartridges worked for low-pressure loads and were utilized in the Henry and Spencer rifles, but centerfire ignition provided a much stronger gas-retaining system. The paper and foil cartridge designed for the Snider conversion allowed a more rapidly loaded cartridge to be employed in the same .577 barrel used in the original muzzleloaders. In time, the action and barrels were improved, but the Snider rifle always retained its large bore.

In the U.S., the flip-up Allen action was first employed using .58-caliber rimfire cartridges, but in 1866 the rimfire cartridge was replaced by the centerfire .50-70. In 1873 the caliber was further reduced to .45 caliber, and the .45-70 cartridge was employed through the Indian War period and the Spanish-American War. Rifles chambered for the .45-70 Government have been made ever since and produced in low-pressure black powder equivalent loads and high-pressure smokeless versions.

How did these cartridges perform compared to the muzzleloaders, and how do they work today when loaded with black-powder equivalent loads?

Cartridges were more accurate than muzzleloaders because of more uniform compression of the powder and more consistent bullet lubrication. This issue was hotly contested in several international rifle matches, and the cartridge guns ultimately won.

A different situation arises when comparing these old black-powder cartridge loads with those which may be shot in modern muzzleloaders. Muzzleloaders routinely use larger charges of powder, 90 to 150 grains compared to 60 to 110 grains for the cartridges which also used lighter weight, more efficient, expanding bullets. This combination performs better on game if no, or little, bone is hit as in a double-lung shot on a deer. The bullets from the slow moving black powder cartridges plow straight through doing comparatively little damage. On large animals where the desire is to break bone, the old bullets will still perform adequately.

The Snider rifle

A swinging-block action submitted by American inventor Joseph Snider to alter millions of Civil War muzzleloaders to shoot cartridges did not win any U.S. contracts, but his action was used by the British to convert their .577 Enfields. The design employed a swinging block with a hinge on the left-hand side of the barrel. When the release button on the left of the block is pressed the block can be swung up and over, exposing the loading channel. Using the muzzleloading rifle's stock, lock barrel and production machinery resulted in a new cartridge gun that could be provided to troops faster and made much less expensively than a new design.

It was soon discovered that guns employing a separate breech threaded onto the cut-off muzzleloader barrels shot better than those with welded-on breechblocks, and all Snider guns issued to British troops employed screwed-on breeches. In latter production, new barrels were made of steel and these guns were so marked. The final evolution of the Snider was the Mark III which used a plunger on the back of the block to lock the action. Sniders were used by Native

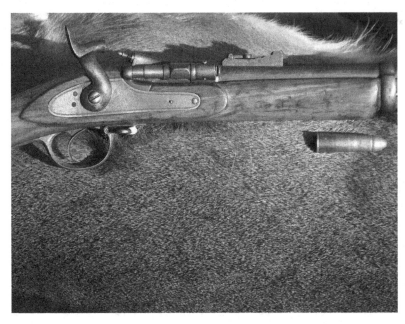

*Snider Rifle with cartridge. This rifle is a later design that has a locking rod in the breech that seats into the tang.*

troops in India as late as 1893.

Snider cartridges had a straight case with a slight bottleneck around the bullet. They were loaded with 70-grains of black powder and a hollow-based 480-grain bullet. For better ballistics, the bullet's length was increased by using a hollow base and a closed cavity in the nose. For a more complete description of the evolution of this early cartridge refer to Frank C. Barnes' *Cartridges of the World.* Barnes reports that the cartridge loaded with from 70-to-73-grains of FFg black powder develops 1,250 fps. and 1,666 ft.lbs. of muzzle energy. He also stated, "The big bullet has ample power for big game, but the very curved trajectory (13-inches of drop at 100 yards and 57 at 200) make it a short-range proposition."

Early .577 cartridges used a composite construction with a brass head and cardboard case, much like paper-cased shotshells, but even the weak Snider extractor could pull the heads from stuck cases. Later, a built-up brass-paper case was made of coiled brass foil and paper. This case was designed by Col. Boxer who also invented the Boxer primer. Although stronger than the previous cases, the coiled brass construction still gave problems.

Sniders, in rifle, short rifle and carbine lengths, were used in the British Abyssinian Campaign of 1868. Its most telling use was when 300-400 men armed with the new breechloaders repulsed a force of 7,000 natives at Arogi. The Sniders were fired at a rate of 6-8 rounds a minute, compared to the 3-4 rounds a minute possible with the muzzleloading Enfields. The guns were rugged and gave good service, but the cartridges were a continual source of problems.

Although some batches of Snider rifles have entered the U.S. since the 1950s, the most recent arrivals have come via Nepal. These guns are being sold by Atlanta Cutlery strictly as collector's items. The company makes no claims that these rifles are safe to be fired and assumes no responsibility if they are shot. These guns are a mixed lot of rifles, short rifles and carbines with some originating in England, while others were made in Indian arsenals and have Indian-character assembly numbers. The Nepalese also added their own numbers.

Looking superficially like the muzzleloading Enfield, the rifle I have has a 36-inch barrel, an over-all length of 55-inches and a weight of 8¼-pounds. The barrel is retained in the full-length walnut stock by three bands and a tang screw. The rifle's breech block is of the later Mark III type with a spring-loaded plunger that locks the block closed. As was the case with its parent, the lock is a side-action lock with a massive hammer that strikes an offset firing pin (like the Sharps and Allen-action Springfields). The firing pin is spring loaded to automatically retract when the hammer is re-cocked.

Pulling the hammer back to half-cock is the first step towards opening the block. Once the block has been swung aside, an extractor fitted into the barrel catches about 15-percent of the rim and partly withdraws the case when the block is pulled the rear. The partly extracted case must then be pulled into the loading trough with the fingers to clear the chamber. The case may be withdrawn with the fingers or dumped on the ground by turning the rifle upside down.

To ready for firing, a fresh cartridge is placed in the loading trough, pushed into the chamber, the block closed and the hammer is pulled back to its full-cock position. Finally, the trigger is pulled to shoot the rifle. If the preceding steps sound slow, they were. Nonetheless, it was an improvement over the muzzleloading rifle it replaced, although not nearly as efficient a battle rifle as the Martini-Henry that succeeded it. The Snider could be fired at about six times a minute - about twice the rate of fire for the muzzleloading Enfield. In addition, the gun could be reloaded with less motion and even from prone, although the infantry was still fighting in ranks, as they had in Napoleonic times.

As received, the Snider had been partly cleaned from an encrustation of black grime that was a combination of grease, dust, insect parts and rust. I cleaned the parts some more with a brass scaling tool, solvent and brass brushes to remove even more material from the operating parts. Surprisingly, the bore was not pitted and the slow twist (about 1:74 inch) rifling was bright and clean. The massive lock was soaked in solvent, disassembled, cleaned and reassembled as was the block. After cleaning, I was pleased to discover that all of the parts had matching numbers.

Now that the Snider was in a somewhat better state, I could more readily evaluate the gun. It had been hard used, but was fully functional. The heads on the breech block screws had been enlarged, but the threads still held. The stock was sound and showed no signs of rot or splitting. There appeared to be no mechanical reasons that this gun could not be shot. The problem was ammunition. The original military ammunition had been shot up decades ago, and although once loaded by Kynoch and others, these rounds were considered collector's items if they could be obtained at all.

The first glimmer of hope came when I saw that Cabela's offered black powder loadings of the .577 Snider with 500-grain .575 bullets in their now apparently discontinued "Obsolete Ammunition" line. The .577 ammo that I received was loaded in 24-gauge Berdan-primed brass cases. Things were not looking very promising as three of the first five rounds struck the target sideways. After this disappointing result, I cleaned the gun and put it away for several months.

Later I tried a little rapid-fire exercise with my gun using the .577 ammunition from Cabela's. If nothing else, this would give me some empty cases that I could reload with round balls. After 10 rounds in rapid succession the block became uncomfortably warm and the empty cases had to be pulled from the chamber with the fingernails. By the time 12 rounds had been fired, the brass cases were sticking in the chamber and the bolt required a tap with the foot to free them. The barrel was so hot that linseed oil was seeping from the stock. Surprisingly, the rifle now shot with fair accuracy even though the barrel, breech and fired cases were too hot to manipulate.

Apparently, shooting and the following cleaning had taken more gunk out of the barrel and allowed the bullets to be spun by the rifling instead of being blasted out of the bore like peas from a straw. I also discovered that the powder charge was very loose in the case and left an unusually large amount of sticky black fouling in the barrel and on the operating parts. The gun was disassembled, and the barrel, block and hammer washed with soapy water. Just like muzzleloaders, the Snider requires cleaning with soapy water and water-based solvents to remove corrosive black powder combustion products.

Searching on the net, I found two other sources of .577s. Gad Custom Cartridges in Medford, Wisconsin, looked particularly attractive as this company would reload customer brass and reprime Berdan cases. If all else failed, I thought that I could shoot a patched round ball from the slow twist barrel with a sufficient powder charge to kill deer-sized game.

Speaking with Gad's owner, I was informed that loading the cartridge required black powder, wads to keep the powder under compression and sometimes a solid-based bullet to give acceptable results. He also mentioned that a Canadian shooter had managed 3-inch groups at 100 yards with the shooter's own design of solid-based bullets. A new mold had been made, and Gad could reload .577-cases with these bullets. Arrangements were made to send 20 of my cases for reloading and for him to load 20 more rounds in new Boxer-primed cases all with the new bullets. With what remained of the Cabela's cartridges, this would give me 60 rounds for testing and hunting in addition to some Boxer-primed cases that I could reload with round balls. One way or another, I was going to have some hunting ammunition.

Although I have deer here in Georgia, I could not think of a better place to hunt with the refurbished Snider than to return it to a Commonwealth country where it had once been used. Perhaps this opportunity will present itself.

Like muzzleloading guns, the Snider bullet has a very steep trajectory, the guns yield a lot of smoke, they must be cleaned just as rigorously and they have a

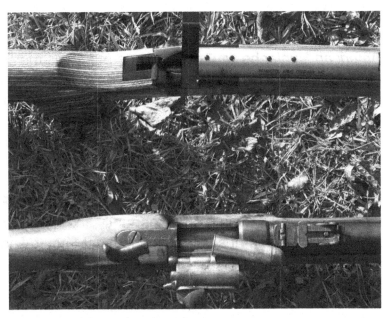

*After first introducing a muzzleloader based on its Model 700 rifle action, Remington's next venture was with a swinging block design.*

very similar appearance and handling characteristics to their front-loading siblings. They differ in that they do use waterproof self-contained ammunition and are a bit faster to reload.

The question is, "Why try to hunt with them?"

They are a bit of a challenge, they are reliable, they are historic guns which, I think, have earned a bit of time in the field, and most of all, they are just plain fun to use. When you have "Snidered" your animal, you have had to work at it a bit and have earned your deer.

Remington introduced a new side-swinging block muzzleloader at the 2006 Shot Show. This rifle, like the Snider, employs a swinging block, external hammer and retracting firing pin enclosed in the block. These components permit the muzzleloader's 209-primer to be easily inserted into the barrel's breech. This adaptation of the Snider's action is part of a trend in modern muzzleloaders that recognizes that simplified breech-loading systems work very well in guns where the firing pressures are contained by a screwed-in breech plug. The functions that the breech block serves are to allow primers to be loaded and removed as well as to protect the shooter from blow-back from the charge. The modern version of the old Snider system performs these functions very well.

Ironically, the side-swinging Snider action of this "almost muzzleloader" has reemerged as a key component of a modern muzzleloader design.

Bean pot bullets in the 1886 Winchester

Carrying the new Browning ExtraLite 1886 Winchester lever action loaded with my .45-70 black-powder equivalent loads through the Georgia woods reminded me of countless others who used this gun to hunt Arizona's mule deer, Alaska's big bear, Maine's moose and Minnesota's big whitetails. Produced from 1886 to 1935, the '86 Winchester was one of the most popular guns for taking heavy game during the first quarter of the 20th century – and for good reason.

Teddy Roosevelt thought well of the .45-70. In his *Outdoor Pastimes of an American Hunter* he wrote, "For some purposes the old .45-70 or .45-90, even with black-powder loads is as good as any modern weapon." During the black-powder era, 300-grain bullets were preferred for deer, 400-grain bullets for elk and 500-grain bullets for buffalo. The long, slow, heavy bullets had excellent penetration, but did not expand in soft tissue. Bone had to be hit to bring an animal down.

During the dozen years I worked in Alaska, I owned a pair of 1886s lever guns. These were shot-out relics that were smooth-functioning, but heavy. The reintroduced 1886 is far superior. At 7¾-pounds the ExtraLite '86 carries well and mounts smoothly. Even more importantly, the new rifle could digest every variety of .45-70 flat or round-nosed ammunition that I could find or make. Each of 100 shots fired hit within the area of a deer's vitals at 50 yards.

One feature that the ExtraLite retained that was dammed by all the gun writers of the period is the game-hiding buckhorn rear sight. However, the new rifle is factory drilled and tapped for a Lyman peep sight. If I could have kept the test gun, I would have installed one of these effective receiver sights. Other new features include a tang safety and a rebounding hammer.

Wanting to recapture something of a turn-of-the-century hunt, I built a wood fire on my charcoal grill, melted lead in a cast-iron bean pot, and cast my bullets in the back yard. I also used an old Winchester mold that threw 300-grain bullets to enhance the experience. I had considerable trouble keeping the lead hot enough for casting. By the time the mold warmed up and was dropping good bullets, the pot cooled and the lead lost its fluidity. This required that I add more wood, remelt my rejects and wait for the pot to heat up again.

After spending an entire afternoon casting a few good bullets an hour, I finally made enough 300 and 405-grain bullets for testing and hunting. This same

*Wood and charcoal fire with pot holding molten lead and dipper ready for casting.*

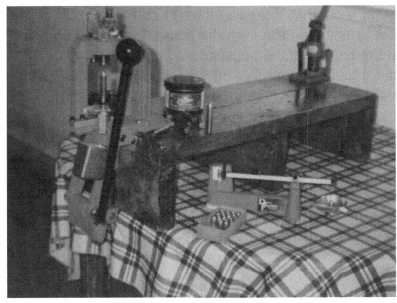

*Loading set up with press, lubricator-sizer and scales.*

process could have been completed in an hour with an electric casting furnace. This exercise taught me that those old buffalo hunters who cast their own bullets, had to allocate a fair amount of time and care for this vital operation. I sized the bullets to .457-inches and lubricated them with a Lyman Lubricator-Sizer.

Something I had in common with the old-time hunters is that I was casting the bullets I needed almost within 300 yards from where I planned to hunt. On a rifle range this doesn't seem far, but in thick Georgia woodlands, it is a considerable distance. I hoped that conditions would be favorable for me to take a home-grown deer with my home-cast bullets.

I went hunting eight times with the '86 loaded with my .405-grain bullets with Hodgdon's recommended charge of two 30-grain Pyrodex pistol pellets. Seven times I saw no deer. At 11:00 A.M. on my 8th hunt, I was about ready to give up when I heard the sound of deer running behind me. This was not in the hunt plan. I wanted a shot at a feeding deer so that I could place one of my 405-grain hard-

*Georgia doe taken with Browning ExtraLite 1886 Winchester and handloaded .45-70 cartridge.*

cast bullets in its spine. Twisting around in the deer stand, I could see part of the back of a doe through the thick brush 40-yards from the stand. I thumbed back the hammer, took a "fine bead" in the bottom of the buckhorn sight and fired.

As the smoke cleared, I could see that the '86 with its antique-style bullets had done its job. My deer was down, but lively. It took four follow-up shots through the brush at infrequently exposed bits of the deer's neck to kill it. The old cast-bullet loads worked as they always had, but modern expanding bullets would have finished the deer faster. I have shot Winchester's new loads on block gelatin and beef joints, and they have much improved performance over the black-powder loads.

How did my experience differ from those described in the late 1800s? Not much. The typical advice for hunters was, "Shoot for the biggest part of the animal,

## Table 4. 45-70 loads in the ExtraLite 1886 lever action

| Bullet type | Velocity | Muzzle energy | recommended for |
| --- | --- | --- | --- |
| Cast 300* | 1283 | 1097 | target & plinking |
| Cast 405* | 1188 | 1066 | target & deer |
| Win. 300 jhp | 1750 | 2040 | deer |
| Win. 300** | 1749 | 2038 | elk and moose |
| Rem. 405 jhp | 1120 | 1128 | deer |
| Rem. 500***Pb | 1200 | 1599 | elk and moose |

*Author's reloads using two Pyrodex pistol pellets, .44-.45 caliber Wonder Wads (two with 300-grain bullet, one with .405) and cast bullets. Velocities taken with Competitive Edge Dynamic Chronograph.
**Nosler Partition Bullet
***Pre-1940 high speed factory load

and keep shooting until the animal is dead." The 405-grain bullet I used (Lyman 457124 lubricated and sized to .457-inches) is a middleweight .45-70 bullet. Keeping in mind that the .45-70 was designed to use 405 and 500-grain bullets, it is not surprising that these heavier bullets shoot more accurately than the 300-grain bullet in every original .45-70 rifle that I have owned. Nonetheless, the 300-grain bullets are sufficiently accurate to take deer at ranges of up to 100 yards.

A favorite deer bullet of the day was a 300-grain cast hollow-pointed bullet similar to Lyman's 457122 HP which weighs 322 grains. The Lyman 47th Reloading Handbook lists loads for the 1886 using this bullet with velocities ranging from 1,000 to 2,100 fps. As velocity is increased, the greater is the probability of meaningful expansion in game animals.

Working from the 100-yard range out my back door and shooting at 200 yards from a hunting buddy's tower stand, I tried some new loads with a later batch of Pyrodex Pistol pellets and the new Pyrodex .45-caliber Rifle Pellets with 300 and 405-grain bullets. I added a 50-grain Rifle Pellet to a 30-grain pistol pellet to make 80-grain loads. These loads were fired using a Traditions Replica Sharps rifle with a 32-inch barrel.

In an attempt to keep conditions as uniform as possible, new Starline 45-70 brass was used instead of the hodge-podge of old cases that I had. The Starline cases performed very well. I also used .458-sized Bull-X's CJS High Performance 405-grain and some hard cast 300-grain bullets. Loading was easy with the Dillon AT 500 press and RCBS dies.

The best combination of these components for the Sharps, was two 30-grain Pyrodex pistol pellets, a Wonder Wad and the 405-grain CJS bullet. This load developed 1,281 fps. and a muzzle energy of 1,474 ft./lbs. - similar to PMC and Ultramax cowboy loads.

With one 50-grain Pyrodex Pellet and one 30-grain pistol pellet, the equivalent of 80-grains of FFg could be loaded in the .45-70 case with either 300 or 405-grain bullets. These loads gave no indications of excessive pressures. Leading was seen with the CJS bullet at a velocity of 1,565 fps., but the 300-grain hard-cast bullet at 1,734 fps. gave no problems. Again, the 405-grain bullet with a .44-caliber Wonder Wads between the pellets and bullet was more accurate than the 300-grain bullet.

A year later the '86 and the Sharps were long gone. I still wanted to see how stable the Pyrodex Pellet-Wonder Wads loads were after a year's storage in a hot loft. I dug out my old Harrington & Richardson Shikari with its 24-inch barrel. I could not hope to match the velocities achieved by the other guns' longer barrels, but at least I could determine if the loads had deteriorated to a significant degree. Five shots using the CJS 405-grain bullet and two 30-grain pellets averaged 1,117-fps. with a standard deviation of 16. Three shots were fired with a load using the 300-grain bullet and one 50 and one 30-grain pellet and gave 1,554, 1,567 and 1,555 fps. The loads were fine, and I would not hesitate to use them.

Pyrodex and Pyrodex Pellet residue corrode steel and brass. Pyrodex recommends cleaning guns with their EZ-Clean Pyrodex solvent. I follow this with soapy water, drying and oiling. The company has a different recommendation for the brass cases. They say to rinse the cases in white vinegar for a few seconds to neutralize the residue as soon after firing as possible followed by washing the cases in soapy water. I deprime the cases first so that the neutralizing acid will have access to the primer pocket.

After washing and drying the cases can be reloaded almost indefinitely. Usually the first sign of failure will be a small split at the ends of frequently resized cases.

With limited production and a suggested retail price of $2,000, the ExtraLite '86 is beyond the reach of most hunters, even though it is in my opinion the best lever .45-70 ever made. My advice to those fortunate enough to purchase that '86, and to others shooting the .45-70, is to use black-powder equivalent loads at targets, but use today's expanding-bullet loads on game. Your shots on game, like mine, cannot always be perfect and modern loads give faster kills.

Black-powder revolvers

Because of the restricted capacity of revolver chambers, black-powder loaded revolvers are restricted to be small game guns even through they may shoot .44 and .45-caliber balls. I consider 85-grains of FFg black powder and a round ball to be a minimal load for taking-close range deer when fired from a rifle-length barrel. When the powder charge is reduced to between 20-45 grains and the bullet is fired from a pistol barrel, this is a load that is only effective for point-blank shots on big game (see Chapter 18 where I use the Ruger Old Army to kill alligators), a back-up or a small game gun. TripleSeven loads in all steel-framed guns with adjustable sights can be effectively used on smallish deer and hogs. These can develop 500 ft. lbs. energy from the Ruger Olda Army and Cabela's Buffalo revolvers.

I enjoy hunting squirrels and small game with these revolvers. Over the years they have accounted for many squirrel and rabbits as well as an occasional rattlesnake.

*Articles and mentions of black-powder cartridge guns include one in Mississippi Sportsman published in December, 2008, titled Mississippi's "new" primitive weapons as well as mentions in the 2010 Gun Digest. The article, Bean pot bullets, appeared in the Fall, 2004, issue of Mule Deer Magazine.*

*Accessories to maintain and clean a black-powder gun include rods, jags, lubricants and rags as well as containers for components.*

## Chapter 22. Maintaining your black-powder firearm

Any muzzleloading firearm will need accessories, spare parts and cleaning to get it, and keep it, shooting. These needs will change depending on the particular gun although some items (like jags) and range rods may be used for all. It is not unusual to purchase a gun and then spend $100 on accessories. Often, muzzleloaders are sold as packaged sets. These are reasonable deals as the costs of the guns with the kits are less than purchasing the individual components.

Items needed for the guns include a range rod, usually aluminum or stainless steel with a handle that will accept a variety of screw-on components. These components need to include a worm for withdrawing a lost patch, a ball puller for pulling wads and balls and at least one spare jag for holding the cleaning patch and seating the ball. With each different-caliber gun a different set of bullet seating and cleaning jags should be used, although in a pinch a .50-caliber gun may be cleaned with a .45-caliber jag at the risk of having a patch pull off in the bore.

Cleaning patches are sold, but I prefer to use worn out T-shirts and old flannel that is cut to size. If round-ball muzzleloaders are in your future a tough patch cloth made of cotton or linen will also be required. Pillow ticking is a traditional material although I have also used thin canvas from a painter's drop cloth with excellent results. Among the best cleaners and lubricants is Thompson/Center Arms' Bore Butter. This is an all natural lubricant that will help softening black-powder fouling and season the bore.

Speed loaders of some description should be purchased. These enable, as the name implies, the rifle to be reloaded more rapidly. Often these are nothing more than tubes with the bullet contained at one end and the powder charge at the other. Some also have provisions for carrying a percussion cap. Even the worst are better than none, and should be incorporated in every muzzleloader's kit.

Although users of pelletized powders can carry their components in the factory plastic boxes, those who use loose powders will need a flask. These are available in traditional horn, plastic or brass containers. Choose whatever style is appropriate for the gun you have selected. Flintlock shooters will also need a smaller priming flask to hold the FFFFg powder used to prime their guns.

Possibles pouches or larger shooting bags are handy for containing all of the accessories and loads in one place. Because of the bulk of shotgun components (shot, powder, wads and priming) a good shooting bag is a necessity. In a pinch an old computer bag may be pressed into service. These are usually rugged enough even if they are not waterproof.

Flintlock guns require their own subset of equipment. In addition to the tools mentioned above, spare flints, a pan whisk, prick, screwdriver that fits the cock's jaws and leather for holding the flint are necessary. I also carry a small container of alcohol to clean the frizzen and pan of any oils before and after firing to foster the generation of a good spark.

Almost any variety of bullet or ball that is desired may be purchased, but it is sometimes convenient to cast your own. If so, a casting pot, ladle and pouring dipper will be necessary. For round balls, pure plumber's lead is preferred, but some tin and/or antimony alloy at a ratio of about 1:16 is used to harden bullets used in black-powder firearms. Bullet casting is an interesting activity in its own right and Lyman has an excellent handbook on methods as well as on different bullet molds for muzzleloading and cartridge firearms.

Spare parts

The ultimate in spare parts would be to purchase a duplicate gun. This is obviously not possible for most of us, so it is wise to accumulate the parts that are most likely to be broken or lost. For traditional side-hammer percussion guns the part most often damaged is the nipple. On guns that will function with musket caps, I very often replace the no. 11 nipple with a musket cap nipple for faster cap replacement and to provide a more powerful jolt to the powder charge. Having the capabilities of using two sizes of nipples also enables me to utilize any percussion caps that I might be able to purchase anywhere in the world.

Some makers, notably Thompson/Center Arms, CVA, Winchester, Knight and Austin & Halleck offer conversion kits to enable their 209 primer-fired guns to also be used with either size of percussion caps. Some Knight and New England firearms require that special plastic primer holders be used. Without these plastic elements to support the primer these guns may not be fired.

For my own use I have both the rifle and shotgun versions of the Austin & Halleck guns and a spare interchangeable bolt. This comes in handy during a long shooting session at the range. Should the bolt body become too fouled to function, all I need do is to install a fresh bolt and continue shooting. With my Knight .45-caliber Ultra Mag, I have made an "international gun" out of it. I carry extra bolt and breech plug assemblies that enable me to use either no. 11 or musket-sized percussion caps or 209 primers. Anywhere in the world I can find something to make this gun "go bang," although velocities and trajectories will change with substitutions in the priming system. Even different makes of no. 11 caps can make a significant difference.

A magnet is good insurance against losing small parts in the field while assembling, field stripping or cleaning. Just be sure to store it well away from your camera, disk or other electronic media.

Springs will sometimes weaken on traditional guns and will need replacing. I have one flintlock pistol, for example, that I have to replace the spring on an annual basis. With each new spring it shoots fine, but after a year's storage the spring loses its strength. Fortunately, replacements are available from Dixie Gun Works who carries a complete line of components for most replica guns. Even if you have an original, send in the broken spring and they will make the best match from what they have. Some grinding and refitting of these springs will be necessary for the locks to function properly. Care must be taken not to over-compress investment-cast springs. These are much less forgiving than drawn and tempered springs.

Cleaning

More muzzleloaders are ruined by improper cleaning, or lack of cleaning, than by shooting. Modern barrel steels are much more forgiving than the soft barrels of yesteryear, but even stainless barrels will not withstand the onslaught of being put away from one season to the next without cleaning. New black-powder substitutes such as Clean Shot and Clear Shot seem to imply that these products shoot "clean." In fact they do leave less residue than black powder but are even more corrosive to brass and steel than black powder.

I can't remember how many times that I have been handed an old muzzleloader, run a ramrod down the barrel and found a charge or something else in the bore. I have found sand, dirt dauber nests, bullets, bolts, and segments of broken-off ramrods in the barrels. Many old guns were put away loaded and still are. Although now caked solid in the bore, those black-powder charges are just as dangerous now as they were a century or two ago.

If you have a gun with a barrel obstruction, take it to a gunsmith that

*Rodger Kicklighter cleans a Thompson/Center Arms Scout muzzleloading rifle with a rod, water and rags by "pumping" water through the barrel.*

specializes in black-powder firearms and pay him to remove the blockage and clean the barrel. This will help insure that the barrel is extracted from the stock without damaging either part, that the powder is safely removed and the gun is returned in the best possible condition. Do not attempt to shoot an unknown load out of a gun.

The first cleaning step is to make sure that any gun, even one of your own, is unloaded. If the gun was put away cleaned at the end of the last hunting season, run a patch that is lightly lubricated with Thompson/Center's Bore Butter or other "natural lube product" in and out of the bore. It should run down smoothly and come out with perhaps a bit of light-gray discoloration. Don't be too shocked if it is lightly coated with rust. This is common and a uniform coating of light rust in a bore is not too damaging. What it means is that the barrel needs to be more thoroughly cleaned and dried next time.

If the gun has been fired, I dismount the barrel (an easy task on most modern replica muzzleloaders) and remove the nipple. Next I take the lock out of the stock and, if possible, remove the hammer. Place the butt end of the barrel in a bucket of water into which a squirt of Dawn Dishwashing detergent has been added and run patches in and out of the bore until they come out clean. If fouling appears to be particularly stubborn, a bore brush can also be used between the wet patches.

Wipe the outside of the barrel down with a bit of old toweling paying particular attention to the rear of the barrel around the nipple. It may be necessary to brush this area with a stiff toothbrush to remove caked-on fouling. Then stand the barrel on its muzzle and allow it to drain for a few seconds while you cut some patches from old T-shirt material or other absorbent cloth. Dry the outside of the barrel with the towel and run as many patches down the bore as necessary to remove any excess water. Take a Q-tip and clean out the nipple seat and put a twist of cloth in the nipple to absorb any excess water. Lubricate patches with Bore Butter and work them up and down the bore until they come out clean. Twist the cloth to a point and twist it in the nipple seat to mop out all moisture.

Lubricate the outside of the barrel, the threads of the nipple seat and place the barrel on the top of a heating stove or next to a fireplace until it becomes hot to the touch. Then wipe the bore and barrel exterior with more lubricated patches. Run a lubricated patch or two down the bore again the next day.

Commonly, black-powder residue will be blown into the interior of the lock and the exterior of the lock will be partly coated with black-powder residue. Place the fully assembled lock in a basin of warm soapy water and brush it thoroughly until it is clean. If the hammer can be removed, brush all surfaces of the hammer paying particular attention to the inside of the hammer nose. Also brush and thoroughly clean the nipple using a twist of paper or cloth to insure that the nipple vent is clean and unobstructed.

Rinse the parts in cold water. Place the small parts in a pan of water, heat to boiling and then remove the parts and put on a towel. Dab any free water off the parts, and shake any droplets from the interior parts of the lock. Allow the latent heat of the metal to finish drying the parts and while still warm lubricate the outside with Bore Butter and the inside with a free-running gun oil such as Knight's or Remington's.

For flintlocks, go through the same steps, making sure that the flint, frizzen, cock and pan are thoroughly cleaned. Retouch your flint with a knapping hammer or replace it before the next hunt. I always go hunting with a new flint and take along a spare.

Shooters of patched round-ball guns can "season" a bore by using patches lubricated with Bore Butter or bear grease. This is the same thing that is done with a cast-iron frying pan. The result will be a barrel that can be easily cleaned, is much more forgiving about being put away dirty; but the trick is that no harsh solvents, heavy soaps or synthetic oils may be put down the bore. The barrel is washed and cleaned with clear water. After drying it is relubricated with a patch saturated with Bore Butter and no other solvent is ever put down the bore.

(Hint: If you own only a few muzzleloaders, it pays to grind screwdriver heads to fit the screws of your guns and keep any punches, etc. needed to take the gun apart in a plastic bag with that gun's name on it to keep from having to search for them every time you service the gun.)

In-lines have the reputation of being easier to clean than traditional sidelocks, but I am not so sure that this is true. The bolts of in-lines must be disassembled and cleaned between each shooting session and the breech plugs of most in-lines also need to be removed and cleaned. Because the bore can be completely exposed, black-powder solvents are typically employed to clean in-line guns, although the traditional soap-and-water method described above will always work. Good results can be obtained by using solvents on the barrel and cleaning the bolt, breech plug, trigger assembly, etc. with soapy water.

After removing the breech plug, put an extension on the ramrod, a solvent impregnated patch on the jag and run the patch completely through the bore. Remove the patch and withdraw the ramrod. Use an appropriately-sized brass bristle brush and run it completely through the barrel and draw it back again several times to loosen all fouling. Put the jag back on the ramrod and run solvent-impregnated patches through the bore until they come out clean. Use a brush to clean the breech plug threads. Wrap a patch around the brush and twist it through the threads until all fouling is removed. Run a dry patch down the entire barrel noting if more solvent-impregnated patches are needed. Follow up with patches impregnated with Bore Butter, or other natural lubricant, until they come out light gray.

Disassemble the bolt and wash the parts thoroughly in soapy water. Use a brush to clean the threads of the breech plug and breech plug nipple (if any). Dry and lubricate using breech-plug grease on the threads and a light coating of gun oil on the bolt parts. Clean the receiver area of the barrel, using a brass brush if necessary to remove any stubborn fowling. Then the gun is ready to reassemble. Wipe the exterior of the barrel with solvent-impregnated patches followed by patches soaked in lubricant. Run a few lubricated patches in and out of the bore the next day to remove any residual fouling.

As a group, black-powder revolvers are the most troublesome of all muzzleloading firearms to clean. Soapy water, properly fitting screwdrivers, having the correct nipple wrench and patience are the keys to success. You can usually

*Circulating air around guns in this homemade rack help prevents moisture build up and rust. Even gun safes require a means to keep them dry or to move air around the guns.*

get away with leaving the action parts of the gun assembled in the frame unless the pistol has been shot extensively. Everything except the wooden grip goes into the water and is scrubbed, heated in hot water, dabbed dry and relubricated as described above. Stainless steel parts help prevent rusting, but even stainless guns will require cleaning if you expect to use them more than once.

Cleaned in this manner there is no reason that any modern muzzleloader should not last for generations.

### Gun Storage

In dry climates such as in most of the Western U.S., keeping a gun clean and in shooting condition is much less of a problem than in the East where humidity in the 90-percent range can linger for weeks. Guns need to be kept in areas that are dry where air can circulate around them. Military guns were typically packed in heavy grease for storage. This grease preserved the metal, but seeped into and softened the wood over time. For storage from one hunting season to the next, Thompson/Center Arms' Bore Butter works well on the metallic parts and appears to be less damaging to wood than traditional greases. I put Bore Butter on the metallic parts and use a good grade of paste furniture wax on the stocks. For longer storage a special micron-sized conservationist wax is used on both the wooden and metallic parts as well as on polished steel items like swords.

Long exposure to hot conditions such as over an active stove or fireplace will cause most original finishes to crackle or fade and is not recommended for any firearm. Also avoid plugging a barrel with an oiled rag and this restricts air circulation and can promote rust. Similarly, do not store the firearm in gun cases in long-term contact with cloth linings. These cases are best for carrying the firearms and not for storage. The more humid the weather the more problems will result from storage in contact with cloth or fabrics. There have been in the past, and are now, special waxed papers used to preserve guns during shipping. These offer temporary protection and are not suitable for long-term storage.

Hunting in and near salt water, such as in coastal waterfowling, is particularly rough on muzzleloading guns. At the conclusion of such a hunt I remove the barrel and lock and completely immerse them in fresh soapy water following by a rinse in clean water to dissolve any salts that may be on the gun. I also wipe down the stock and attached metallic parts with a wet rag followed by drying with an absorbent towel. Then I go through the regular cleaning and lubrication steps.

*An article, A vertical gun rack for muzzleloading rifles and shotguns, published in the December, 2004, issue of Muzzle Blasts described building the rack shown in this chapter. More on cleaning, restoring and shooting historic guns also appeared in Muzzle Blasts in November, 2004; August, 2009 and in other issues.*

*Although no sane person would take on a buffalo with a bayonet, it does provide a means of last desperate defense.*

# Chapter 23. Knives and bayonets for muzzleloading guns

My interest in the connection between knives and muzzleloading guns is not only because their use was historically authentic, but because the blades were useful for servicing the guns and for hunting. Through most of the long era of muzzleloading guns, two types of knives have been employed. The first was the patch knife which was/is a small-bladed knife commonly held in a sheath around the neck used to cut patches for round-ball rifles. The second, the rifleman's knife, was a longer bladed belt knife that was employed for butchering game, cutting up meat and as a secondary self-defense arm for the hunter after he had discharged his gun. An interesting derivation of this knife was the hunting bayonet. This knife was first slid into the gun's barrel and was later attached to the barrel by means of a lug.

The patch knife

While any sharp blade could cut a piece of patch cloth from the muzzle of a gun, most patch knives have fixed blades about 3-inches long that are often affixed to a deer-horn handle. Frequently, these were held in a leather sheath suspended from a thong around the neck. Alternatively, patch knives could be carried in the possibles bag or even in a smaller sheath attached to the belt knife. In the later part of the muzzleloading era, it was more fashionable to use a pocket knife which, although slower to deploy, tended to be less troublesome than having something around the neck.

Patch knives were capable of accomplishing other important task. They were often used to "bleed" the animal by slicing its neck after the kill. This practice dates from at least Medieval times and is done in some cultures to render meat religiously fit for consumption. Nowadays slicing the throat only serves to make more work for the taxidermist who must very carefully patch a long rip in the hide where it is most visible. Patch knives are also very useful for delicate skinning chores such as around the horns, eyes and lips of the animal. Small game, and indeed much larger animals, can also be skinned with this knife.

Hand forged high-carbon steel is the traditional material for a patch knife's blade, but any paring knife blade that will hold an edge and be fitted to an antler handle can serve. Even some original patch knives are sometimes available for purchase. Most recently some were recovered from the Royal Arsenal of Nepal and sold by Atlanta Cutlery Company. These were apparently made for troops who were issued the Baker and Brunswick rifles which were the last in British service designed to be shot with a patched round ball. The later Brunswick rifle used a "belted ball" to mechanically fit the gun's two-grooved bore and then the Minie ball was adopted which had a hollow base and expanded to fill the grooves of the Endfield rifle.

*A small patch knife and a long-bladed rifleman's knife were frequent companions for users of muzzleloading guns.*

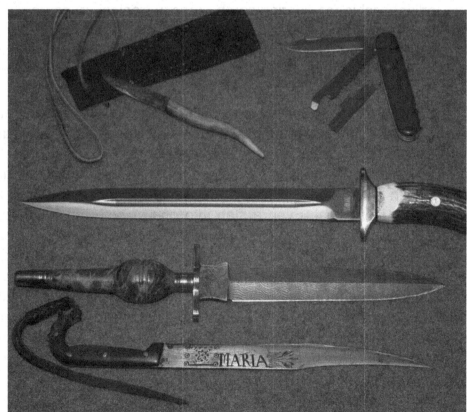

The rifleman's knife

Simultaneously serving the functions of a camp knife, fighting knife and butcher knife, the rifleman's knife was a serious knife which often had a 10-inch blade. These blades were most often single edged with a heavy back so they could be pounded to cut through a heavy pelvis bone, although some had double-edges and were spear-pointed like dirks. Remember, that not only did the eastern hunter's game include deer, but also elk, buffalo and moose. These large knives were useful for skinning as well as cutting up large animals. After the 1840s, the Bowie style became very popular, although there were many variations in size and shape on both domestic and imported knives.

Part of the reason that these blades were longer and heavier than what we would now consider a "hunting knife" was that they could serve as a last-ditch measure of self defense if the hunter found himself suddenly set upon by a wounded animal. Most frequently bears were mentioned in this regard although, deer and other animals would also sometimes beset the hunting party. Even if for some reason his gun would no longer function, a wilderness hunter with dogs and a good knife could still take enough game to feed himself, and this important lesson was not lost on our forbearers.

What about today? Should a muzzleloading hunter carry a big knife, and if so, how should he use it? I once read an observation that went something like, "the further back into the wilderness, the bigger the knife that is carried." Machetes are indispensable for clearing camp areas in tropical areas and in some cases just to hack through the heavy growth by the rivers to reach the more open forests in areas shaded by the canopy of the tall trees. This long blade is too much for most North American use and the rounded blunt points make them ineffective for thrusting.

In fighting with knives and swords, the thrust is more effective than the slash. In addition, a slashing stroke leaves the person who delivered it more exposed as he recovers from the backstroke.

Matadors use a long thin sword to kill the bull that faces him by cutting the spine with his blade. To slash randomly at these large animals would be completely ineffectual. Even a stab into one or both lungs would leave these big animals wounded, but still able to fight.

A double-edged blade is more effective than a single edge and a sharp point more useful than a blunted one when used for killing game. When knife hunting it is prudent to have the animal under some restraint either being held by dogs (most common), other hunters (less common) or trapped in nets as was done historically. The thrust is made behind the shoulder driving down and forward to either puncture the heart or cut the blood vessels coming from it. This is the primary reason for the 10-inches of blade.

In Central Europe the favored tool is the hirschfanger, or stag stabber, which is a short sword with a thin double-edged 14-inch blade. This blade was lighter and much less cumbersome than a full-length sword for hunting on foot and had sufficient length and strength to reach deep into the body cavity of a red deer. Highly decorated versions are still made and sold, but are more often for presentation pieces than for actual use.

A good swordsman was agile, quick of wit and speedy of limb; and anyone who is going to take game with a knife needs to have the same attributes. In short, if you can finish off a piece of game with another rifle or pistol shot do so. If for some reason you cannot shoot the game, a stout knife is a handy tool to have; but to use a knife is to invite injury as you close with the animal or even after delivering a killing thrust.

The hunting bayonet

Long before the invention of the first firearms, man had to confront the European wild boar. Not only did these large pigs sometimes weigh over 600 pounds and have formidable teeth, they often foraged in large family groups and would eat, destroy and root up fields and vineyards. Present nearly everywhere on the Eurasian continent, big boars were rightly feared.

Defending one's property against these beasts fell to the aristocracy of their respective cultures as Greek heroes and English lords alike fought these beasts with whatever weapons were provided by the technology of the day. Heavy spears were preferred over crossbows, bows, swords and knives because none of the other instruments impacted with more than 100 ft. lbs. of energy. Only a pike-like spear could reliably turn the charge of a large boar.

Heavy-caliber matchlocks offered the promise of being able to deal a lethal blow from a safe distance by transmitting over 1,000 pounds of energy to the mound of black fury in front of the hunter. Their successful use was conditional on the cumbersome guns being brought into action fast enough and fired when, and not before or after, they were needed. By the end of 1500s the matchlocks were considered to be "perfected," and were more user friendly than the heavy arbacusses that Columbus had brought to the New World a century before.

While still heavy, 10 pounds or so, late-period matchlocks could be taken on hunts with lit matches carried in vented metal boxes. Valuable time was still needed to blow up a good coal, affix the match in the cock and rotate the pan cover to one side before the gun could be fired.

I can attest to the problems involved with shooting a matchlock. If the match is too long or dropped forcefully down on the prime, it can snuff itself out. Then the match must be removed, relit and reattached prior to another attempt. Military musketeers lit both ends of their matches so that the other end could be attached more quickly without having to "borrow a light" from one of their fellows (I don't light both ends and don't recommend it.) With everyone carrying black powder, this second unwatched ignition source was a hazard, and unwanted explosions were common. These guns were dangers to both friends and foes. Not only this, once the match was positioned over the powder, ignition could occur at any instant should a spark fall into the power exposed in the pan or even on a grain crushed between the closed pan cover and the barrel (I've had this happen too.).

Putting all of this aside, assume that the hunter had fired his one shot at a big boar and fatally hit the animal. Big hogs, then and now, are tough animals. Instantaneous kills are uncommon. Frequently the animals will make a determined final charge at whoever is nearby. With no time to reload the cumbersome gun, the hunter is left with a not-too-effective club.

### The plug bayonet

Instead of carrying both a heavy gun and a spear, a knifemaker in the town of Bayonet, France, is widely credited to having modified a knife so that it could be forced into the muzzle of an empty gun to convert it into a pike. The utility of this tool as a back-up weapon for sporting and military uses became so obvious that it was quickly adopted throughout Europe. The plug bayonet evolved into a standard form with a twin edged spear pointed blade and a grip that had a crossbar, a bulbous section that was much larger than the muzzle diameter, a tapered section and finally a metal end cap.

Although made technologically obsolete by the first socket bayonets which fitted around the barrel that allowed the gun to be loaded and fired with the bayonet attached, plug bayonets continued to be made throughout the 1700s as parts of highly ornamented hunting sets produced for the nobility. Preserved as works of art rather than historical tools, most of the surviving plug bayonets belonged to these sets and show few signs of use.

Plug bayonets employed by hunters might be expected to be often lost during the fight, knocked from the gun's barrel or were so useful as knives they were resharpened until there was nothing left. Few have been made in recent times. I wanted to see what one was really like and had a plug bayonet crafted by Swedish knife maker Micke Andersson so that I could determine the capabilities of this historic hunting tool.

Andersson was interested in making a historic knife pattern that had probably not been produced in Sweden for hundreds of years. He hand forged the Damascus blade and fitted it to a burr-wood handle that had been stabilized with resin to give it added durability.

Often handling an object will reveal characteristics that are not apparent from a picture. The tapered grip allowed the knife to fit into .69-to-.75-caliber muskets. To apparently allow for moisture expansion of the wood and ease insertion into the barrel, the grip was purposefully tapered. Once installed, the end of the muzzle did not touch the bulbous portion of the wooden grip as might be expected. The purpose of the bulb was most likely to be a hand stop so the user could also use the bayonet as a knife and exert a powerful thrust against a beast or a man. These wooden "thrust bulbs" appeared on the Brown Bess musket as well as on an original Central African throwing and thrusting spear in my collection.

Function testing

Fitting the plug bayonet to Bess, a Dixie Gun Works "Indian Gun," I found that the friction fit provided by the tapered grip was sufficient to hold it into the barrel provided that the blade did not forcefully hit another object. I suspected, which later proved to be the case, that if the blade were stuck into something that provided resistance that it would be pulled from the gun's barrel.

To test the capabilities of this bayonet against the other weapons of the day, I gathered a modern spear, Silver Stag Boar Sword (sold by Cabela's), Browning double-edged hunting knife and triangular bayonet mounted on an Indian-made British 1842 musket. The bayonet had the same shape as those used on the Revolutionary War Brown Besses, but the 1842 musket added a spring-loaded catch on the bottom of the barrel to hold the bayonet firmly into position.

A 5½-inch thick Styrofoam block bowfished from a North Georgia Lake provided the test media. A strong one-handed thrust with the Browning dagger did not penetrate the block. The Boar Sword pierced the block with 1-inch of blade. Three inches of spear point thrown from a range of 5 yards skewered the block. A double handed thrust with the plug bayonet drove the blade through the block up to the hilt and 3¾-inches of the blade extended beyond it. The first try with the triangular bayonet passed through the Styrofoam and stuck into a tree root. On a second try it again penetrated the block and 9¼-inches of soil.

Putting a knife on the end of a rifle increased the penetrative ability of the blade by a significant amount compared to a one-handed knife thrust. This added penetration would have considerably aided a hunter's ability to cut though the tough hide and vitals-protecting gristle plate of an old boar.

Socket bayonets were much more effective penetrators, but the triangular blades provided little cutting action. For hunting, the double-bladed bayonets continued to be preferred even after the socket bayonets were universally adopted by world's military. In some cases during the mid-1800s the triangular bayonet was replaced by the sword bayonet. This heavy weight put on the end of an already long rifle became unmanageable.

Sword-length bayonets were dammed by Richard Burton in his *The Book of the Sword* with the statement, "As a bayonet (the Yataghan-shaped sword) lost all its distinctive excellence: the forward weight, so valuable in cutting with the hand, made it heavy and unmanageable at the end of a musket, and none but the strongest arms could use it, especially when the thrust had to be 'lanced out.' Yet it lasted for a quarter of a century, and only in 1875 was it superseded (in the French army) by the triangular weapon attached to the fusil Gras."

In modern times, bayonets have either returned to triangular shapes or are dagger, rather than sword, length and comparatively light weight much like the original plug bayonets from which they originated.

The Andersson bayonet has accompanied me on several trips and has been used to finish off deer and hogs as well as being on my belt on my flintlock buffalo hunt (Chapter 19). I used the double sided blade to help flesh and trim the heavy buffalo hide (some parts over 2-inches thick) and it performed very well. As the meat from this buffalo was going to be sold on the commercial market, it is customary to bleed the buffalo in the field and I used a spear to plunge deep into the neck which cut the jugular vein and windpipe to perform this function. The bayonet could have also performed this function, but the spear provided deeper penetration in the massive animal.

*The most comprehensive article that I published on the plug bayonet appeared in the March, 2007, issue of Muzzle Blasts. Other coverage on this topic was published in "Knives 2008" under the title, "Bayonet hunting gets the blood pumping."*

*Arriving for a hunt on a Georgia island. Although the author hunts alone, on hunts like this many others share a common camping area.*

## Chapter 24. Solo hunting

Alone. That word is not very comforting to most people. To me, and a small cohort of other hunters, alone means adventure. It is something that I need from time to time to reconnect with the person I am or think that I might wish to be. Whatever the outcome, it is the results of my single-handed efforts, planning, stamina and willingness to stick to the plan, whatever the consequences.

I spent an entire Summer in a backpacking tent in Alaska while I was working on my thesis in the late 1960s. Most of the time, I kept my camp on a creek a few miles from the road and walked out to areas that I wanted to map. Infrequently, I would extend my work further out and take a smaller tent to even more remote areas. For company, I borrowed a husky named Sounder that I outfitted with a backpack which was most often loaded with his own food. He and I got along fine, except that he had a tendency for going after porcupines with predictable results. After the third encounter he learned to leave these prickly rodents alone. At the end of the season it took me three tips to extract my camp, rock samples and trash after a nearly 3-month-long stay.

A few years later I was working as a geologist and spending all Summer in the bush managing a crew of 8-12 people. At the end of the season I would have a bush plane fly me to some remote spot to hunt waterfowl. These hunts were not terribly successful, but they gave me a chance to relax and see different parts of

*Author and Demeter play the waiting game while on a squirrel hunt.*

the state like the Minto and Cordova flats. After I returned from my hunt, I was ready to spend the months-long process of putting together a detailed report on the season's work.

I still go on guided hunts, hunt and bowfish with my buddies and enjoy participating on hunts with some of the pioneers in the black-powder gun-and-hunting industry. Even so, most of the time I am in the woods alone with my muzzleloader trying to bag a squirrel, goose or deer. My motivation has seldom been to replicate a muzzleloading experience from the 1700s, but to enjoy myself, the guns and the woods.

Thomas Jefferson counted as one of life's real pleasures the experience of walking in the woods with his gun. As I am sure Jefferson did, I feel alive when I am out by myself. My senses are finely attuned to catch the distant chatter of a squirrel or perhaps the footfall of an approaching deer. Each trip and experience is different, and each trip into the woods shows me things that I had never seen before even though I might have walked that same trail hundreds of times.

Every so often when I have a good view, I plunk my cushion down and sit in the woods. Demeter, my old Lab, knows this game very well. She lies down beside me and we listen together. Maybe all we will hear is the steady plunk, plunk, plunk of dew dripping off leaves. She puts her head on the gun barrel across my legs and I give her a scratch. We will find something for the old flintlock to shoot and her to find, but for now a scratch, a look and a shared understanding between man and dog is enough.

Deciding on a hunt

Most people don't spend months at the time in the bush or walk for days with packs on their backs as I have done. Just as a first camping trip might be setting up a tent in the back yard, a first solo hunt should be close to home. It would be imprudent to have a first unguided hunt in the Alaskan wilderness, however exciting that might be, that was not prefaced by a body of previous experience. These first hunts should be short and simple, perhaps starting with small game in some nearby woods. These will help imprint in your mind the basic needs that you and your muzzleloader have to conduct a 5-or-6 hour hunt. If something vital has been forgotten, then it is not too much bother to go back and get it

A good first step is to make computer lists of what you need for waterfowl hunting, deer hunting, bird shooting etc. This way if an after-work hunt seems appropriate, a quick check will insure that you have the basics with you. Sometimes too little "stuff" will be taken and at other times too much, but ultimately a reasonable compromise will be achieved. It will soon be discovered, for example, that five changes of clothes are not needed for a 3-day hunt, but a safe supply of drinking water is vital.

Almost all states have specialized management deer hunts on public lands. Some of these might be done from home or motels, while others are best conducted from tent camps on the WMA. While you might be alone, there will be other hunters that you will interact with on a daily basis. Some will hunt adjacent blocks of ground while others will be camped next to you. Should you leave something, there is a reasonable chance that someone in camp has spares or can help you drag your animal back to camp.

A number of decisions need to be made before starting out. Regulations may put restraints on the muzzleloaders or components that might be used. Some states, and some hunts, restrict ignition systems, gun calibers, use of scopes and so on. Others require that the hunter bring all game back to camp, and in wilderness areas no carts or wheeled vehicles may be used. Equipment will be needed to kill, field dress, transport the deer and process it for the trip home. If no cooler is available, ice chests will also be needed if it is not possible to make a quick trip to a cooler or nearby processor.

Topography will dictate hunt strategies. Most often this entails driving or packing to some point, setting up camp and hunting from that camp using a day pack. The camp gear is a significant load in a pack, and it is cumbersome to hunt carrying a heavy pack. If the camp location is accessible by vehicle, then more materials may be taken, but if it is a several hours pack from the trail head to the camp, this adds another degree of difficulty. The concept is to spend the maximum amount of time hunting, not packing stuff to and from camp. On the trip out it might take multiple "backs and fourths" to extract the camp and game. The ideal would be to make one trip in with the gear, and two or three trips out with the meat and camp.

Deer are bad enough to get out of the woods, but moose and elk are much worse. The added bulk of animal necessitates the solo hunter get help in extracting it or hiring additional packers to go after it. The typical fee for horse packers to retrieve an elk is now about $500. Often western ranch hunts include retrieving the animals after a kill, but on public-land hunts the hunter is responsible. When there are no other options, butchering the animal on the spot and relay-packing it out is an appropriate decision. On occasion, other hunters may be willing to help out for a "packer's share" of the meat.

A prudent approach would be to hunt smaller animals in the beginning and as more gear and experiences are accumulated set your sights on larger species. Just always keep in mind that the fun stops when the skinning knife comes out. Then the hunt becomes nothing more than a considerable amount of very hard work.

Personal conditioning is another important consideration. Strenuous backpacking and climbing hunts undertaken at 26 take on additional difficulties at 62. Even if in condition, altitude changes can severely impact any hunter's ability to do hunts that require a large amount of climbing. Being in physical shape for a hunt often translates into success when it is necessary to make that extra half-day effort on the last day or crawl over that next ridge to glass the valley beyond. This is especially important when hunting alone. In short, choose a hunt that you know that you can do. If you make a mistake, it could have deadly consequences when you are by yourself.

At 69, I don't have any problems doing hunts here in Georgia where I may walk 4 miles to the stand and drag a deer back to camp. This is at near sea level, there are reasonable trails near my hunt area and I use a plastic sled to transport the (cut-up) deer. Move the scene to Idaho's Snake River Canyon, and a different picture emerges. I can make it 2,000 feet to the ridge top once and walk along the crest, but the down and back up and down and back up trips over loose rock and steep slopes are no longer within my capabilities. With much training, perhaps they could be, but this is not something that I would jump into right now without considerable physical preparation.

Choices of solo hunts hinges on legal issues, selection of firearms, topography, duration, game to be taken, physical condition and the equipment that is needed. Other factors such as weather can also have major impacts on the hunt and gear selection. When everything is being carried on your back, this reduces the options of packing for widely variable hunting conditions. The onslaught of an early-season blizzard can make the difference between a challenging hunt and a race for survival.

Gathering gear

Every time I think of camp gear I remember those on the "trail of '98" who packed tons of gear over the Chilkoot Pass into Canada on their way to the Alaskan gold fields. This included cast-iron cook pots, canvas tents, cross-cut saws, axes, hardware and thousands of pounds of food and prospecting equipment - everything needed to build boats, a cabin and survive harsh Winter weather.

Even with a helicopter to put in a tent camp, I can attest that boating or flying in plywood floors and tent frames and all of the rest of the gear necessary to keep a crew dry, well fed and happy for months at the time is not a small undertaking.

Modern backpacking gear began to be developed after World War II, and by the 1950s great advances had been made over traditional materials. Down sleeping bags replaced heavy animal-hide robes and blankets, rip-stop nylon became the fabric of choice for tents and aluminum components reduced the weight of cookware and packs. Not only were these components lighter, they were also compressible so it became possible to have a tent, stove, fuel, and a sleeping bag in a single backpack.

Food, always a bulky item, became available as freeze-dried components to supplement the traditional beans, rice and noodles which had been the mainstays of yesteryear's campers. A handful of rice, a can of tuna, a dash of salt and pepper and a few dried mushrooms could produce an eatable, sustaining food product that would keep one going even if it was not of four-star restaurant quality. This was supplemented with fresh berries, fiddlehead ferns and perhaps even the occasional grouse or fish if suitable opportunities presented themselves.

Now, foil packets can be purchased that only need to be thrown into boiling water to produce a one-pot meal. The names of some of these products are more appealing than the results, but they will keep a hunter going. Another alternative is military rations which weigh less than conventional foods, and the modern MRE's (meals ready to eat) are better than the C-Rations from the World War II.

Before even buying food, plan each day's meals and measure out the components that are needed and consolidate these in plastic bags. If food is solidly frozen, steaks (or even frozen stews) may be packed in for the first day, but should be quickly consumed. If something alcoholic is desired after a long day, consider 150-proof Hudson's Bay Rum. In concentrated form a tablespoon makes a good drink mixed with hot water and a dash of butter or olive oil.

*A one-man tent and pack-in camp*

A minimalist list for a backpacking hunt would include the following:

For Camp

1 Two man tent with fly and stakes.(The extra space will be needed to help keep things dry.)
1 Sleeping bag. (Down has been replaced by hollow-fill synthetic fibers which will hold heat even if wet.)
1 Sleeping pad. (Roll up compressible pads are desired.)
1 Light-weight stove with fuel. (I used an Optimus which is still available and runs off Coleman fuel, but even lighter-weigh stoves are now available.)
1 Aluminum cook pot with lid and bail.
Fuel for a week's outing. (Plan on cooking two hot meals a day.)
Stainless steel fork and spoon.
Sierra Club stainless-steel cup for hot liquids.
1 hank of ¼-inch nylon rope for tying down tent, hoisting meat, etc.
1 Waterproof container with lighter and matches.
1 Water purification unit. (Water should be either boiled or purified. I consume much of my water as tea.)
1 Lamp with fuel. (This is very nice when you arrive in camp after dark. It also serves to warm a tent for a few minutes, but must be turned off before going to sleep to prevent carbon monoxide poisoning.)
1 Folding saw. (For clearing camp area, gathering firewood and dressing game.)
2 cloth game bags. (For protecting meat while it is hanging.)
3 Plastic trash bags. (To keep clothes and other items dry.)
1 Knife with a 4-inch blade for cleaning game and general utility.
1 Diamond sharpening steel.
1 Flashlight with extra batteries.
1 map.
1 GPS unit with extra batteries.
1 Charged cell or satellite phone.
1 Small first aid kit.
1 Water bottle. (Fill with purified or boiled water.)

Gun and accessories

1 Firearm.
1 Gun case. (A hard case will be needed in many areas to legally transport the gun to the hunting area. I often carry a gun to camp in a gun slip to help protect it on the trip in, but most often hunt with an uncased gun.)
1 Set of cleaning gear including patches, jags, lubricant and solvent.
6 Charges preloaded in speed loaders and packed in separate plastic bags.

2 Separate sets of ignition components. (Caps, 209 primers, or flints packaged in separate plastic bags).
1 Optical rangefinder which doubles as binoculars.


Vehicle-supported camping

When camps can be transported to the area by a vehicle, aircraft or boat, larger tents and comfort items may also be carried. I don't hunt to listen to music - mine or anyone else's. A small receiver that can provide weather and tide information is all that is really needed. Although I may carry a cell or satellite phone, I only use it to check in at home on a prescheduled basis or for emergencies. The easier an area is to access, the more likely that there will be neighbors, and I always throw a couple of pairs of earplugs into my tent just in case. These have bought me many nights of good sleep which would have otherwise been prevented by noisy campers.

Backpack hunts of necessity are restrictive, but a decision needs to be made early on if a vehicle-supported hunt is a "hunting trip supported by camping" or a "camping trip with incidental hunting." If the former relatively more emphasis is placed on the hunting aspects of the outing rather than the camping aspect, and items like camping chairs and folding tables are left behind. The more time and energy that is spent maintaining camp, the less will be available for hunting.

Nowhere was this better illustrated than my and Roger Kicklighter's periodic hunts on Georgia's Ossabaw Island.

"You folks ain't got near-enough stuff," remarked the weather-beaten charter operator as he looked over our modest pile of gear lying in the bottom of his boat. "Sometimes, it takes a full boat just to get two people across. If everyone packed like you do, I could take four camps a trip."

I'll admit that on the wide white deck of the 22-foot outboard our hunt camp resembled a group of rubber ducks left on the bottom of a tub after the water drained.

This was Kicklighter's and my first trip to muzzleload hunt on Georgia's Ossabaw Island, and frankly I thought we had packed a bit on the heavy side. My previous experience had been in backpack hunting where everything had to fit into a pack or be carried on the body.

"What else do we need," I thought as I re-inventoried our gear. "Two man nylon tent with fly, poles, stakes and tie-cord – check. Cook pot, stove, fuel, matches, lid, plate and two cups – check. Sleeping bags and air mattresses – check. Collapsible water bottle – check. Wet weather gear and a change of shoes and clothes – check. Hunting license, management area stamp and drawing ticket – check. Freeze-dried food and snacks – check. Insect repellant and mosquito coils – check."

In addition, I had brought a cooler the size of a small coffin to put our deer in, a cast iron frying pan (a necessity for Southern cooking), a hibachi with charcoal, onions, potatoes, assorted soft drinks and a 12-pack of beer for our 3-day hunt.

The possibility that I might be wrong was reinforced when the next group arrived at Kilkenny Marina. They resembled an upwardly mobile mob of Gypsies. The four of them were in two pickup trucks. Both trucks were loaded cab-high with gear secured by a spider web of lashings. The full-size truck also towed a four-horse trailer packed to the roof with chairs, deer stands, propane stoves and cots.

Roger remarked, "Maybe they know something that we don't."

"Maybe they do. I do know that all that gear and six people are not going to make it to the island on one trip," I responded.

When we reached the island we found that ancient oaks with 6-foot diameter trunks and limbs bearded with Spanish moss now served as anchors for ropes supporting plastic sheets which covered the hunters' tents. Stately palms likewise held ropes to guy a canvas A-tent that would have been familiar to veterans of Valley Forge. Yellow, red and orange back-pack mountain tents resembled beetles foraging among the dead palmetto fronds.

Nothing about the island's campsite resembled a classic military bivouac with arrow-straight rows of uniform tents arranged in blocks. This more nearly resembled the annual campout of the "Free-Spirit Campers of America," if there were such an organization.

That first year Roger and I each shot our deer, got a little wet and weren't as comfortable as we might have been. All told, we did O.K.

Each time we hunted Ossabaw or nearby Sapelo and Cumberland islands we learned. We soon added a larger tent, a cook box and a twin-burner propane stove. Folding chairs came next along with a propane lantern. Then we needed a cart to haul our stuff. Finally with the addition of a ground blind, a wheeled deer transporter, a roll of plastic and a coil of rope we had it all.

Ultimately we achieved a weatherized camp and hunting setup where we

*A tented hunt camp on one of Georgia's offshore islands.*

could sleep, eat and hunt under conditions which commonly brought insects, rain and mud. Besides the equipment for hunting and camping, we discovered a way to simultaneously bring a large quantity of ice to the island and reduce food preparation time.

Some of the pervious year's deer was cooked into deer steaks with tomato sauce, deer stew and deer chili. These precooked meals were frozen in plastic milk jugs. When combined with jugs of frozen drinking water the frozen containers provided us with both good water and heat-and-eat meals. Keeping these in a small cooler inside the larger one kept everything solidly frozen until we were ready to use it.

Camp List

1 Five-man sleeping tent.
1 Sleeping bag.
1 Sleeping pad.
1 Cot.
1 Bag of re-bar tent pegs.
1 Hatchet.
1 Wrench for propane bottle.
2 Screw drivers: flat head and Phillips.
1 Hank ¼-inch nylon rope for tent support.
1 Entrenching tool.
1 Cooking knife.
1 Cooking spoon.
1 Spatula.
1 Set knife, fork and spoon.
1 Set plate, bowl.
2 Pots.
1 Frying pan.
1 Coffee pot.
3 Plastic trash bags.
1 Bar soap.
4 Ounces dishwashing soap.
1 Scouring pad.
1 Dish rag.
1 Dish towel.
1 Roll paper towels.
1 Pack mosquito coils or ThermaCell with refills.
1 Washbasin.
1 Folding chair or stool.
1 Two-burner propane stove.
1 Propane bottle.

1 Matches.
1 Folding table.
1 Ice chests for frozen food.
1 Big ice chest for game.
Precook frozen foods.
Frozen drinking water.
Propane lantern.
Large tarp.
Rope to suspend tarp over tent and camp area.
Come-a-long for tightening tarp rope.
Two-wheeled garden cart (36-inch hub to hub).

Personal

1 Duffel bag or pack for clothes.
2 Long sleeve shirts.
2 Mosquito-proof trousers.
1 Pair hiking boots.
1 Pair rubber boots.
Change of socks for each day.
Underwear change each day.
Liquid mosquito repellant.
1 Twin-bladed pocket knife.
1 Set snake gaiters.
1 Set rain gear.
2 Flashlights with extra batteries.
1 Compass or GPS unit with batteries.
Plastic bags for maps, matches and percussion caps.
Reading materials.
Small sewing kit.
Compact first aid kit.
Aspirin or equivalent and medications.
Ear plugs.
Hunting license.
Big game license.
Game management stamp (signed).
Hunt permit card.
Driver's license.

Guns and accessories

Rifles – including one spare.
Percussion caps and/or flints.

Nipple prick.
Magnet. (For recovering small dropped parts.)
Powder.
Priming powder. (If shooting flint.)
Powder horn or flask.
Priming horn. (If shooting flint.)
Powder measure.
Balls. (Or whatever bullets are being used.)
Patch material.
Nipple wrench or knapping hammer.
Hunting bag.
Cleaning rod with jags and tips.
Black powder solvent.
$CO_2$ ball discharger with accessories for flintlocks.
Ball puller.
Cleaning patches and rags.
Gun oil.
Day pack.
Camera.
Rangefinder.
Film.
Light meter.
Compass.
Map.
Deer scent.
Deer stand.
Safety harness.
Pocket saw.
Grunt call.
Deer sled.
Deer drag-gun hoisting rope.
Hunting knife.

Archery list

Bow or crossbow with spare.
Case.
Arrows
Quiver.
Stone for sharpening points.
Tool for disassembling point.
Fletching cement.
Fletching waterproofing. (If shooting feather-fletched arrows.)

String and crossbow deck wax and lube.
Oil. (For metal parts on crossbow.)
Crossbow cocking rope.
Face paint or covering.

It is always possible that some accident could befall the gun or some part might be left, lost or fail. If on an island for a week-long hunt this can be disastrous. I often take a back-up muzzleloader, or crossbow, to insure that I will always have something to hunt with. This might be nothing more than a muzzleloading pistol with a half-dozen speed-loaders or another style of rifle. If the weather looks like it is going to do nothing but rain, I sometimes also take a bow or crossbow. Always check the hunt regulations to make sure that your proposed tools and methods are legal.

Hunting from home

Because of the progression of the hunting seasons, muzzleloading hunting is more involved than grabbing a gun and box of cartridges and heading into the woods. In July, before everything starts on August 15, I decide what guns I am going to use for that season and put together loading components and accessories for each hunt. In Georgia we start with squirrels in mid-August, dove and resident geese in early September, muzzleloading deer in the second week of October and wind up with deer hunting in mid-January. In addition, rabbit and quail start in mid-November and conclude the last day of February. Following this it is not too long a wait until turkey season cranks up in late March and concludes in mid May. There is also a split duck season with hunting in November, part of December and most of January.

Potentially there is a need for a small-game rifle, shotgun for small game and waterfowling, deer rifle, back-up handgun and perhaps even a specialized gun and/or load for a western elk hunt. To make sure I have everything I need to make the guns function, I do the majority of my load testing in late Summer. Once I have the guns and loads decided upon I pre-assemble hunt kits for each gun and hunt so I am not casting about for some hard-to-get loading component a few days before the hunt.

In my duck-goose hunting bag goes shot, wads, powder, caps, primers, and calls along with extra lines and weights for the decoys. Then all I need to do before a hunt is to make sure that the hunt bag and gun get into the truck. When the hunt is over components are replaced, and then I am ready to go again. Even when I want to change for a dove hunt, this usually only necessitates substituting different shot and wads, which is much less trouble than starting from scratch.

For further simplifications I use only one muzzleloading shotgun (or smoothbore) per season. As shotgun shooting at flying targets is more instinctual than aiming a rifle, using one gun gives the body and the gun a chance to become mutually coordinated. Each shotgun is highly individualistic (even individual barrels on double guns), and it takes time to learn these guns. As mentioned earlier (Chapter 2) my Davide Pedersoli slug-shotgun shoots round balls significantly better from the right barrel and patterns shot much better from the left.

I may select primary and alternate deer guns so that I have two available should I have a malfunction with one of them. Most commonly lost or broken ramrods can be compensated for, but occasionally a part will break. At home this is no problem, but when away this can end a hunt and leave a person messing around camp while others are killing game.

Often, I put my duck boat on the pond, build a tree stand or install a ground blind before season. Typically, I hang my climbing tree stands the same mornings I hunt; but I will have already cut shooting lanes in areas I hunt each year. Even so, I only hunt these areas a few times a season when wind and weather conditions are favorable.

A downside of hunting near home is that after several hours of sitting in a tree and seeing absolutely nothing, it is tempting to go home. The mind can think of many more useful things that could be done back at the house or maybe you just can't sit for 6 hours at the time. Stay. Take a good cushion and a pocket book, and plan to stick it out. Persistence kills deer, particularly when they are in rut and may be intermittently active throughout the day. Plan your hunt the night before and stick to it. This is more difficult when hunting by yourself, for who is there to care if you came in early? I have killed many deer around noon, after most hunters had gone back to camp.

There is a powerful temptation to move to another spot, even when sitting on the ground. Sometimes a move towards an active deer trail can be successful. The procedure is to move, pay attention to the wind, blind up again and sit. Walking around will most often only push deer to someone else. Still hunting, which is walking a few steps standing for ten minutes and then walking again, can work if conditions are damp or very windy; but tromping through the woods covering miles will likely yield nothing but sore legs and tired feet. The great majority of game animals will be spotted while sitting or at least standing still. Several times I have had game animals approach after I had stopped to take a photo of something else. The deer never knew I was there.


The interpersonal side


One advantage of solo hunting trips is that time consuming coordination with potential hunting companions is necessary. The trip becomes, "I'm going. If you want to come, that's fine. If not, maybe next time." There is no closer bonding that two straight guys can have than sharing adventures of the hunt trip after trip. Over a period of decades you come to know each other very well, become an ex-offico "uncle" to their kids and a "drop-in" member of the household. To say to a buddy, "I'm doing this one alone" may elicit some feelings of rejection and/or conflict with the hunting buddy who wonders, "What did I do?"

A likely answer for readers of this book is, "I just want to try something new with my muzzleloader. If it works out, maybe you will want to join me next year. I'll tell you how it went when I get back." That will usually work and is all that needs to be said.

Post-hunt activities

Getting the game back to camp, butchering it and putting it in the freezer is something that must be learned and preferably practiced before going on a solo hunt. These topics are covered in my book, Backyard Deer Hunting: converting deer to dinner for pennies per pound. Other post-hunt tasks will be cleaning the gear that was used, drying it out and packing it up for the next trip. I keep a cooler loaded with all of my cooking and camping stuff ready to go and replenish it after I return. The tents and seeping bags are dried for a few days and then rolled, put into their stuff bags and made ready for another adventure.

Quality gear that is well taken care of will last for decades. The same backpack that I used in the 1970s now has replacement straps and belly band, but I still use it every year. The same can be said of my tents and cooking outfit. Take care of your gear, and it will do well for you.

*Perhaps the most descriptive article that I published on camp-out hunts was Hunting camps Golden Isle style, which appeared in the Spring 2004, issue of Blackpowder Hunting. Solo hunting carries the risks that the participant might not return from a hunt and his fate might never be known. This occurs with some frequency in Alaska. Satellite telephones are good insurance, but be prepared to pay for the costs of your rescue.*

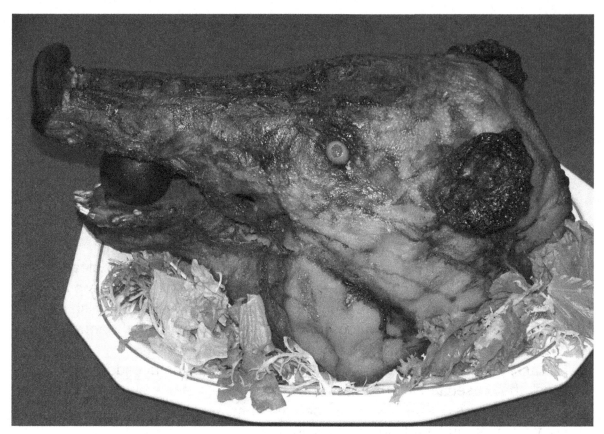

*A roasted hog's head makes a striking, and traditional, centerpiece for a holiday meal while also providing the starting material for Brunswick stew. This head had been frozen, which made hair-scraping impossible. I skinned it, boiled it and smoked it before salvaging the lean meat for the stew.*

## Chapter 25. X-treme wild game recipes

Recipes for this chapter are among the more unusual that I have developed. Some have been previously published in my books, *Practical Bowfishing, Crossbow Hunting and Backyard Deer Hunting: Converting deer to dinner for pennies per pound* or on my web site or blog (www.hoveysmith.com and http://hoveysmith.wordpress.com.). The 50 recipes in Backyard Deer cover the basics of getting started with wild game preparation and cooking. They include detailed cleaning and cooking instructions as well as items that are needed to set up a kitchen. If a potential user can turn on a stove, he, or she, can cook the Backyard Deer recipes.

Game cleaning instructions are also given in *Crossbow Hunting* along with a selection of general recipes for wild game, fowl and alligators. As would be supposed, *Practical Bowfishing* has cleaning and cooking instructions for fish species and alligators.

The recipes given below are unusual in that they are for game and fish species that most people do not cook (but are nonetheless excellent eating) or are

*This carp salad is shown with the boiled cleaned ribs of the carp being used as cocktail picks to hold ripe olives.*

unusual modifications of common recipes. Recipes are provided for everything from salad to dessert, with each featuring wild game or fish components. Several start with homemade deer or wild hog sausage. Detailed instructions for sausage making are found in Backyard Deer Hunting. I also post recipes on my blog, http://www.hoveysmith.wordpress.com.

## Salad

Carp salad

Mixing sweet pickles, mayonnaise, dill salt and pepper with picked leftover baked fish make a simple and tasty carp salad. This dish keeps well under refrigeration, but I would recommend eating within 3 days. A variation is Mexican carp salad in which salsa is poured over the carp salad and the mixture served wrapped in flour tortillas. Carp salad does not have the aftertaste common to more oily fish, such as tuna.

2½ cups baked, picked carp meat
½ cup finely chopped sweet relish
2 tablespoons mayonnaise
  2 teaspoons white vinegar
1 boiled egg, finely chopped
1½ teaspoons dill
1 teaspoon salt
½ teaspoon black pepper

Mix the ingredients in a large bowl. Add additional salt and pepper to taste. This can be eaten immediately, but is better if refrigerated in a covered container overnight. This may be served over fresh lettuce or spread on crackers. For decorative effects it may be pressed in a fish mold and adorned with olives speared with the clean, washed rib bones of the fish.

Dill deer potato salad

Dill weed goes very well with deer, and I often dust dried dill on deer cube steaks or stew meat prior to browning. Although any potato may be used, I frequently substitute a skin-on red potato in place of the more expensive baking potato. Italian sausage works well in this recipe, but strongly sage-flavored sausage does not.

    3 pounds potatoes cut into 3/8ths-inch cubes
    2 chopped boiled eggs
    1 cup cooked, granulated and drained deer sausage
    ½ cup diced sweet pickles with liquid
    1 finely chopped large Spanish onion
    4 tablespoons mayonnaise
    1 tablespoon dried dill weed
    2 teaspoons mustard
    ½ teaspoon salt
    ½ teaspoon black pepper

Boil cubed potatoes to the point where they are done, but still firm. Premix other ingredients except salt and pepper in a separate bowl. After potatoes are drained and cool, fold in mixture to the point of coating the potatoes. Add additional mayonnaise as needed. Taste and adjust salt and pepper as necessary to complement that used in the sausage mix. Cover and chill overnight. Re-mix immediately before serving.

*This meaty wild game stew can be a meal in itself when served over rice or toasted bread. Much variability is allowed in the meats and vegetables that might be used.*

## Soup

Brunswick stew

I frequently employ the boiled, smoked head of a wild hog, or bear, as the starting point for Brunswick stew. Commercial versions of this dish use chicken, but the original Georgia recipe called for wild hog meat, deer meat along with other game meats as might be available. This is a rich, thick stew, rather than a soup, that is typically served with bar-b-que. As I most often use and smoke a fresh hog's head, I usually skin mine to start with, rather than scraping it in the traditional manner to remove the hair.

1 cleaned hog or bear head
1 lb. deer or other meat
2 14 oz. cans cut corn (not cream style)
1 cup freshly shelled butter beans
1 medium Spanish onion finely chopped
1 6 oz. can tomato paste
4 tablespoons white vinegar
4 tablespoons Catalina salad dressing
1 teaspoon salt
½ teaspoon black pepper

Place skinned and washed head into a large pot and cover with water. Boil until meat is tender. Remove lean meat from skull and neck and chop finely. Discard fat, the membranes from the tongue, and anything else you deem a little too exotic to eat. Let boiled brains remain in skull. Pour about half the water into a smaller pot and add other ingredients except corn and butter beans. Continue boiling until meat almost completely separates. Add corn and butter beans about an hour before taking up. The stew should be very meaty and thick. This recipe is for an animal that has a live weight of about 100 pounds. Scale up accordingly for bigger hogs or bear. This may be eaten as is or served over toast or rice.

Bear-bean soup

This is a simple recipe that is a break from the traditional camp chilies, although it uses many of the same components. In this case the meat is trimmed of fat, cut into 1/2-inch cubes and browned. I usually use a little of the fat in the frying pan to brown the meat, although a small amount of any frying oil will serve.

1-2 pounds bear meat cut into ½-inch cubes
2 14 ounce cans red beans
2 14 ounce cans stewed tomatoes
1 finely diced medium Spanish onion
½ bell pepper
½ teaspoon black pepper
1 teaspoon salt
1 cup white flour

Cut up bear meat and dredge in flour. Brown in bear fat or cooking oil in fry pan. Before taking up add cut-up onions and bell pepper and cook until onions are transparent. Allow meat to drain and pour off excess oil. Put frypan scrapings and meat into pot and add other ingredients with sufficient water to make a thick soup. Heat until beans are tender and serve. To make this into a chili, add 2-tablespoons of chili powder and another ½-teaspoon of black pepper. Serve with toasted sourdough garlic bread. A Burgundy wine goes best with the soup, and a cold Pilsner beer complements the chili version of this recipe.

Buffalo tongue soup

Ground and cut meat from buffalo may be used in any deer recipe. I was particularly interested in the historic dish of buffalo tongue which was enjoyed by Buffalo Bill and other settlers of the western plains. Buffalo tongues were salted and sent by the thousands to diners in the east. The tongue is a long organ on a mature buffalo and the one from my buffalo was nearly 2-feet long. It had a bulbous spongiform section on the rear and a thin muscular section on the front.

The only thing necessary to make this into a tasty meal is to boil it with a little salt and pepper until it is tender. Since I would likely kill only one buffalo in my lifetime, I split mine in half and boiled half of it and lightly smoked the other half in a Little Chief smoker over hickory chips. Before smoking I soaked the tongue in a brine made from 2-quarts of water, and ½-cup each of salt and brown sugar. The smoked product was too tough to eat, and I also boiled it until it was tender.

Both the smoked and unsmoked tongue yielded a thick, rich broth to which I added rice, and the skinned and finely cut-up portions of the muscular front of the tongue. The result was rich tasty soups having slightly different flavors between the smoked and unsmoked versions. This is perhaps the easiest to prepare of all wild game dishes as it only requires a pot, water, the tongue, rice (or beans) and a little salt and pepper.

Coot soup

I once thought that I had rather eat a coot than be one. Now that I am approaching the age where I might be considered to be an "old coot," that alternative does not seem so bad. The reason I developed this recipe is that the limit on coot is usually 15 birds, they are abundant throughout North America and it seemed reasonable to harvest and eat them. The secret in cooking coot is to skin the birds and remove all visible fat from the carcass. Coots also have the largest gizzards of any waterfowl. These may also be split, cleaned and eaten as a boiled or fried product.

    3 coot, skinned with fat removed
    1 14 oz. can stewed tomatoes
    2 stalks celery
    1 large Spanish onion finely chopped
    ¼ cup rice
    2 tablespoon chopped garlic
    1 tablespoon margarine
    1 teaspoon salt
    ½ teaspoon black pepper

Place three coot in large pot, cover with water and boil until meat falls from the bones. Add additional water as needed. Pick bones and return finely chopped meat to the pot. Add other ingredients and cook until rice is done. Adjust seasonings adding additional garlic salt (or garlic) and margarine as desired. I like a garlic taste in this soup and "smooth it out" with a little margarine. This is one of the few dishes that is complemented by a dark beer or stout.

"Dear Heart" soup

This soup is so-named because I wooed my wife with it. When I met Thresa she had a gall-bladder problem and could tolerate very little fat in her diet. This was a nutrient-rich soup that she could eat and enjoy. Like the coot soup described above it has so little fat that a little butter substitute is used to carry flavor.

    1 deer (or other animal) heart
    1 14 oz. can whole kernel corn with liquid
    1 14 oz. can stewed tomatoes
    1 large Spanish onion, finely diced
    1 tablespoon margarine
    ½ teaspoon salt
    ½ teaspoon black pepper

Wash and pump any congealed blood from the chambers of the heart. Put in pot and boil. When cooked, remove and cut away large blood vessels and fat from top of heart. Dice meat very fine and return to pot. Add other ingredients to boil water and cook. Taste and add additional salt and pepper as desired. The meat and soup will have a slightly sweet taste.

Gator paw soup

Alligator paw soup is not a dish for everyone, but for those who wish to try something a bit unusual, the paws make a fine hot dish. This soup makes an unusual prelude for a wild game dinner and will be a pleasant surprise to those whose tastes run towards adventurous foods. If the alligator is small, use as much meat from the legs as necessary to make a meaty soup. On larger individuals the four paws by themselves will be sufficient. Before skinning wash the paws and forelegs down with a solution made of 1-cup of Clorox added to 5-gallons of water taking care not to get any of the solution on the meat. This will kill any surface bacteria on the hide. Skin the legs and paws, cutting and pulling the hide off the fingers and toes. Cut the hide free just back of the claws.

    4 skinned alligator paws
    1 large Spanish onion
    1 14-oz. can cut corn
    ½ teaspoon coriander
    ½ teaspoon salt
    ¼ teaspoon black pepper

In a large pot with sufficient water to cover, add the skinned paws, other ingredients and boil until meat is fork tender. Remove paws and continue boiling until the soup thickens. Serve while hot with paws on side plates. Yields four servings.

Gazpacho

This is a cold soup that is very good when served ice cold in mid-Summer. It may be thought of as a V-8 Juice on steroids. Instead of tomato juice, I start with 2-cans of tomato sauce and go from there. I put no added fat in my deer sausage. When the soup is chilled the fat will solidify on the top of the soup and is then skimmed from the liquid. As might be supposed the result is a very low-fat product. Commercial sausages might also be used, although more fat will be poured off when the sausage is fried or skimmed from the soup.

2 14 oz. cans tomato sauce
1 small Spanish onion finely chopped
1 celery stalk finely chopped
3/4 cup alder smoked Italian deer sausage cooked, drained and granulated
¼ bell pepper finely chopped
¼ teaspoon salt
sprinkle black pepper
sprinkle powered red pepper

Wash and chop vegetables. Place tomato sauce and four cans of water into pot. Add ingredients and heat to boiling, maintaining this temperature until the vegetables start to soften, but do not become fully cooked. Chill and serve. This with a bread product and a small glass of red wine makes a delightful summertime lunch.

## Chili

Vermillion chili

Purist decry putting anything in chili but meat, onion, tomatoes and chili powder, but I like the taste and texture of beans in chili. When starting from scratch, I pre-cook pinto or red beans so that the water soak-up by the beans can be more closely controlled. Once I found myself with only one of the two cans of stewed tomatoes that I customarily use and a surplus of canned beets. I like beets and thought that his would give the chili an interesting twist in flavors. Indeed, it did by making it a bit sweeter and somewhat cut the harsh bang that chili powders give the pallet. Children and adults who do not like pepper-hot chilies will often find the beet-added recipe more palatable. This also makes the dish less acid which is also helpful to those with digestive problems.

1-2 pounds ground deer meat with no added fat
1 14-oz. can stewed tomatoes
1 14-oz. can beets
1 large Spanish onion cut medium fine
1 bell pepper cut medium fine
1 ounce chili pepper (Different brands have different  strengths. Often it is necessary to experiment a bit to derive the optimum taste.)
¼ teaspoon red pepper flakes
¼ teaspoon black pepper
½ teaspoon salt

Open canned products and dice the beets into small pieces. Add canned products to Crock Pot and put on high heat. Cut up onions and bell peppers. Brown deer burger in frying pan. Pour off any liquid. Add onions, peppers and chili powder to pan and continue cooking until onions start to clarify. Add to Crock Pot along with sufficient water (about a cup) to liquefy the mix to the consistency of a thick soup. Add seasonings. Cook until boiling point is reached and then turn down to low to continue cooking. If in a hurry the product may be eaten as soon as it boils for about 5 minutes, but it will be better after slow cooking for about 3 hours. When the product has reached a boil, taste and add additional seasonings as desired. Be cautious because chili powders and peppers have a delayed heat. The harshness of the taste may be reduced by the addition of a tablespoon of margarine which will tend to somewhat mask and smooth out the flavors. If the chili taste too "fresh," this is an indication that it needs a touch more salt, but proceed cautiously. An ice-cold beer goes well with chilies as will any red wine. This is not the place for a timid wine, but even the harshest Italian reds will work with this traditional Tex-Mex dish with the beets providing a central European touch to this truly international dish.

## Curry

Curries from the southern half of the Indian subcontinent are noted for being spicy and, like much Indian music, for having a complex blend of competing flavors in contrast to the typical European dishes which are usually just salty, peppery or sweet.

1 lb. diced deer backstrap lightly browned in oil
1 pod dried chili pepper about 6-inches long
2 tablespoons graded fresh ginger root
1 tablespoon fresh garlic
1 medium onion chopped
¼ cup vegetable oil
5 tablespoons Indian spice mix
1 cup white rice
1 teaspoon butter
1 teaspoon lemon juice
1 teaspoon lime juice

Cube deer while partly frozen, complete thawing and dredge in flour. Cook 1-cup of rice in 2-cups of water and 1-teaspoon of butter. Allow to steam and keep warm. While rice is cooking lightly brown deer adjust space        meat in canola oil and drain. Pour all but a small amount of oil out of the pan and allow to cool. Reheat oil to warm, but not frying temperature, and add graded ginger, chopped onions, graded chili pepper and garlic. Heat until onions are transparent. Return meat to pot and mix with Indian spice mix. Add ¼-cup of water along with lemon and lime juice to moisten the mix and allow to thoroughly mix and heat. Let stand for 5-minutes over low heat stirring occasionally. The mixture should be pasty, but not runny. Ladle over rice and serve with a robust red wine.

There are many available spice mixes at Indian markets. Most of them will contain varying amounts of salt, ground red pepper, garlic, cumin, cinnamon, mace, nutmeg and black pepper. The amount of added spices will control the heat of the mix. If a batch is too hot for family consumption the best remedy is to dilute the entire mixture with rice until a palatable result is achieved, and next time adjust the recipe accordingly. It is not a requirement that curries be unpleasantly hot. It will sometimes take a few experiments to get the family recipe exactly right, but the efforts will be well worth the trouble.

*Ground meat and sausage loafs are nice changes from the usual deer burgers. In this recipe puff-ball mushrooms are used in place of the bread that is usually employed to provide an interesting variation on a classic recipe.*

## Meat

Deer puff ball meat loaf

This dish is a nice mix of all natural products with the usual bread often mixed in a meatloaf being replaced by the puff-ball mushroom. These are common throughout North America and may grow to the size of basketballs. If you want to keep some around, harvest those that are ready to be picked, but allow the others to disperse their spores to insure a continuing supply throughout the season. Puff balls will usually be prime in warm weather about three days after a rain. When picked they should be firm to the touch and yield a white, moist meat. There is a similar-appearing mushroom that is poisonous. This one has a rough corrugated skin. Pick only puff balls that have smooth rinds that are white or buff-colored.

1½ to 2 pound package of ground deer meat
1 puff ball 6-8 inches in diameter or several smaller ones
1 large Spanish onion chopped
½ green bell pepper chopped
2 tablespoons margarine
1 teaspoon salt
¼ cup catsup
2 tablespoons mustard
½ teaspoon black pepper
¼ teaspoon cumin

Cut off puff ball roots, skin and dice firm white flesh into masses smaller

268

than 1-inch square. Heat margarine in frying pan and add mushroom. Cook until mushrooms are reduced to about 20 percent of original volume, and lightly browned in spots. Finely chop onion and bell pepper. Mix all ingredients in large bowl and form into a loaf in a large frying pan that has been wiped in vegetable oil. The loaf should sit in the middle of the pan with open space on both sides. Stripe top of loaf with catsup. Cook in 350- degree oven for about an hour. The juices from meatloaf with began to char in the bottom of the pan and the top of the loaf will brown when done. Serve with mashed potatoes and a rose wine.

Whole roasted wild pig with three-sausage cabbage stuffing

Wild hogs of any age are taken because they breed so rapidly and are destructive to the landscape. In this case a small pig was shot, and I decided that this would be the time to experiment with a whole-roasted stuffed animal. I had on hand some alder-smoked and Italian deer sausage as well as a commercial Jimmy Dean sausage roll that needed to be cooked. To cut the sausage I also incorporated some chopped cabbage, onion and a pepper adding two eggs to help the mix stick together. The result was that I had more "stuffing" than hog, and I cooked the left-over stuffing as a meat loaf. The quantities here are vague, because they would depend on the size of the animal. After the initial eating, the remainder of the meat was picked off the bones and mixed with bar-b-que sauce. The extra stuffing was mixed with cans of string beans and stewed tomatoes and converted into an impromptu soup.

1 wild pig trimmed to fit a large roasting pan
3 varieties of wild-game sausage
chopped cabbage
chopped onion
eggs
bell pepper

Clean and wash skinned wild pig. Trim to fit available roasting pan. Salt exterior of animal and stuff rib cage with sausage-cabbage mix. Put 1-2 cups of water in bottom of pan and add pig. Put in pre-heated oven at 350-degrees roast until legs pull easily from the carcass. Remove, drain and serve on large platter. Trim away top layer of ribs to allow easy access to the stuffing.

Peached bear

The sweet taste of fruit goes very well with bear meat and wild pork. I used fresh peaches in this recipe, but cut-up apples or pears (preferably the hard canning pear) do very well.

1 pound bear meat cut into ½-1 inch cubes
1 cup cut fresh peaches
1 cup water
1 medium Spanish onion
Sprinkle crushed red pepper

Mix cut fruit with 1-cup water and boil until fruit is tender. Put cut meat into cast iron frying pan and mix with fruit and seasonings. Put in oven and bake at 350-degrees until fluid is nearly evaporated and meat is cooked done (about 20 minutes). Serve with Rhine wine.

Curse of the zucchini deer loaf

It is now late Summer. Your zucchini squash plants have produced beyond all immediate needs, and you have given away as much of them as you can. Here is one more, delicious and unusual, way to use a couple more of them.

2 unpeeled zucchini squash (6-7 inches long) sliced and boiled until tender
2 pounds ground deer meat
2 14-oz. cans stewed tomatoes drained (fresh tomatoes may be
 substituted)
1 medium Spanish onion finely diced
¼ green bell pepper finely diced
¼ cup tomato catsup
4 tablespoons tomato catsup
4 tablespoons granulated Parmesan cheese
½ teaspoon oregano
½ teaspoon salt
¼ teaspoon black pepper

Slice and boil the zucchini until tender. Drain. Add stewed tomatoes, onion and bell pepper. Dice the mixture and drain off the excess liquid. Place in bowl and mix with deer meat and catsup. Mound into a loaf and put in middle of large cast-iron frying pan lined with aluminum foil on the bottom of the pan. (Most meat loafs use eggs and bread crumbs, these are not necessary in this recipe). Put in 350-degree oven. As meatloaf cooks it will shrink about 20-percent and liquid will accumulate in bottom of pan. Allow to continue to cook as liquid boils away. When a black char starts to form, the meatloaf is done. Cool and remove from pan. Reheat before serving and serve with tomato catsup sauce made by mixing catsup with ¼- teaspoon of horseradish per ½-cup of catsup. Mashed potatoes and butter would be a traditional side dish as would English peas. A red wine would complement this dish.

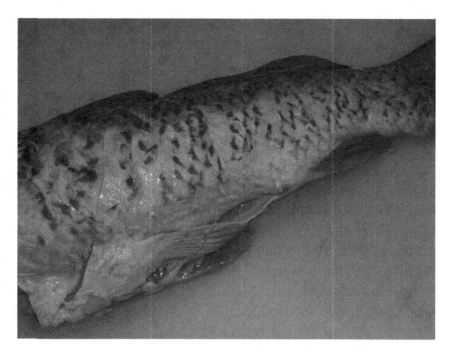

*A nice-size carp, scaled, gutted, beheaded and ready for baking. This particular fish was bowfished from a Georgia lake. This is about an average-sized German, or common, carp.*

## Fish

Baked carp

There are now five species of carp in North America, all of which were ultimately derived from Asia. These include the common (or German) carp, bighead (jumping) carp, Amur, silver (grass) carp and the largest and most recent arrival is the black carp. All of these fish are eatable when taken from clean waters. Although somewhat more bony than many fish, on fish that are between 2-3 feet long, these bones are no real problem. They make an excellent baked fish and the left-over product may be made into carp salad (see under salad section), using the same recipe as tuna fish salad.

 1 carp, cleaned and scaled with head removed
 1 medium onion chopped
 1 teaspoons margarine
 1 teaspoon salt
 1cup water

Wrap scaled, cleaned carp in aluminum foil. Add water, salt and dot margarine over top of fish. Sprinkle onion over fish. Bake at 350-degrees for about an hour. When slightly cooled remove from foil, remove skin and place fish on platter. Rub with 1-teaspoon of butter and sprinkle with salt and lemon juice. Serve hot. Carp taken from clean waters makes for an excellent baked fish. Remove the red medial line from the center of both sides of the fish before serving. Avoid cutting carp into sections as this cuts through the small bones. Guests should use their forks to pull meat from one side of the fish. Then turn fish over and pull from the other side. Uneaten baked carp can be used to make a carp salad. Serve baked carp with a semi-dry white wine.

Gefilte fish for the rest of us

Gefilte fish, the famous and traditional Jewish Passover dish, has many variations. Common to most renditions is boiling the ground fish with carrots and onions; reserving of the broth to make a gelatin sauce; and serving the dish cold with the sauce poured over it. Carp was the traditional fish used for this dish; but other fish, including pike and whitefish are often added to it. Other regional additions include the use of beats, parsley and sugar depending on whether the preference is for a sweet or non-sweet product.

To make the gelatin sauce in the traditional way the skin, head, bones and fins were boiled to produce this product. This is usually a bit much for modern taste. In this recipe the boiled fish heads and skin are omitted and a commercial gelatin is substituted.

> 1 carp, cleaned, beheaded and scaled but in bones (1, 5½ lbs. carp yields 3 cups cleaned, picked fish weighing 1 1/8-lbs.)
> 2 large carrots
> 3 medium Spanish onions (leave peelings on for a darker broth)
> ¼ cup matzo meal (or bread crumbs)
> 2 eggs
> 2 tablespoons salt
> 1 teaspoon pepper
> 1 tablespoon sugar
> 1 sprig parsley
> 1 package plain gelatin
> 1 small jar red or white horseradish sauce

Boil the fish in a large pot with cut-up vegetables until the meat flakes off the bones. Grate enough carrots to yield ¼-cup of raw carrots. Remove meat from bones, carefully picking out the small bones. (This is tedious, but nothing about the Passover experience was ever said to be easy.) Return large bones to pot and continue to simmer vegetables and bones. Mix the matzo meal, fish, eggs and sugar with ½-cup of grated carrots. Salt and pepper to taste. Roll fish mixture into balls. (Dipping the hands into cold water will keep the mixture from sticking to the hands.) Remove bones and vegetables from broth and allow broth to return to a boil. Drop in fish balls. They will sink and rise to the top. Boil gently for 1 hour. Place one-layer deep on platter. When fish balls are done, reduce the broth to about 4 cups and dissolve gelatin in broth. Taste and add additional salt and pepper if desired. Allow mix to stand until gelatin starts to set. Spoon enough gelatin over gefilte fish balls to coat them and give a thin layer on bottom of platter. Chill and serve with the boiled carrots and garnish with parsley (the bitter herbs of the Passover meal). Gefilte fish is typically eaten with red or white horseradish sauce. Makes 13, 1¼-inch gefilte fish balls.

Carp grits

Carp roe are traditionally deep fried in the South, but a healthier use for the roe is to mix with grits where the roe adds a mild butter flavor. DO NOT SUBSTITUTE GAR ROE. THE ROE FROM GAR IS TOXIC AND MAY BE DEADLY TO SOME INDIVIDUALS.

1 skein carp roe
1 cup grits
2 cups water
1 teaspoon salt
¼ teaspoon pepper
1 teaspoon butter or margarine
1 block of sharp Cheddar cheese about 1/2-inch square

Remove roe from fish and wash. Boil roe in salted water in separate pot until roe turns dark yellow. Remove roe and allow to drain and cool. Put 2-cups of water, salt pepper, margarine, butter and grits into a pan and bring to a boil. Separate roe and add ¼-cup of roe to cooking grits. Stir to keep from sticking, and add a little additional water if necessary. When grits are done, add cheese, allow cheese to melt, mix thoroughly and serve. Remaining boiled roe can be frozen for later use.

Gar steaks, nuggets and scallops

Gar is one of the best fish to be found in North America. There is hardly anything that can be done with gar meat (backstraps) that does not turn out well. I use it battered and fried, smoked, in fish soup and as a ground product for fish sandwiches. Cut away and discard any meat that has been contaminated with stomach contents from a bowfished gar. Cleaning instructions are found in Practical Bowfishing.

2 pounds gar meat cut into steaks, nuggets or 1-inch cubes for scallops
3 cups canola oil
1 cup flour
1 teaspoons salt
1 teaspoon black pepper
1 teaspoon dill weed

1 large brown paper bag

Heat oil. While oil is heating mix dry ingredients in plastic bag and flour cut pieces of gar. Use tongs and drop into oil one at a time taking care to avoid the splatter. Cook to golden brown and drain on brown paper bags. Serve while hot. Do not overcook, as this toughens the meat. Gar is very versatile. It may also be used in stir frys or ground, made into patties, battered in an egg-flour-milk batter and deep-fried for an excellent fish sandwich. Serve with a semi-dry white wine, such as Italian Pescevino (A white wine particularly blended to complement fish).

*This is a fine roasted swan, ready for Christmas dinner.*

## Fowl

Christmas turkey, goose or swan
with cornbread dressing and giblet gravy

This recipe for a Christmas turkey dinner may also be used to roast a goose, swan as well as a wild turkey. This is a 3-day process. Three days before I cook eggbread, hoecake and toast for the dressing. The day before Christmas, I cook the turkey, and on Christmas morning the dressing goes into the oven so that it will be warm when put on the table.

1 plucked wild turkey with giblets
6 stalks celery
2¾ cups of yellow corn meal (or yellow corn meal bread mix)
2¼ cups white flour
2½ cups milk, sour milk or buttermilk
4 tablespoons Crisco shortening
2 large onions
1 boiled egg, pealed and chopped
1 tablespoons olive oil
1 teaspoons salt
1 teaspoon baking powder (if using plain corn meal add 1 teaspoon baking soda)
1 teaspoon black pepper

Egg bread: In a large bowl pour in yellow corn meal, flour, and 1-teaspoon

275

of salt, sugar, baking soda and baking power (if using a corn meal bread mix add flour, but omit other ingredients). Melt 1-tablespoon of shortening and pour over mixed, dry ingredients. Add eggs and sufficient milk to make a thick liquid paste. It should be thin enough to pour freely. Coat fry pan with olive oil and pour in mix shaking it to allow bubbles to rise. Place in 350-degree oven and cook for 15 minutes until brown on top and bread starts to pull away slightly from edges of the frying pan. When done and cool, crumble into a very large bowl. This egg bread is excellent when buttered and eaten warm or even served with syrup and butter for breakfast.

Hoecake: This is a simple bread consisting of 2-cups of flour to which are added 3-tablespoons of Crisco shortening and sufficient milk to make a soft paste. If self-rising flour is used there is no need to add baking powder. If using plain flour add 1- teaspoon of baking powder and one of baking soda. Use a spoon to layer the mix in the bottom of a thick cast iron frying pan that has been whipped with Crisco or oil. Cook in oven with eggbread. The hoecake will be white on top with lightly browned points when done. Crumble with eggbread into bowl, taking care to break the crust into fine particles.

Roasted turkey: Thaw turkey. Initially the turkey may be set out on a counter the day before it is to be cooked at room temperature until the surface is soft to the touch. Then move to cooler spot and allow to continue the thawing process. Put in refrigerator overnight. The next morning place in a sink of cold water. When possible pull out the frozen bag of giblets and change the water. Place giblets in a 3-quart pot to boil and wash turkey thoroughly inside and out with clear water. Wild turkeys have very tall breasts and may not allow the lid of a conventional turkey roaster to close. Line the bottom of the roaster with heavy-duty aluminum foil leaving at least 2-inches protruding from the top of the roaster. Rub turkey breast with butter and salt. Cut up a large onion and 3-stalks of celery and place inside the body cavity. Place turkey into foil-lined roaster. Add 3-cups of water. Take another sheet of foil and place over top of turkey crimping the edges. Put in oven at 350-degrees and cook. Cooking time will vary depending on the size of the bird. Check after 3 hours adding additional water if necessary. The bird is done when the legs move freely and start to tear away from the body. Do not brown the bird, as this merely dries it out. When done remove from oven, save "drippings" from pan and place turkey on large platter to cool. When still warm, cover with a clean cotton towel and place in refrigerator. Slice when cold immediately before serving.

Dressing: Dressing is cooked in a separate pan compared to stuffing that is placed inside the bird. A vital component of dressing is the turkey "drippings." For this reason these drippings are saved, refrigerated overnight and used to make the dressing Christmas morning. (Sage in stuffing and dressing is not part of the Southern tradition. If your family has traditionally used it, it may be added. Sage is a strong spice and a teaspoon in a pan of dressing is sufficient.) To crumbled egg bread and hoecake add three slices of crumbled wheat toast. Mix with 2-teaspoons of black pepper. Crack 6 eggs on top. Take turkey "drippings" and re-liquefy them by placing in a boiler and heating. Now add finely cut celery and onions. Start pouring in liquefied "drippings," mixing as you pour. The dressing mix should be moist, but not liquid. Reserve 1-heaping tablespoon of raw dressing to add to giblet gravy.

Spoon into large greased pan in a layer not over 1-inch thick. Cook excess, if necessary, in smaller fry pans. Smooth top of dressing in pans. There should be no free liquid, but all of the particles should be wetted. Place in oven at 350-degrees and cook approximately 20 minutes. When the dressing is browned at the edges and the celery is soft it is done. When cut it should still be slightly moist. Cut, put on platter and serve warm.

Giblet gravy: Remove boiled liver, gizzard, heart and neck from pot and allow organs to cool. Add remaining pan "drippings" from turkey to pot. Chop up one boiled egg and place in pot. Pick meat from neck and cut longer strings with scissors until none is longer than ½-inch. Cut up organ meat and add back to pot. Simmer for 30 minutes before serving. The product is quite lumpy and is best dipped with a ladle rather than poured.

Road warrior pheasant (or other fowl) and purple rice

This dish was inspired when I was on a Western hunt and one of my stops had resulted in my shooting a Nebraska pheasant. Being on the road with Thanksgiving Day approaching, I considered ways that I could conveniently cook this pheasant into a tasty meal using a charcoal grill. Simply breasting the bird and putting it on the grill would have dried it out, and I wanted to try something different to more nearly resemble a traditional roasted fowl.

The cock bird had been cleaned and plucked in the round. I decided what I would do would be to purchase a Pyrex dish, put the pheasant in a marinate sauce and use the grill to roast the bird. The result was a moist, juicy bird that I cooked in the parking lot outside of my motel.

    1 plucked pheasant or other game bird
    2 cups burgundy wine
    2 cups Italian dressing
    1 cup soy sauce
    1 medium onion diced

Marinate bird in the mixture of wine, dressing and soy sauce for 4 hours. Prepare charcoal and heat grill. Place pheasant in Pyrex loaf dish and cover with aluminum foil or grill lid. Allow to cook until legs pull freely and juice from the bird is clear. Serve hot and dip meat into marinate sauce. For anyone who would want to serve purple rice, use some of the extra sauce as make-up water for a cup of white rice. The resulting rice will taste good and look a little different on the dinner table.

## Pasta sauce

Golden State pasta sauce

As California is the home of much of the nation's fresh vegetables and particularly of avocado production, it seemed fitting to name this pasta sauce after it. While customary to use Roma tomatoes in pasta sauces, this recipe also uses an avocado and a zucchini along with more traditional components.

1 pound of ground deer meat with no added fat
1 14 ounce can stewed tomatoes
1 4 ounce can tomato paste
4 bay leaves
1 fresh avocado pealed and seeded (this substitutes for a tablespoon of
 butter)
1 zucchini squash diced
1 finely chopped Roma tomato
1 medium Spanish onion, medium chopped
1 quarter bell pepper, chopped medium fine
3 medium mushrooms
½ teaspoon salt
½ teaspoon oregano
¼ teaspoon black pepper

In deep frying pan brown deer meat to which has been added the onions and bell pepper. After the meat is mostly browned add the remaining vegetables and continue to stir. When onions are clarified, add the can of stewed tomatoes. Mix well. Fold in tomato paste and one 4-ounce can of water. Drop in the bay leaves and cover with sauce. Simmer, tasting and adding water if necessary. The pasta sauce should be slightly salty, as the rather bland-tasting pasta will dilute it. To complete the California theme, use this sauce with a Spinach tagliatelle or other vegetable-based pasta. A medium-strength to robust red wine complements this sauce.

Cranberry bog pasta sauce

This recipe derived from one of those "O shit" moments when you are well into a recipe and find that you are out of some key ingredients and are too far from town to go for replacements. That was the circumstance when I was making a pasta sauce to go on some vegetable-(spinach, carrot, etc.)-based pasta. I had only one can of the usual stewed tomatoes that I would add, no oregano and no tomato sauce. I did have some Pace Medium Salsa and two Roma tomatoes. After these were added the sauce tasted too acid (from the vinegar in the salsa). About ½-cup of cranberries and 2-tablespoons of margarine took care of that, and the result was an exceptionally smooth pasta sauce without the wham-bang hits from the strong spices.

    2 pounds ground deer burger (without added fat)
    1 14 ounce can stewed tomatoes
    1 finely diced Spanish onion
    2 cut up Roma tomatoes
    1 cup Pace Medium Salsa
    ½ half cup cranberries
    ¼ diced bell pepper
    2 tablespoons margarine
    1 tablespoon crushed garlic
    1 tablespoon Italian pizza spices
    1 teaspoon salt (Be cautious and taste before adding
    as the salsa and stewed tomatoes are pre-salted.)
    ½ teaspoon black pepper

Brown deer meat with onions and bell pepper in large electric frying pan. When meat is browned add remaining ingredients and simmer. Additional water may be added from time to time to keep from drying out. After mixture has reached a boil and starts to thicken, transfer to a Crock Pot. Continue to heat for half-a-day at "low" heat setting. Adjust seasonings by adding more salt if needed. Serve over any pasta or on toasted multi-grain bread.

*This is a fun dish. I used a commercial pepperoni, but any spicy wild game sausage might also be used.*

## Vegetables (mostly)

Hunter's ratatouille

On of the first times that I served this dish was after parts of my family, including some kids, had just viewed Ratatouille, the Disney feature film. Although the version as made in the film used a red, presumably tomato-based, sauce as the bottom layer I prefer the less acid taste of either sour cream or cream cheese as the base layer. I also employed pepperoni and raisins to give some spice and sweet to the mixed selection of grilled vegetables. If impossible to find the vegetables of approximately the same diameter to make a presentation of evenly-sliced round products they may also be diced and then poured over the cheese base. There will be no practical difference in taste. I also found no appreciable difference in the taste of the dish made with sour cream or cream cheese. Either of these will work very well in this tribute to the Disney movie and French cooking.

1 small eggplant
3 Roma tomatoes
2 long yellow squash 1-2 inches in diameter
2 Irish potatoes
2 medium onions
1 zucchini
1 cucumber
¼ pound thinly sliced pizza pepperoni
½ cup sour cream or cream cheese
¼ cup raisins
2 tablespoons mayonnaise
sprinkle red pepper

280

Select vegetables that have approximately the same diameter. Wash vegetables, but do not peel except to defoliate onion. Slice thinly. In bowl mix sour cream or warmed cream cheese with mayonnaise and raisins. Coat 12-inch Pyrex dish with butter and spread layer of cream-mayonnaise mixture on bottom. Alternate vegetables using 2-slices of pepperoni to separate the zucchini and cucumber slices. Place in 350-degree oven and cook approximately 30 minutes. Dish is done when the vegetables are soft and the protruding tips of the eggplant are starting to brown. Serve with a Burgundy. Any of a variety of elongate squashes might be used in this recipe. I generally reduce the fat loading of this dish by using low-fat cheese products and mayonnaise. Alternatively, any of a variety of smoked wild game sausages might also be employed.

Sausage potatoes

Any sausage whether made of pork, venison or bear goes well with this recipe. In this version canned potatoes is used as the starch, but dried potatoes, white beans, rice or cut up fresh potatoes might be substituted. The fat content is considerably reduced by cooking the sausage first and then pouring off the excess fat. This is also a recipe that can be used with leftover sausage that was made up fresh in camp.

1 pound cooked, drained and granulated sausage
2 15-ounce cans sliced boiled potatoes
½ Spanish onion cut fine
½ bell pepper cut fine
1 diced Roma tomato
¼ teaspoon black pepper
½ teaspoon salt
1 block Cheddar cheese about 1-inch square and 3-inches long.

Put all ingredients except cheese and tomato in a 2-quart sauce pan along with 2-cups of water and bring to boil. When onions are transparent, add cheese and stir to insure that it goes into liquid. Taste and add additional seasonings as desired. When ready stir in tomatoes and cook an additional five minutes. Serve with Town House crackers. Either as a soup or a one-pot meal for any occasion, this makes a good breakfast dish for a cold morning along with a cup of hot coffee.

Wild hog pork and beans

I was called upon to cook at a public event and made up a 5-gallon pot of chili and had 5 cups of beans left over. These were a mix of 4:1 Pinto and Black beans that I had already soaked overnight. I was given a wild hog shoulder which I had skinned, removed the fat, sliced the leaner meat, and soaked in a brown sugar-salt brine overnight. The morning of the cooking I put it in my smoker and used some hickory chips. The concept here was not to completely smoke the meat, but to give it some smoke flavor. I hand ground the meat that I needed for the chili and still had some remaining. This I sorted into 1-pound packets and froze for seasoning meat for use with vegetables and other dishes. I already had more than enough chili so I used one package of meat and the excess beans for homemade pork and beans.

6 cups presoaked pinto and black beans
1 pound smoked, seasoned wild hog meat with excess fat removed
3 tablespoons brown sugar
2 14 oz. cans stewed tomatoes
1 large onion finely diced
1 tablespoon margarine
½ teaspoon salt
½ teaspoon black pepper
sprinkle red pepper

Start beans in large pot adding tomatoes, margarine, sugar, salt, pepper and sufficient water to cover at least 1 inch. Cut hog meat into approximately ½-inch squares separating excess fat. Brown meat in frying pan with diced onions. Add meat to pot and bring to boil. Continue heating until beans are very tender. Adjust seasonings to taste. I like to put this into a Crock Pot on low heat for half-a-day to completely tenderize the beans.

Navy buttons

Kids like to call this dish "Navy Buttons" because the large white beans are an interesting contrast to the eggplant, yellow and green squashes and red tomatoes. This is a colorful dish with a tasty mix of flavors. The best result is from cooking in a heavy boiler that will evenly distribute heat and prevent scorching while the vegetables are cooking down. I have an enameled cast-iron cooking pot that I prefer for this dish use because of its even heating characteristics.

1 eggplant with skin on diced in ½-inch cubes
1 medium yellow squash diced in ½-inch cubes
1 small zucchini squash diced in ½-inch cubes
1 cup dried navy beans
1 cup browned deer burger
½ bell pepper
1 14 oz. can Italian stewed tomatoes
4 oz. Colby-Monterey Jack cheese
2 table spoons olive oil

½ teaspoon salt
¼ teaspoon coarsely ground black pepper

Soak beans for 3 hours. Put in pot and boil until soft. Brown deer burger in fry pan and set aside. Cut up vegetables and mix. Wipe large heavy pot add olive oil and add vegetables. Use moderate heat and allow vegetables to stew until they have been reduced to half their volume. Add beans, burger, canned tomatoes and stir in seasonings except for cheese. Cook until vegetables are done and stir in cheese while mix is hot enough to allow cheese to melt.

Deer guacamole

Green and deer are not often thought of as going well together as the majority of deer dishes are either brown or reddish. This is a simple dip that takes only some avocadoes, a little mayonnaise and some fried deer burger. The recipe is for 2 medium-sized avocadoes and can be proportionally increased. Avocadoes very quickly turn brown if exposed to air and once made this dish must be tightly covered and refrigerated. It is best if made up immediately before serving. If a little heat is desired it can be sprinkled with a very light dusting of red pepper.

1 cup browned deer burger
2 ripe avocadoes, pealed, deseeded and mashed
2 tablespoons light mayonnaise
sprinkle of black or red pepper

Brown 1 cup of deer burger in fry pan and pour off liquid. Peal and mash avocadoes with mayonnaise. Mix in browned meat. Serve cold with beer.

Fortified Hoppin' Jon

Hoppin' Jon is a traditional New Year's Day meal that is a mixture of beans and rice with more-or-less seasonings depending on whether the dish originated in Louisiana or South Carolina. This recipe adds ground deer sausage, cheese and catsup to make this a one-pot meal for the deer camp that is both tasty and filling.

1½ cups cooked granulated deer sausage
1 cup pinto (or other) beans
1 cup white rice
½ minced Spanish onion
4 oz. low-fat cheese
6 tablespoons catsup
1 tablespoon minced garlic

Start soaking beans in large pot. When ready to start cooking put on stove with two quarts of water with onion and garlic and start cooking until beans are nearly done. Brown granulated deer sausage and add to pot. Thirty minutes before serving add rice. When rice is cooked, but while contents of pot are still hot, stir in cheese and catsup and continue serving until cheese is melted. If reheated, add additional water, stir and warm slowly to keep from scorching. On a cold morning, this makes an excellent hot breakfast.

*Good hot or cold and with or without whipped cream or a splash of maple syrup on top, this deer recipe will elicit some surprised expressions when guests discover that it contains deer sausage.*

## Dessert

Sausage sweet potato stuff

I often serve this with maple syrup for Christmas breakfast or on New Year's Day. It can be made in advance and then only requires a few minutes in a microwave to be ready to serve. The sausage is precooked, drained and granulated before adding to the sweet potatoes.

2 pounds cubed sweet potatoes boiled until soft
1 pound browned and drained granulated sausage
5 large eggs
1 tablespoon Sweet Thing or other non-sugar sweetener
1 teaspoon cinnamon powder
1 ¼-pound stick low-fat butter substitute
½ teaspoon nutmeg
1 teaspoon vanilla extract
1 teaspoon salt
1 small finely chopped onion

Place deer burger, chopped onions and salt in frying pan. Brown deer meat. Chop sweet potatoes and boil until fork tender in a large pot. Drain off water. While still hot pour into large bowl beating in eggs, margarine, spices and sweetener. Fold in browned deer meat. Pour into buttered oven-proof one-serving bowls. Cook in microwave for 10 minutes. The soufflé will be done when it pulls away from the sides of the bowl. Serve hot covered in reduced-sugar warm maple syrup. This goes equally well with hot coffee or skimmed milk.

Tasty pumpkin pie

Garrison Keeler's comment that, "Pumpkin pies are a study in mediocrity as the best pumpkin pie you ever had does not taste much different from the worst. Pumpkin pies are just an excuse to eat nutmeg," prompted me to consider ways to improve this classic American dessert. One thing is that other squashes will "pie" too. I have made pies out of Hubbard, butternut and acorn squashes that turned out well. There are two things to look out for with pumpkin pies. Some people do not tolerate cinnamon and nutmeg very well. Repeated exposure to cinnamon will give me heart burn and Thresa, my wife, could tolerate very little nutmeg and no mace without instantly purging her system of it. If some member of your family always gets sick after holiday meals, the innocent-appearing pumpkin pie may be the culprit. We are all different creatures in what our bodies can tolerate. Making your own pumpkin pies will allow adjustments of the seasoning and sweetening agents to suite personal needs. Much tasting, trying and adding additional ingredients should go on before the eggs are added to the mix to arrive at an acceptable balance of flavors. A general rule is to use 1-teaspoon of nutmeg per tablespoon of cinnamon. For each pie a starting mix is ¼-teaspoon of red pepper, ½-teaspoon of salt, 1-cup of combined raisons and coconut, ¼-stick of butter and ½-cup of sugar equivalent. There is no milk in this recipe.


Spice mix (per pie)

> 2 tablespoons cinnamon
> 2 tablespoons all purpose flour
> 2 teaspoons nutmeg
> ½ teaspoon salt
> ¼ teaspoon powered red pepper

Pumpkin

> 1 12-inch pumpkin (or 5, 6-inch pumpkins)
> 6 pie crusts
> 3 eggs per pie
> ¾ cup sugar or ½ cup most sugar substitutes
> ½ cup shredded coconut per pie
> ½ cup raisins per pie
> ¼ pound butter (or substitute) per pie

Break up the pumpkin with a hatchet. (You may save, wash and dry the seeds for the birds if you like.) Put broken pumpkin pieces into large pots and boil until meat is tender. Drain, allow to cool, and cut meat from rind with a knife. While pumpkin is cooling estimate the number of pies and mix up spices (These will want to clump, so mix well on a board.) Place pumpkin meat, while still warm, into large bowl. Add butter and mix, allowing butter to melt. Sprinkle spice mix over pumpkin and mix. Add fruit, half of sugar and mix again. Taste. Add additional spices and sugar as necessary. Add eggs and remix. Fill pie crusts, but not over 1-inch thick. Bake in 350-degree oven until crust is brown. (For pies are likely to be frozen and re-heated, cook until crust is light brown. If to be eaten without freezing, cook until crust is well browned.) Very lightly sprinkle with nutmeg. Serve with whipped cream.

# Index

291

# Our Product Testing Grounds.

The authentic black powder that helped build a nation.

Made in the U.S.A. for more than 200 years. GOEX. The tradition continues.

Phone 913-362-9455

www.goexpowder.com